JRD Tata

J.R.D. TATA

Editors
M.A. Shewan
A.C. Akela **N.P. Sharma**

Himalaya Books Pvt. Ltd.
'Ramdoot', Dr. Bhalerao Marg, Girgaon, Mumbai - 400 004
Tel : (022) 23863863. Fax : (022) 23877178
Email : himpub@vsnl.com

First Edition : 2011

Published by : **H.B.P.L.**
"Pooja Apartments", 4-B, Murari Lal Street, Ansari Road,
Darya Ganj, New Delhi-110 002
Phones : 23270392, 23278631 Reliance : 30180392 to 396
Fax : 011-23256286 Email : hphdel@vsnl.com

Sole Distributers : HIMALAYA PUBLISHING HOUSE PVT. LTD.

Branch Offices

Mumbai : "Ramdoot", Dr. Bhalerao Marg, Girgaon, Mumbai-400 004.
Phones : 23860170/23863863 Fax : 022-23877178
Email : himpub@vsnl.com
Website : www.himpub.com

Nagpur : Kundanlal Chandak Industrial Estate, Ghat Road, **Nagpur - 440 018.**
Phone: 2738731, 3296733 Telefax : 0712-2721215

Bengaluru : No. 16/1 (Old 12/1), 1st Floor, Next to Hotel Highlands, Madhava Nagar, Race Course Road, **Bengaluru - 560 001.**
Phone : 22281541, 22385461, Telefax: 080-22286611

Hyderabad : No. 3-4-184, Lingampally, Besides Raghavendra Swamy Matham, Kachiguda, **Hyderabad - 500 027.** Phone: 040-27560041, 27550139, Mobile:- 09848130433 Telefax: 040-27560041

Chennai : No. 85/50, Bazullah Road, T. Nagar, **Chennai - 600 017.**
Phone: 044-28344020, 32463737, 42124860

Pune : No. 527, "Laksha" Apartment, First Floor, Mehunpura, Shaniwarpeth, (Near Prabhat Theatre), **Pune - 411 030.**
Phone: 020-24496323/24496333/32326733

Lucknow : Jai Baba Bhawan, Near Manas Complex, Church Road, Aliganj, **Lucknow - 226 024.** Phone: 0522-2339329, 9305302158, 9415349385

Ahmedabad : No. 114, "SHAIL", 1st Floor, Opp. Madhu Sudan House, C.G.Road, Navrang Pura, **Ahmedabad – 380 009.**
Phone: 079-26560126, Mobiles: 09327324149,09314679413

Ernakulam : No. 39/104 A, Lakshmi Apartment, Karikkamuri Cross Rd., Ernakulam, **Cochin – 682011**, Kerala. Phone: 0484-2378012, 2378016, Mob.: 09344199799

Bhubaneswar : 5 Station Square, **Bhubaneswar (Orissa) - 751 001.**
Mobile: 9861046007, E-mail:- orissa@himpub.com

Indore : Kesardeep Avenue Extension, 73, Narayan Bagh.Flat No. 302, IIIrd Floor, Near Humpty Dumpty School, Narayan Bagh, **Indore (M.P.) 452 007**
Mobile: 09301386468

Kolkata : 108/4, Beliaghata, Main Road, Near ID Hospital, Opp. SBI Bank
Kolkata - 700 010. Mobile: 09910440956, E-mail:- nkmitra@himpub.com

Guwahati : House No. 15, Behind Prajjyotish College, Near Sharma Printing Press, P.O. Bharalumukh, Guwahati - 781009 (Assam
Mobile: 07439040301; 07439040302

Printed by : A to Z Printers, New Delhi

Preface

Biography, is now a form of literature, very much in vogue. In fact, biography is a description or account of someone's life and the times, which is usually published in the form of a book. A biography is more than a mention of personal facts (life, education, work, relationships and death), it also portrays the subject's experience of events. Technically speaking, a work is biographical, if it covers, all of a person's life. Biography writing has a long history. A biography is real. Ancient Greeks developed the biographical tradition, which we have inherited, although until the 5th century AD, when the word 'biographia' first appeared, in Damascius' "Life of Isodorus," biographical pieces were called simply "lives". It is quite likely that the Greeks were drawing on a pre-existing eastern tradition. Certainly Herodotus' "Histories" contains more detailed biographical information on Persian kings and subjects. The earliest surviving pieces, which we would identify as biographical are Isocrates' "Life of Evagoras" and Xenophon's "Life of Agesilaos," both from the fifth century BC. "Parallel Lives" by Plutarch, a Greek writing under the Roman empire, is a series of short biographies of eminent men.

The Golden Age of English biography emerged in late eighteenth century, the century in which the terms "biography" and "autobiography" entered English lexicon. The classic works of the period were Samuel Johnson's "Critical Lives of the Poets" and James Boswell's "Massive Life of Johnson". Generally American biography followed English model. By World War I, cheap hardcover reprints had become popular. The decade of the 1920s witnessed a biographical 'boom'. Later, biographical writings developed a lot and today biographies are written and compiled in the finest form of the genre. In India too, biography, as a form of literature has been evolved, cultivated and polished over the years. Here is an effort to promote this tradition further.

This series of biographies of great men, great women and celebrities in all walks of life is an adventurous academic endeavour, in its own right. A team of researchers and compilers has worked for a good period of time to accomplish the project. For this purpose, hundreds of books by eminent authors and editors have been consulted and referred to. We have benefited from various works, liberally, in order to illustrate and enrich this effort of ours. Present book is devoted to the great personality of J.R.D. Tata.

One of the pioneering industrialists of India, Jehangir Ratanji Dadabhoy (J.R.D) Tata was a legend in his life time. He raised Tata Group to new heights, during his long tenure as its head. Under him, the Tata Group diversified into a large number of sectors, from airlines to hotels, trucks to locomotives, soda ash, heavy chemicals to pharmaceuticals, and financial services to tea, air-conditioning etc. He was not only an industrialist, but was a pioneering aviator too and brought commercial aviation to India. Besides being a patron of the arts and a philanthropist, he was a great leader and motivator. He was also the longest serving member of the Atomic Energy Commission. He was honoured with Bharat Ratna, besides other prestigious awards and honours.

This is a compact and comprehensive account of the above mentioned great life, which is bound to attract the attention of scholars, researchers, students and the general readers, alike. Let's hope this humble effort would receive a warm welcome and due applause.

— *Editors*

Contents

1

Introduction

India's first pilot; established Air India International as India's first international airline; Chairman of Tata Sons for 50 years; recipient of Bharat Ratna in 1992... there are many personas of this one personality. Enterprising, indomitable and undaunted – JRD Tata is the pioneer who was driven by the spirit of the skies.

Born on July 29, 1904 in Paris, Jehangir Ratanji Dadabhoy Tata, was fondly referred to as JRD by commoner and king. Representing an exalted idea of Indianness: progressive, benevolent, ethical and compassionate, JRD Tata is recognised as the most enterprising Indian entrepreneurs of all times. Recognised as the fourth Chairman of the Tata Group at the young age of 34 only, JRD is credited with placing the Tata Group on the international map.

On the personal front, flying was a passion with JRD. He was the first person to qualify within India to fly. He got his license, which bore on it Number 1, on 10 February 1929. As an aviator and pioneer flier, he was the one who brought commercial aviation to India. JRD went on to establish Air-India International in 1948 and became the president of International Air Transport Association (IATA) within 10 years of its establishment. He remained as the helm of Air India till 1978, making it one of the most efficient airlines in the world.

Nobody could have guessed that this is how destiny would unfold, when JRD was born to R.D. Tata, a business partner and relative of Jamsetji Tata, and his French wife Sooni. JRD, the second of four siblings, was educated in France, Japan and England before being drafted into the French army for a mandatory one year period. JRD wanted to extend his stint in the forces (to avail of a chance to attend a renowned horse-riding school), but his father would have none of it. Leaving the French army saved JRD his life, because shortly thereafter, the regiment he served in was wiped out while on an expedition in Morocco.

JRD then set his mind on securing an engineering degree from Cambridge, but his father summoned him back to India (JRD would forever regret not being able to attend university). He soon found himself on the threshold of a business career in a country he was far from familiar with.

JRD entered the Tatas as an unpaid apprentice in December 1925. His mentor in business was John Peterson, a Scotsman who had joined the Group after serving in the Indian Civil Service. At 22, soon after his father passed away, he was on the board of Tata Sons, the Group's flagship company. In 1929, aged 25, he surrendered his French citizenship to embrace the country that would become the central motif of his life. In the same year on February 10, JRD became the first Indian to pass the pilot's examination. With this distinctive honour of being India's first pilot, he was instrumental in giving wings to India by building Tata Airlines, which ultimately became Air India. His passion for flying was fulfilled with the formation of the Tata Aviation Service in 1932.

At the age of 34, in 1938, JRD was elected Chairman of Tata Sons making him the youngest head of the largest industrial group in India. His leadership at Tata Sons, at the beginning, had 14 enterprises which half a century later had expanded to a conglomerate of 95 enterprises. During his tenure, the group expanded into diverse fields such as chemicals, automobiles, tea and information technology. Breaking with the common practice of having members of one's own family run different operations in a business, JRD urged to bring in professionals to the table. He turned the Tata Group into a business federation where entrepreneurial talent and expertise were encouraged to flower.

During his tenure, JRD initiated a programme of closer "employee association with management" to give workers a stronger voice in the affairs of the company. He, for the first time, pioneered the system of developing 'employee welfare schemes' in corporate India and steered the principles of an eight hour working day, free medical aid, workers' provident fund and accident compensation schemes, which were later, adopted as statutory requirements in India.

Under JRD's aegis, in the year 1979, Tata Steel instituted a new practice; a worker is deemed to be "at work" from the moment he leaves home for work till he returns home from work. Hence the company is financially liable to the worker if any mishap takes place on the way to and from work. JRD stepped down from his position as Chairman in 1991, to hand over the baton to Sri. Ratan Tata.

Self-effacing, modest, wistful and endearing are a few of the adjectives used to describe JRD. During the 89 years of his life and as an established corporate citizen of India,

JRD Tata was honoured with a number of awards. He received the Padma Vibhushan in 1957 for his remarkable contribution to the aviation industry, the Guggenheim Medal for aviation in 1988. In 1992, because of his selfless humanitarian endeavours, JRD Tata was awarded India's highest civilian honour, the Bharat Ratna-one of the rarest instances in which this award was granted during a person's lifetime. In the same year, JRD Tata was also bestowed with the United Nations Population Award for his crusading endeavours towards initiating and successfully implementing the family planning movement in India, much before it became an official government policy.

JRD and his wife, Thelma, whom he married after a Paris romance in 1930, did not have any children, but JRD always appeared most comfortable with kids. Be it adult or children, to him, it was people who mattered. With his demise on November 29, 1993, in a Geneva hospital, an epoch had come to an end. A noble bit of India — and Indianness — was gone forever.

2

An Illustrious Life

Birth and Early Life

JRD Tata was born in Paris, France, the second child of Ratanji Dadabhoy Tata, an Indian of Parsi-Zoroastrian heritage, and his French wife Suzanne Briere. His father was a first cousin of Jamsetji Tata, a pioneer industrialist in India. 'Jeh', or 'JRD' as he was commonly known, came to be regarded as the most famous industrial pioneer in modern India. As his mother was French, he spent much of his childhood in France and as a result, French was his first language. He attended the Cathedral and John Connon School, Bombay (now Mumbai).

JRD Tata was inspired early by aviation pioneer Louis Bleriot, and took to flying. In 1929 Tata got the first pilot licence issued in India. He later came to be known as the father of Indian civil aviation. He founded India's first commercial airline, 'Tata Airlines', in 1932, which in 1946 became Air India, now India's national airline.

Days in France

JRD was an interesting product of two continents. Born in Paris in 1904, JRD schooled in Paris, Bombay and Yokohama. Most of his education was in France. In order to improve his

English before going to Cambridge, he was sent to an English Grammar School.

According to JRD, his mother was a very resourceful, intelligent and adaptable lady who — with five children — single-handedly packed up her household items in France and came to India to be with her husband, who was in the House of Tatas. As she went back to her home country every year or two, JRD's education was regularly disrupted.

His grandmother was a very formidable lady. 'Her husband was a humorist and after some time with her,' says JRD, 'the gentleman ran away as anyone would have, had he been married to my grandmother.' Perhaps JRD inherited his sense of humour from his French grandfather.

Louis Bleriot, the first man to fly across the English Channel, had a house on the coast of France near the Tata's country home. Bleriot's pilot, who used to land a small plane on the beach, once gave JRD a joy-ride. It was then that the fifteen-year-old boy decided that one day he too would fly. He had to wait ten years for it to happen.

After school, he was drafted for a year into the French army and assigned to a regiment in France called *Le Saphis*. At the end of his time there, he expected to go on to Cambridge where a place was reserved for him. But his father summoned him back to India to join the Tatas.

It was to rankle with him for decades that he never went to a university. His father must have had a premonition, for he died nine months later and JRD took his place as director of Tata Sons, which controlled India's largest industrial group. JRD was twenty-one.

Though he missed his college education, he undertook his own education after office hours, studying books on various aspects of business. When he was in his early twenties, while recovering from typhoid, he would come to his room, throw himself in bed and study. When his sister Rodabeh pleaded, 'Why don't you rest Jeh, you are tired and unwell,' JRD replied, 'I want to be worthy of Tata's.'

Beginning at Tata

In 1925, Mr Tata arrived at Bombay House to work under John Peterson, the director-in-charge of Tata Steel. In 1938 when Sir Nowroji Saklatvala, the Chairman of Tata Sons expired, JRD Tata was catapulted to head the country's largest industrial empire. He was barely thirty four! And he guided the destiny of India's largest Industrial house for well over half a century.

In 1939 Tata Chemicals started its struggle towards pioneering a self reliant, basic inorganic chemical industry for India, in the face of repeated crises. Just before India's Independence, Tata Steel promoted the Tata Engineering and Locomotive Company (TELCO) in 1945 with an objective to produce locomotives for the Indian Railways. Today Telco has emerged as India's largest Commercial Vehicle producer.

Successful Career

JRD Tata joined Tata Sons as an unpaid apprentice in 1925. In 1938, at the age of 34, JRD was elected Chairman of Tata & Sons making him the head of the largest industrial group in India. For decades, JRD directed the huge Tata Group of companies, with major interests in Steel, Engineering, Power, Chemicals and Hospitality. He was famous for succeeding in business while maintaining high ethical standards— refusing to bribe politicians or use the black market.

Under J.R.D's chairmanship, the assets of the Tata Group grew from Rs. 620 Million to over Rs 100 Billion. He started with 14 enterprises under his leadership and half a century later on July 26, 1988, when he left, Tata & Sons was a conglomerate of 95 enterprises which they either started or in which they had controlling interest.

JRD was the trustee of Sir Dorabji Tata Trust from its inception in 1932 for over half a century. Under his guidance, this Trust established Asia's first cancer hospital, the Tata Memorial Centre for Cancer, Research and Treatment, in Bombay in 1941. It also founded the Tata Institute of Social Sciences (TISS, 1936), the Tata Institute of Fundamental Research (TIFR, 1945), and the National Centre for Performing Arts.

In 1948, JRD Tata launched Air India International as India's first international airline. In 1953, the Indian Government appointed JRD as Chairman of Air-India and a director on the Board of Indian Airlines — a position JRD retained for 25 years. For his crowning achievements in Aviation, JRD was bestowed with the title of Honorary Air Commodore of India.

In 1956, JRD Tata initiated a programme of closer 'employee association with management' to give workers a stronger voice in the affairs of the company. He firmly believed in employee welfare and espoused the principles of an eight-hour working day, free medical aid, workers' provident scheme, and workmen's accident compensation schemes, which were later, adopted as statutory requirements in India. In 1979, Tata Steel instituted a new practice: a worker being deemed to be "at work" from the moment he leaves home for work till he returns home from work. This made the company financially liable to the worker for any mishap on the way to and from work. Tata Steel Township was also selected as a UN Global Compact City because of the quality of life, conditions of sanitation, roads and welfare that were offered by Tata Steel.

Great Businessman

JRD Tata studied engineering at the University of Cambridge. He returned to India and started the Tata group in a workshop in Jamshedpur with a group of 10 workers. Several years later, when the Tata group became quite successful in India, he financed the building of the new engineering department at Cambridge University.

For decades, Tata directed the huge Tata Group of Companies, with major interests in many industries in India, including steel, engineering, hospitality and electrical companies. He was famous for succeeding in business while maintaining high ethical standards refusing to bribe politicians or use the black market. His contributions to founding many famous institutions of higher learning in India are also well recognised.

Among a host of awards, he received the Padma Vibhushan in 1957 on the eve of silver jubilee of Air India. He was awarded the Bharat Ratna in 1992 for his service to industry and nation building. He also received the Guggenheim Medal for aviation in 1988. He died in Geneva, Switzerland in 1993 at age of 89.

Expansion at a Large Scale

During the last half of the twentieth century Tata entered several new businesses, many of them unconventional, and produced a vast range of products — from airlines to hotels, trucks to locomotives, soda ash and other heavy chemicals to pharmaceuticals and financial services, tea and air conditioning to lipsticks and cologne.

The group seemed to make everything and do everything. One of Tata's earliest achievements was to cajole ten rival cement companies to merge and form the Associated Cement Companies, run by the Tata's.

JRD strengthened existing businesses such as steel, power and hotels. At the same time, the group lost interest in some of its older core businesses.

As an industrialist, JRD Tata was credited with placing the Tata Group on the international map. As an aviator and pioneer flier, he brought commercial aviation to India.

The Strong Group

JRD's respect for his managers bound the group. 'I am a firm believer that the disintegration of the Tata Group is impossible,' he once declared.

Most business groups have disintegrated or drifted apart because of family ownership and management, with rival family members wanting to go their own way. In contrast, the Tata Group companies are run by professionals who firmly believe in the trusteeship concept laid down by J.N. Tata as also by Mahatma Gandhi.

A university dropout, JRD was something of a self-taught technocrat, and died long before the phrase 'war for talent' was coined. Yet, almost every senior Tata director from the 1930s onwards held a degree from a foreign university. Tata willingly financed bright young boys who wanted to go abroad for further education.

He was also a vital bridge between the scientific establishment and the government through his founding of the Tata Institute of Fundamental Research, and as the longest serving member of the Atomic Energy Commission.

Tata's personal interest in technology, combined with India's isolation in the 1950s and 1960s, spurred several group companies, particularly Tata Steel and Tata Chemicals, to innovate in their fields. At Tata Steel, a Research and Control Laboratory had been opened in 1937, and its researchers developed an extensive variety of special steels for applications as varied as parachute harnesses and razor blades.

The lab also developed a high-tensile alloy steel — Tiscrom — which made it possible for the Howrah Bridge in Calcutta to be built entirely from Indian materials. Another corrosion resistant, low-alloy high-yield strength steel — Tiscor — was used for the manufacture of all-metal steel coaches on the Indian railways.

Key to Success

A company, which uses the name Tata, shares a tradition. The symbol 'T' has to be a symbol of quality.' The achievements of the Tata Group would not have been possible without the support of its workforce. Before JRD took over, the labour situation at key Tata plants was frequently tense despite the fact that management had poured millions into subsidised housing for workers, offered free medical and hospital treatment, as well as free education and was miles ahead of government legislation in terms of labour practices.

For example, Tata Steel pioneered the eight-hour day in 1912, long before the principle had been accepted in the United States or Europe (Britain introduced the twelve-hour day in 1911).

Tata Steel introduced leave with pay in 1920, and in India this was established by law in 1945. Tata Steel set up a provident fund in 1920, which was not legalised until 1952. Tata asked the question: if the workers were being treated exceptionally well, why were they frequently discontented and mistrustful and hostile towards the company?

According to Tata, the crux of any successful labour policy lay in making workers feel wanted. One of the inherent drawbacks of modern industry with its large and concentrated labour forces was that each man felt 'that instead of being a valued member of a friendly and human organisation, he was a mere cog in a soulless machine.'

'Because of this, a worker's attitude towards management becomes one of indifference, mistrust and coldness often tinged with hostility. He is easily led to feeling himself the victim of callous and unfair treatment and little is needed to make him look upon his employers as his enemies and break out into open conflict.'

Tata Steel became one of the earliest companies in India to have a dedicated human resources department. Expressing surprise that the company had functioned for so long without one, Tata commented: 'If our operations required the employment of, say, 30,000 machine tools, we would undoubtedly have a special staff or department to look after them, to keep them in repair, replace them when necessary, maintain their efficiency, protect them from damage, etc.'

'But when employing 30,000 human beings each with a mind and soul of his own, we seem to have assumed that they would look after themselves and that there was no need for a separate organisation to deal with the human problems involved.'

Jehangir Ratanji Dadabhoy Tata died in Geneva on November 29, 1993, and made his money in India. Few addressed him with the full pomposity of the name with which he was born; he was simply 'JRD' to the world, and Jeh to his friends.

JRD was India's most well known industrialist, widely respected for his enormous contribution to the development of Indian industry and aviation in particular.

Tata headed India's largest industrial conglomerate with uncommon success. But this was only one aspect of his life. He was also a man of great sensitivity and was pained by the poverty he saw around him and sought vigorously to alleviate it.

He also was a philanthropist who wanted India to be a happy country and did all he could to make it so; a patron of the sciences and the arts; and a man with a passion for literature, fast cars, skiing, and flying.

Despite all Odds

As an industrialist, JRD was credited with placing the Tata Group on the international map. He proved his mettle by saving it from disintegration in an era when family ownership and management or family rifts were ripping apart family businesses. He was a redoubtable visionary under whose regime the group entered into several new streams of business, many of them unconventional and produced a vast range of product. As an aviator and pioneer flier, he brought commercial aviation to India. He was greatly revered by artists, sculpture and performing artistes as he generously patronised Indian art and culture.

And as a philanthropist, he was respected for building and keeping alive the tremendously active Tata charitable trusts. His achievements have to be seen through the lens of India's economic and political history. Under British colonial rule until 1947, India was straitjacketed by a foreign exchange crunch for almost 40 years after Independence, which gravely limited industrial entrepreneurship.

From 1964 to 1991, stiff government control through the licence-quota regime further curbed the growth of the group. Despite all these bottlenecks, he expanded the Tata Empire manifold and made it India's biggest business group. JRD Tata reigned over the Tata group for more than three decades. He started his stint as chairman at the tender age of 34 in 1938. Under his leadership, the Tata assets grew from Rs 62 crore in 1939 to over Rs 10,000 crore in 1990. At the same time, the number of companies under the group grew from 14 to 50 large manufacturing ones, besides innumerable holding, investment, subsidiaries and associate concerns.

According to JRD, quality had to match innovation. He disliked the laid-back Indian attitude, and much of his fabled short temper was triggered by the carelessness of others. He stressed: "If you want excellence, you must aim at perfection. I know that aiming at perfection has its drawbacks. It makes you go into detail that you can avoid. It takes a lot of energy out of you but that's the only way you finally actually achieve excellence. So in that sense, being finicky is essential... A company, which uses the name Tata shares a tradition..."

JRD was an expert in managing human resource. At his behest, Tata Steel became one of the earliest companies in India to have a dedicated human resource department. Expressing his surprise that the company had functioned for so long without one, JRD commented: "If our operations required the employment of, say, 30,000 machine tools, we would undoubtedly have a special staff or department to look after them, to keep them repair, replace them when necessary, maintain their efficiency, protect them from damage, etc. but when employing 30,000 human beings, each with a mind and soul of his own, we seem to have assumed that they would look after themselves and that there was no need for a separate organisation to deal with the human problems involved". As the saying goes, all good things must come to an end, and so did JRD's brilliant life. JRD died in Geneva on November 29, 1993. He left behind an indelible mark on the Indian business terrain as also a huge business empire we all know as the House of Tatas.

The First Flier

Flying was a passion with JRD. He was the first one to qualify within India to fly. He got his licence, which bore on it Number 1, on 10 February 1929. When one asked him what was the greatest adventure of his life, he replied, 'The flying experience. None can equal that.' He added, 'When you are on your own in that little plane at the control without an instructor, and the plane speeds on the runway and finally takes off — you know you are in the air on your own.'

In 1930, the Aga Khan Trophy was offered for the first Indian to fly solo from India to England or vice versa. JRD competed, taking off from Karachi to London. When he landed at Aboukir Bay in Egypt, he found that Aspy Engineer, the other contender, flying from London to Karachi, was stranded in the desert airfield for want of a spark plug!

JRD sportingly parted with his spare one and they continued their journey in opposite directions. Aspy beat him by a couple of hours. 'I am glad he won,' said JRD, 'because it helped him get into the Royal Indian Air Force.' Later Aspy was to be the second Indian to be the chief of the Indian Air Force.

JRD recalled that in 1932, 'one October morning as the sun rose on the eastern horizon, a single-engined Puss Moth plane took off from Karachi with a load of mail for Bombay. As the plane hummed and rose the pilot said a word of prayer.' And so India's first airline - the Tata Airlines - was inaugurated.

In 1948, JRD went on to start Air-India International. Within ten years he was president of International Air Transport Association (IATA). Though the airline was nationalised in 1953, he remained at the helm of Air India till 1978, making it one of the most efficient airlines in the world.

In 1938, at the age of thirty-four, he had become the chairman of the largest industrial group in India, which he led with distinction for fifty-two years.

When one asked him why he was appointed at such a young age as chairman of Tata Sons, when senior, more distinguished men like Sir Homi Mody and Sir Ardeshir Dalal were on the board, he shrugged it off and said, 'It was an aberration.' When pressed for a reply, he said, 'Perhaps, because I was hard working.'

With his limitation of formal education, how did he discharge his responsibilities? 'Because of a lack of technical knowledge, my main contribution in management was to encourage others.'

He elaborated on how he dealt with each man in his own way and brought out the best in people. 'At times, it involved suppressing yourself. It is painful but necessary... To lead men, you have to lead them with affection.'

With more than sixty years of experience in top management, he developed his own philosophy and method where leadership was concerned. 'One of the qualities of leadership is to assess what is needed to get the best results for an enterprise. If that demands being a very active executive chairman, as I was in Air-India, I did that. On the other hand, in one of our other companies where I know that the managing director likes to be alone and will get the results that way, I argue with myself and decide that it will be stupid for me to come in the way when the other person has a capacity for focusing his genius and producing the results. Often a chairman's main responsibility is to inspire respect.' And then he added, 'Don't forget, I like people.'

The Demise

He breathed his last in Switzerland on 29 November 1993 at the age of 89. The Indian Parliament was adjourned in his memory in a gesture rarely accorded to non-Members of Parliament. He was buried at Père Lachaise Cemetery in Paris.

3

Multifaceted Personality

An Unmatched Character

Jehangir Ratanji Dadabhoy Tata was not an easy man to write about. With his iconic status and corporate accolades, JRD the businessman could have overshadowed JRD the man and yet the book "Forever Jeh" details the humanitarian side of the astute entrepreneur. Instead of showcasing his by now legendary impact on the country's commerce, the book picks up strands from his social and public commitments. A collection of interviews, photographs and quotes, "Forever Jeh" describes a gentleman tycoon who could "look beyond labels". Clarifying that "this is not another biography of JRD Tata" in the preface, author Surekha Tenneti Venugopal pledges the emotive tribute to a subjective analysis of the Bharat Ratna awarded and first airline pioneer of India.

Born on June 29 1904, in a pretty house in Rue de Halevy in Paris to French girl Sooni and Indian Parsi R.D. Tata, JRD was named Jehangir - conqueror of the world. When he was a teen he was sent to the Tata Iron and Steel Company in Jamshedpur and, at just 34, became the chairman of Tata Sons.

Aloo Bhartania, JRD's former secretary, reminisces: "He was most perturbed about the way people carelessly used articles - 'a', 'an' and 'the'. An article has such significance, he often said."

The non-chauvinist and romantic Jeh surfaces now and then. When asked whether he missed having a son, JRD had famously replied: "I miss not having a daughter."

She adds: "Each day from the large bouquet of fresh flowers in his room, he'd pick a rose and take it home for his ailing wife (Thelma who he married in Paris in 1930)... every single day."

"He loved to live dangerously," says Bhartania, asking, "Had he not piloted a plane at '78, skied on the mountains and performed the most difficult workouts in the gym in his house nearly till the end?"

Russi Lala, who has written multiple biographies of JRD, says: "He was in essence a very great human being. There was this undeniable aura about him wherever he went."

The private letters between JRD and his father, too, are touching testimony to his affection and ambition even as a little boy. In one letter, he writes: "Papa I am sure that you merit the legion de'honeur in your business because you work as no many persons did work. When I shall be big I shall be like you... and I kiss you so much that I can't tell you."

Anonymous pals vouch for JRD's provocative sense of humour while top officials of Tata Steel remember an irreplaceable mentor. On his death on Nov 29, 1993, the Parliament, in an unusual gesture for a private citizen, was adjourned in his memory and Maharashtra declared three days of mourning.

The author, who was married to a Tata Steel engineer and was a columnist for "TISCO News", quotes Sir Homi Mody as saying, "JRD had a very keen intellect... his versatility is truly amasing. Whether it is a blast furnace or an ice-cream freezer, an aircraft engine or a cigarette lighter, he is equally at home with all of them." A cross between a coffee table book and a research treatise, "Forever Jeh" is a veritable photo album with rare footage of JRD in both personal and professional spheres. The book is a must not just for die-hard Tata fans but for anyone who is in need of a motivational fix. India's JRD Tata: Can he hand-pick a successor to carry on a corporate legend? By dubbing his nephew, Ratan, heir apparent, JRD had taken a step that could split up the famed house of Tata.

As the nephew of the childless JRD, and the son of deputy group chairman Naval Tata, Ratan was the obvious choice as heir apparent to the Tata throne. A graduate of Cornell University in Ithaca, New York, he worked in both Tisco and Telco before assuming a role as the group's unofficial troubleshooter. Over the last 10 years, he has been given credit for turning around two group companies, the National Radio and Electronics Corp. (Nelco) and a 100 year old textile mill. Still a bachelor, he remains wedded to his work. He believes that his primary task as chairman of Tata Industries is "to try to encourage the directors of the different companies to work together towards trying to rebuild a closeness of the group that has diminished over the years.

Jehangir Ratanji Dadabhoy (JRD) Tata, head of India's huge Tata industrial empire, was renowned as a cautious man who always listened to other people's counsel. So when the 78 year old industrialist recently decided to make a solo flight in a vintage aircraft from Karachi to Bombay, refusing to listen to warnings that it was "the harebrained idea of an old fool", it was clear that he had not lost his sense of determination.

JRD's 600 mile flight in October was a re-enactment of his pioneering effort 50 years ago, when he began Air India's first commercial airmail service. The touchdown in Bombay was witnessed by crowds of admirers, many of them young people. One reason for making the flight, explained JRD to a battery of microphones and clicking cameras, was "to rekindle enthusiasm among the younger generation".

Although observers might have viewed JRD's sudden change of behaviour as a second childhood, what it really signalled was his recognition that after 45 years as chairman of Tata Sons, the group's parent company, he would soon have to hand over the reins. A long period of government-imposed restraints on the growth of big business houses such as Tata was now giving way to opportunities for massive expansion, and JRD would like a younger man to take over the helm.

The apparent crown prince in the wings was his 45 year old nephew, Ratan. JRD had startled trusted colleagues by stepping aside as chairman of Tata Industries, the group's major policy-making body, and named Ratan as his successor. The move catapulted Ratan to the front of the succession queue for the chairmanship of Tata Sons. The decision created consternation among several expectant, more experienced and longer-serving Tata executives.

But the matter was far from settled. JRD hastily smoothed the ruffled feathers of the group executives by ensuring them that when he retired, or died, his successor as chairman of Tata Sons would be chosen by the board of Tata Sons. Virtually all of the senior Tata executives who laid claim to the top job sat on the board of the parent company.

At stake was arguably the most prestigious corporate post in India. As the head of Tata, JRD guided the activities of 30 autonomous companies employing more than 237,800 people, a payroll that was a tribute to Tata's efforts to help keep India's unemployment rate down. Indeed, Tata had become a modern-day legend for its commitment to look beyond the needs of its own business interests and address the wider concerns of a poverty-stricken nation.

All of the Tata companies were bound by common ideals and goals that strive to carry on the founder's tradition of social responsibility — often at the expense of profits — that was established before the turn of the century. JRD's successor will be expected to carry on the Tata legacy of mixing big business with philanthropy.

Historically, the Tatas had also been at the frontier of the development of India's heavy and basic industries. The group's two largest companies, which combined account for well over half of last year's total group sales of $2.9 billion and pre-tax profits of $321 million, were Tata Iron and Steel Co. (Tisco) and Tata Engineering and Locomotive Co. (Telco). Tisco was India's first steel mill and was the only one left in the private sector. Telco was the country's largest motor vehicle manufacturer. Other group interests included power generation, textiles, chemicals, tea, hotels, publishing, toiletries and computers.

Until the mid-1970s, Tata also held indisputable claim to being the largest grouping of companies in the private sector in India.

Since then, years of stagnant growth had allowed it to be overtaken in both sales and assets by its main rival, the Birla group. JRD was quick to pounce on criticisms of Tata's slothful growth record, among other things, during a three-hour interview with International Management that was interrupted by a couple of meetings with key executives and several telephone calls.

Far Ahead of Time

JRD Tata was a visionary far ahead of his time. An industry leader with a deep commitment to India's development, his pioneering efforts in combining nation-building with business growth were instrumental in conditioning the thinking of Indian businesses.

Leaders raise the aspirations of their people to achieve what was previously thought impossible. In this, JRD was a true leader. He headed the country's largest industrial empire whose destiny he guided for over half a century. Under his leadership, the Tata group's assets climbed from Rs. 620 million in 1939 to over Rs 1,00,000 million in 1990. Over the years he helped establish many new enterprises—the number of Tata ventures grew from 13 to around 80, encompassing software, steel, power generation, engineering and hotels, among others.

JRD was among the first to realise that employees are among the most important resources in any organisation. He introduced employee-friendly measures such as the eight-hour working day, free medical aid and workers provident scheme. Many of these subsequently have been adopted as statutory requirements by law. He also believed in leadership through consensus and, in 1956, initiated programmes for closer employee association with management.

Today, when corporate social responsibility is increasingly becoming a norm in India, we must remember that JRD set the trend way back in the early 1960s. He believed that every corporation has a responsibility towards the people of the area in which it is located. He contributed in developing Jamshedpur into a model town. In fact, the Tata group continues to have well-established community development programmes at most of its industrial sites.

It is important that leaders fight for the right cause. JRD saw the country's developmental process as an integral part of business growth. To quote his own words, "No success in material terms is worthwhile unless it serves the needs or interests of the country and its people". JRD undertook several initiatives towards this. For instance, he arranged for training of employees of the three new public sector steel complexes that came up in the '60s. He was among the first to realise the effects of unchecked population growth on the country's developmental efforts. In 1970, he started the Family Planning Foundation jointly with the Ford Foundation.

While building an empire, he advocated a holistic approach encompassing social change. The economic and social development goals in India's development planning owe much to JRD. He crusaded for issues critical for India—women's education and spread of literacy. Further, he was instrumental in establishing Asia's first cancer hospital in Mumbai. In all, JRD Tata was an inspirational business leader who looked beyond narrow short-term benefits. He inspired the Tata group to become one of the most respectable and successful business houses in the country. In the words of Mahatma Gandhi, "Men of character will easily inspire confidence". Indeed, JRD symbolised this.

Motivating Spirit

Leadership, according to JRD meant motivating others. 'As chairman, my main responsibility is to inspire respect.' Sometimes referred to as the 'chairmen's chairman,' JRD adopted a management by consensus style: 'When a number of persons are involved I am definitely a consensus man,' he once said, adding: 'but that does not mean that I do not disagree or that I do not express my views. Basically it is a question of having to deal with individual men heading different enterprises. You have to adapt yourself to their ways and deal accordingly and draw out the best in each man. If I have any merit it is getting on with individuals according to their ways and characteristics. In fifty years I have dealt with a hundred top directors and I have got on with all of them. At times it involves suppressing yourself. It is painful but necessary. To be a leader you have got to lead human beings with affection.'

Be that as it may, JRD spotted talent easily. And once he was confident that a manager would perform, he gave him a long rope. If they wanted to be on their own, like Sumant Moolgaokar, he left them to it. If they occasionally wanted a shoulder to cry on, like Darbari Seth, he was there.

The supportive climate he built developed entrepreneurs such as Sir Homi Mody, Sir Ardeshir Dalal, Sir Jehangir Ghandy, Russi Mody, Sumant Moolgaokar and Darbari Seth, and others who created billions in wealth for the group and the country.

It was an environment where scientists of international repute such as Homi Bhabha, leading lawyers such as J.D. Choksi and Nani Palkhivala, and economists such as John Matthai, A.D. Shroff, D.R. Pendse and Freddie Mehta could flourish.

This attitude contrasted sharply with the prevailing management styles of other Indian business leaders. Large Indian companies tend to fall into three categories: public sector ones run by the government, multinational affiliates, and those promoted by family dynasties. While the Tata Group firmly remained a family concern — to date, four out of its five chairman have been Tatas — JRD's professionalism stood out from the crowd.

Moreover, in most of the family firms, the top management tended to belong to the same community as the promoter family. With the Tatas, it was different: only merit counted.

JRD's role model in management was the British civil service. How was it, he wondered 'that a young Briton straight from college, could come to a foreign country and administer various departments with such distinction?'

The Tata Group faced a constant shortage of managers, and JRD carried out many experiments to expand and improve the pool of talent. His first attempt — the formation of the Superior Staff Recruiting Committee — failed when none of the recruits stayed with the corporation.

Eventually he formed the Tata Administrative Service and the Tata Management Training Centre at Pune. This commitment to professionalism served the group well. In 1971, for example, when the coal industry was nationalised, Mohan Kumaramangalam, the then industry minister, left Tata Steel's coal mines untouched on the ground that these efficiently run mines would provide a model for the nationalised mines.

Generous Credit

From 1964 to 1991 severe government controls on big business further curbed the growth of the Tata Group. Analysing his own performance, JRD Tata insisted that his only real contribution to the group of companies was Air-India. For the rest, he generously gave credit to his executives.

Most Carefree

In the mid-1970s, a convoy of cars and buses sped along a highway in Sweden with motorcycle escorts on either side. A helicopter constantly hovered over it, for the cargo was precious. In this convoy were men of finance and industry who between them controlled billions and who could be held up for vast ransoms.

Every six months they met either in America or in Europe under the aegis of the Chase Manhattan Bank. Among them were Dr. Giovanni Agnelli, president of Fiat; the president of Ford Motors; the biggest shipbuilder in the world, who was from Hong Kong; a member of the House of Mitsubishi; David Rockefeller, president of the Chase Manhattan; and Dr. Henry Kissinger.

The most carefree in this select company was JRD Tata from India. He assured his friends, "Nobody will kidnap me, for nobody will want a ransom in rupees !"

When not on one of his travels in India or abroad, he stayed with his wife in a bungalow that definitely stood its ground when skyscrapers soared all around it. The sprawling bungalow, set amidst scores of shady trees, was a vestige of a by gone era of space and leisure. One room in the home was allocated for a workshop and a gymnasium which JRD proudly showed to his visitors.

Avid Reader

JRD preferred to spend a good deal of his time in what appeared to be his study. There was a whole shelf of books on aviation, another on military ventures and warfare, and one on sport cars and motor racing. He liked to read crime fiction, lighter books like David Niven's *Bring on the Horses,* and books by Louis L'Amour.

JRD was not just a collector of books but was an avid and enthusiastic reader. After one of my first interviews at his home, I returned with three of his favourite books including one by Alexander Woolcott, which JRD was keen I should read.

An Art Lover

As a patron of the arts, he was revered by India's artists, sculptors and performing artists; under JRD's tutelage, the Tatas became the biggest buyers, promoters and supporters of the art world in India. And as a philanthropist, he was respected for keeping alive and building up the tremendously active Tata charitable trusts.

Moral Values

The life of JRD Tata defines ethics and values in their truest sense showing us that it is possible to create a large, successful yet humane organisation.

JRD Tata was the Chairman of Tata Sons, the holding Company of the Tata Group of Companies which has major interests in Steel, Engineering, Power, Chemicals and Hospitality. He was famous for succeeding in business while maintaining high ethical standards. Under JRD's Chairmanship, the number of companies in the Tata Group grew from 15 to over 100. Monetarily, the assets of Tata group grew from Rs 620 Million to over Rs 100 Billion.

In the public mind, ethics in business is mainly identified with financial integrity. Important as that is, the real meaning of ethics goes beyond that. The dictionary defines it as "the science of morals in human conduct, a moral principle or code." It encompasses the entire spectrum of human conduct. Business ethics lays down how a person in business deals with his or her colleagues, staff and workers, shareholders, customers, the community, the government, the environment and even the nation at large.

To him, ethics included gratitude, loyalty and affection. It came about because he thought not only of business but also of people. In dealing with his workers he was particularly influenced by Jamsetji Tata, who at the height of capitalist exploitation in the 1880s and the 1890s gave his workers accident insurance and a pension fund, adequate ventilation at the workplace and other benefits. He wanted workers to have a say in their own welfare and safety, and he wanted their suggestions on the running of the company. A note that he wrote on personnel policy resulted in the founding of a personnel department. As a further consequence of that note came about two pioneering strokes by Tata Steel: a profit-sharing bonus and a joint consultative council. Tata Steel has enjoyed peace between management and labour for 70 years

Financial Ethics

JRD Tata was meticulous when it came to financial ethics. When a colleague pointed out to him in 1979 that the Tatas had not expanded as much in the 1960s and 1970s as some other groups had, he replied: "I have often thought about that. If we had done some of the things that some other groups have done, we would have been twice as big as we are today. But we didn't, and I would not have it any other way."

The well-known tax consultant, Dinesh Vyas, says that JRD never entered into a debate over 'tax avoidance', which was permissible, and 'tax evasion', which was illegal; his sole motto was 'tax compliance'. On one occasion a senior executive of a Tata company tried to save on taxes. Before putting up that case, the Chairman of the company took him to JRD. Vyas explained to JRD: "But sir, it is not illegal." JRD asked, softly: "Not illegal, yes. But is it right?" Vyas says that during his decades of professional work no one had ever asked him that question. Vyas later wrote in an article: "JRD would have been the most ardent supporter of the view expressed by Lord Denning: 'The avoidance of tax may be lawful, but it is not yet a virtue.'"

Always Polite

When he rang his staff in the office he would first ask: "Can you speak?" or "Do you have someone with you?" Except when he was agitated, he would never ask you: "Can you come up?" He was always polite.

In the Words of his Biographer: JRD's strong point was his intense interest in people and his desire to make them happy. Towards the end of his life he often said: "We don't smile enough." When I was writing The Creation of Wealth, he told me about his dealings with his colleagues: "With each man I have my own way. I am one who will make full allowance for a man's character and idiosyncrasies. You have to adapt yourself to their ways and deal accordingly and draw out the best in each man. At times it involves suppressing yourself. It is painful but necessary.... To be a leader you have got to lead human beings with affection." It is a measure of his affection that even after some of them retired he would write to them. He was always grateful and loyal.

Social Obligations

Decades later, Tata Steel workers had received several benefits. Then JRD looked further. In a speech in Madras in 1969 he called on the managements of industries located in rural or semi-urban areas to think of their less fortunate neighbours in the surrounding regions. "Let industry established in the countryside 'adopt' the villages in its neighbourhood; let some of the time of its managers, its engineers, doctors and skilled specialists be spared to help and advise the people of the villages and to supervise new developments undertaken by cooperative effort between them and the company."

To put JRD's ideas into action, the Articles of Association of leading Tata companies were amended and social obligations beyond the welfare of employees was accepted as part of the group's objectives. In the 19th century, Baron Edward Thurlow, the poet, asked: "Did you ever expect a corporation to have a conscience?" The answer from JRD Tata was: "Yes".

Whenever he could, he raised his voice against state capitalism. He never bent the system for his benefit. L.K. Jha recalled in 1986 that whenever JRD came to him when he was a Government Secretary, he came not on behalf of a company but the whole industry. He wanted no favours, only fairness.

In his last years he was very conscious of the environment and industry's part in spoiling it. He wrote in his Foreword to The Creation of Wealth in 1992: "I believe that the social responsibilities of our industrial enterprises should now extend, even beyond serving people, to the environment."

The JRD Tata Centre for Ecotechnology at the M.S. Swaminathan Research Foundation was created in furtherance of his desire.

To him India was not a geographical expression; it was people. When he was awarded the Bharat Ratna in 1992, Tata employees arranged a function on the lawns of the National Centre for Performing Arts in Mumbai. A gentle breeze was blowing from the Arabian Sea. When JRD rose to speak, he said: "An American economist has predicted that in the next century India will be an economic superpower. I don't want India to be an economic superpower. I want India to be a happy country." This was not only his hope, it was also his life. He brought sunshine into the lives of many of us who knew him.

Russi M. Lala was the director of Tata's premier foundation. The Dorabji Tata Trust for eighteen years. His book 'The Heartbeat of a Trust' is based on this Trust. He has authored a large number of books including 'Beyond the Last Blue Mountain: A Life of JRD'. He is also co-founder of the 'Centre for the Advancement of Philanthropy' and has been its chairman since 1993.

Social Service

Despite enormous pressures on his time, Tata took the role of a citizen very seriously and never failed to be of service to the nation. The concept of establishing Asia's first Cancer hospital in Bombay was implemented under Mr Tata's purview in 1941. The Tata Memorial Hospital was the first large contribution of India to the international fight against cancer. Citizen Tata's greatest gift to the scientific establishment came in 1945 when he gave the founding grant to Dr. Homi Bhabha to set up the Tata Institute of Fundamental Research. This Institute has proved to be, in Dr. Homi Bhabha's words "the cradle of our atomic energy programme".

A Humanist

One of JRD's subordinates, once said:

- I vividly remember my first meeting with J. R. D. Tata. I was a trainee in the Tata Trust at Bombay House. The suburban train I used to catch in the morning was delayed, and so I was late to the office. Doubling up the silent corridor of the Bombay House I thought, "why not use the east entrance lift to reach the office?" (This elevator was normally used by J. R. D. Tata.) While I was waiting for the lift, I heard firm, rhythmic footsteps behind me. I turned around to see that it was JRD himself. My heart skipped a beat! The moment I saw him, I gave an apologetic smile and hurried to take the flight of stairs nearby.
- Just a few steps covered; behind I heard the elevator door open, followed by a clap of hands. It was JRD, calling me. I froze. He then gesticulated to me, not condescendingly but with a gentle expression on his face, to join him in the lift. I got in, surprise writ large on my face. He then asked me which floor I wanted to go. When I told him that I was to the second floor, he instructed the liftman to stop there.
- Before getting out at the second floor, I thanked him once again and he, with his characteristic smile acknowledged and went ahead to his office in the fourth floor. This accidental rendezvous and his genuine gesture of concern were an unforgettable experience.
- After my training I joined the PR Department (PRD) at Bombay House. My boss was S. A. Sabavala, PR Advisor to the Tata Group and Executive Assistant to the Chairman. (He became director of several Tata companies later on.) A senior journalist, Sabavala was earlier Editor of *Free Press Journal* and Asia's Chief Correspondent for the *Christian Science Monitor*. It was a great experience working with him. And I had the privilege of working for JRD too on a couple of occasions. Once JRD was invited to be the chief guest for a function at the National Institute of Training in Industrial Engineering, Mumbai, by Air

Chief Marshal P. C. Lal, who was the Chairman of the Governing Body at NITIE. JRD was to deliver an extempore speech as his keynote address.

- Normally whenever the Chairman or any Tata Sons' Director delivered speeches, someone from the PRD would be deputed to cover the function. That time it was I who was on duty and I was told that since there would be no media persons I had to prepare a report to be released to the media later. When I reached the venue, there were half a dozen journalists gathered already in the hall. I wanted to tell JRD about it. But before I could meet him, he was off to the stage. And hence, I gave a chit to P. C. Lal to be handed over to JRD, which unfortunately did not reach him.

- JRD, who was known for his outspokenness and boldness, made some highly critical comments about the economic policies of the Central Government. This I informed to Sabavala, who after meeting the Chairman, told me that it was my duty to see that no newspaper carried the critical remarks of the Chairman the following day. There were six major dailies and I sprang into action meeting their correspondents. Early next morning I picked up all newspapers and read the reports. To my great relief JRD's trenchant attack of the government policies was trimmed down by the reporters of the dailies to appear very natural and constructive. My efforts were appreciated by my boss as well as the Chairman. But at heart I knew from the journalistic fraternity's gesture that it was their highest regard and respect for that towering personality called JRD that did the job silently. It was the same kind of respect from all sections of society that JRD enjoyed throughout his life. Writing speeches for JRD was a tough job. He was a perfectionist to the core. The speechwriters of Bombay House would stay very late flavouring his speech, which in his hands would thoroughly be redone!

- One could see his unique stamp of diction and delivery in every sentence. He never minced words. He was against phrases and slogans. He would clear his final draft speech at the last minute, and the PRD would then spring into action to release it to the press. JRD generally shied away from media exposure and honours. Once Venkatnarayanan, then Editor of *Onlooker and Free Press Journal* (Sunday Supplement) wanted to interview JRD and requested me to get an appointment. I took up his request with the Chairman's office. But I was told that JRD had gently declined it. I conveyed this to Venkat.

- That Sunday morning however I was surprised to see a front-page exclusive interview report with JRD. When I checked with the Chairman's Secretary, she said that Venkatnarayanan phoned up JRD that evening at his residence for a casual conversation. (Normally, at home JRD would pick up the telephone when it rang). Then I knew that the chat had been converted into an exclusive interview.

- There was another unforgettable incident with the media. This time it was Mrs. Bhatia of AIR, who came to interview JRD as a part of their feature on Family Planning programmes in India. JRD was then the Chairman of the Family Planning Foundation of India. Mrs. Bhatia with all her entourage entered JRD's office and started setting up mikes and so on. This annoyed JRD, who commented, "This is the whole problem with we Indians, we unnecessarily waste time on things like this."

- The interview started. Mrs. Bhatia asked her first question without addressing "Mr Tata". Indicating a pause, JRD politely suggested to her that she could begin the question addressing him as "Mr Tata". But Mrs. Bhatia tried to explain to him that only his statements in edited format would be aired and not her questions. But when JRD insisted on this formality, I asked Mrs. Bhatia, why she couldn't do what JRD wanted.

- What I intended as an intervention to cool down tempers, on the contrary, infuriated JRD, who shouted at me to mind my own business. Finally, the programme was aired. JRD's interview was edited to sound as only statements from him, as just a part of a larger feature on family planning. That was my last meeting with the Chairman.

- As a student activist, I had a totally negative view of industrial houses in the country. But later, working with the Tatas, I found that they belonged to a different kind of industrialists with their philosophy of nation-building through industrial revolution, constructive philanthropy, etc.

- In 1968, I interviewed JRD for *Mathrubhoomi Weekly*, a leading Malayalam publication, in which I had reported the enterprising industrial initiatives of the House of Tata, the dynamism of JRD and how the Tatas were good corporate citizens. This surprised many of my former Communist colleagues and even enraged some hardcore elements. When my interview saw print, I was on my annual leave at my native place, a village on the outskirts of Thallassery, in North Kerala. That weekend I went to Thallassery town, blissfully unaware of the storm brewing in the teacup of the extremists. I got down from the bus only to land in front of some Naxalite leaders.

- The legendary K. P. R. Gopalan was among them (K. P. R. Gopalan, a well-known Communist leader, during his days in the Congress as a freedom fighter was decreed to be hanged by the British rulers, but was saved from the gallows on Gandhiji's appeal).

- As soon as he saw me, he caught me by my collar and scoffed at me, "When did you become the mouthpiece of capitalists, young man? Are you not ashamed?" The others too jeered at me. I quietly took KPR aside and sat with him for half an hour explaining about the Tatas and the good work they were doing. He might not have been fully convinced by what I told him but I could see a change in his eyes and facial expression.

- There were innumerable incidents and anecdotes quoted by many writers from the life of JRD that reflect the great personality of this Captain of Independent India Inc. One such happened years back during his visit to the Lockheed aircraft factory in the US. Feeling thirsty, JRD saw two water dispensers at the factory — one for blacks and the other for whites! JRD went straight to the one for blacks.

The officials of the factory tried to lead him to whites' side. But he declined and drank water from the black's side, stating that he too was a non-white!

- This act reportedly prompted the authorities of Lockheed to discontinue the practice of providing separate water facilities for blacks and whites in their premises. J. R. D. Tata's simplicity, honesty, fairness, fearless demeanour, patriotism, service mentality are all exemplary characteristics to be emulated by the entrepreneurs and industrialists alike.
- Do we ever realise that most Westerners are Karma Yogi's par excellence. They may not be aware of the subject meaning of the word (or the word "Karma Yogi" itself)... Yet they have practiced and followed Karma Yoga since times immemorial, not willingly but inherently. They were not even aware of the purport of it! To be or not to be is not the question but inherently following a form of Yoga best suited to needs of today, what more could a person of the present Materialistic World ask for!!
- Karma Yoga stands for doing your duties towards your own self, family, society and masses without a feeling of doubt, obligation or lust but as a duty one has to perform in the service of God. Karma denotes one's capability to think (invoke positive or negative thoughts) followed by action (thoughts in crystallised form). None can perform even a single act without a thought preceding it! Can you?
- The correct approach towards the path of Karma Yoga is living in the present (now or never). The fleeting seconds passing by are the true actual moments within your grasp. You have absolutely zero control over the past events. You can exercise 100 per cent control over the future by controlling your present!!.
- Yoga denotes trying to communicate with the Almighty through various means. Means or paths are only three... Jnana Yoga, Bhakti Yoga or Karma Yoga. When you try to follow the Karma path... you are called a Karma Yogi for, in fulfilling the requirements of self, family and society

you are doing an act of His (God). Satisfaction obtained by such deeds is thus, a prayer completed!!

- Those who make prayers as their only solace of Life like Priests, Swamis, Sadhus and Munis, etc.... are called Bhakti Yogis. Those who embrace Jnana as their chief aim of Life... through introspection and Self Realisation reach their destined goal of Life are followers of the Jnana Yoga path.
- The path of Karma Yoga is simpler and easy to follow for you neither have to leave your family and more so enjoy all comforts of Life but via this path you can never reach the goal in one Life span (Who knows what we shall be in our next Life! It is always desirable to divert ourselves from the path of Karma Yoga to Bhakti Yoga or Jnana Yoga in the present life).
- At every stage of Life you also invariably follow the path of Bhakti Yoga while making your prayers (though inherently). Bhakti Yoga alone is capable of taking you towards God but in Jnana Yoga you have the added advantage of solving all your queries before you realise God. A Jnana Yogi is competent enough to guide the whole Humanity towards the Ultimate goal of Life... The culmination of all your prayers... God - Realisation!

Jehangir Ratanji Dadabhoy Tata conjures up the memory of a man whose life and achievements could be best described in the words of Shakespeare: " His life was gentle and the elements so mixed in him that nature might stand up. And say to all the world,' This was a man!". JRD Tata was born in Paris 1904 and his father was Ratanji Dadabhoy Tata and his mother was a French lady. From a very young age he imbibed the ideals and philosophy of the Tatas which were refreshingly different from those of other industrial houses. Money-making or profit-making always remained secondary to the attainment of higher objectives in life. And JRD's life was a saga of such a life. He was just not the Emperor of the business kingdom of Tatas he was a multifaceted personality, a far-sighted, sagacious captain of the industry, an adventurist, a visionary and above all a great philanthropist.

JRD Tata received his education in France, England and Japan and served in the French military and on his return to India he became the head of the Tata group at fairly young age and continued in the position as chairman for five long decades heralding a new chapter in the success story of Tatas.

The pioneering philanthropic work that he planned and executed with missionary zeal led to foundation of institutions which are household names today. In 1941 came into existence India's first cancer hospital in Mumbai The TATA Memorial Centre for Cancer Research and Treatment which is the destination for thousands of cancer-stricken patients all over the country. Similarly he founded the Tata Institute of Social Sciences which is premier institution in this field. Perhaps the establishment of Tata Institute of Fundamental Science was one of his monumental achievements which scientists of the country would always remember him in great reverence.

He was a true humanist who would inspire the future generations to dedicate themselves to the cause of humanity and let bow our heads to the memory of this greatest son of India.

Progressive View

In the field of labour welfare and relations, Tisco pioneered concepts long before they were practised in the West. It introduced the eight-hour work day in 1912. Three years later, employees were given free medical aid. By 1920, benefits such a leave with pay, a pension and accident compensation were provided to Tisco's workers. Maternity benefits were added in 1928 and a profit-sharing plan was instituted in 1934.

In 1957, Tisco set up a joint consultative worker-management council to handle employee grievances. Two and one-half years ago it became the first Indian company to conduct a social audit of its activities.

Ratan, however, might take a more pragmatic view than his uncle Tata's social role, and this might work against his aspirations to succeed JRD. Questioned over the costs of the social commitments at Jamshedpur and whether he would emulate JRD in spending as much time managing the various trusts as managing the business, he replied, carefully hedging his words: "I do believe that the founder's traditions should be continued. But I also recognise that profit motives must also be met. One issue cannot be isolated form the other. "In short, perhaps there is scope for a little more hard-boiled look at some of the facilities we are giving. Times do change."

Passion for Flying

JRD's passion for flying was fulfilled with the formation of the Tata Aviation Service in 1932. The first flight of Indian Civil Aviation took off at Drigh Road airfield in Karachi on October 15, 1932, with Mr Tata at the controls flying the Puss Moth solo to Ahmedabad and on to Bombay. In its first year of operations, the Tata Aviation Service, achieved cent per cent punctuality and chalked up a profit of Rs. 10,000.

On every flight which Tata flew, he made key observations and suggestions to emphasise on the quality of service. Even though, over the years, Air India International had struck a high note for Indian Aviation, the domestic airline scenario was in a mess. The government decided in 1953 to nationalise the entire airline business and invited Mr Tata to chair the enterprise. He devoted a disproportionate time with Air-India while his group companies were all run by efficient chief executives he had personally recruited.

In 1978, Tata's services in Air-India were terminated by Morarji Desai, India's Prime Minister. This was a body blow for JRD and compared the experience to losing a child he had nurtured for years.

4

Architect of Modern India

The doyen of Indian industry Jahangir Ratanji Dadabhai Tata was popularly and lovingly known as JRD Tata. He was called so because of his vast industrial empire. Apart from industrialist par excellence, he was a keen and active supporter of modern science and technology, a connoisseur of arts, an expert manager who supported excellence in education in all branches and above all, a fine example of a rare combination of scientific temper, humility and the milk of kindness.

'No Secret' JRD Tata replied once when he was asked what was the secret of his success in business, "Just Long hours", he used to put in seventy five to eighty hours of work a week. That makes good about twelve to thirteen hours in a day.

Contribution to Country's Development

Jehangir Ratanji Dadabhoy Tata, JRD to the world, remained the undisputed doyen of Indian industry, widely respected for his contribution to the development of Indian industry and aviation in particular. Apart from being a businessman par excellence, he was a patron of the sciences and the arts, a philanthropist and yet a man with a passion for literature, fast cars, skiing and flying. For his unparalleled excellence in business management, he came to be referred to as chairmen's chairman.

Outstanding Contributions

JRD's outstanding contributions to India were the Tata Airlines he pioneered in 1932, and TELCO (Tata Engineering and Locomotives Company; now simply Tata Motors) and the TIFR (Tata Institute of Fundamental Research) in 1945. In the 1930s, flying was a rich man's sport and few could afford, or even took, commercial flights. Hundred days after launching the airline, in an address to the Rotary Club of Bombay, JRD conceived the future of aviation, as one that would knit India closer. It may be noted that at that time, the Tata Airline was only carrying mail received at Karachi from England to Bombay and South India.

Telco began with locomotives, but he foresaw it becoming a great engineering company of which Tata Iron and Steel Company (Tisco; now Tata Steel) was the springboard. When JRD started Air India International in 1948, there were no international commercial airlines except those of Europe and America. JRD made Air India's presence felt internationally. He never expected to compete in size with the giants who flew across the Atlantic, but he had the conviction that Indians, with their tradition, could excel in hospitality and service. He established that point when, at one time, three out of four passengers on Air India International were from foreign lands.

When Morarji Desai dismissed JRD as Chairman of Air India in 1978, there was an uproar. *The Daily Telegraph* of London said that JRD had made Air India "one of the most successful airlines". It called JRD "a legendary figure known to legions of executives around the world and envied by most for his success." The dismissal, the paper added, was apparently for political reasons and "it brought Desai some of the worst publicity since he took office (as Prime Minister)".

In his book, *Empires of the Skies*, Anthony Samson called JRD "the most long lasting of all pioneers" who insulated his airline from favouritism in appointments. The highest aviation awards came JRD's way, including the Daniel Guggenheim Award first given to Orville Wright. He was active in Air India from 1932 to 1978 — a record. He gave India and Indians pride in the first company to make its mark internationally — a faith that they could hold their own in the comity of nations.

Sadly, JRD's dream and recommendation that government enterprise and private industry should participate in ventures with the private sector, as happened with Air India, was not accepted. State capitalism was the path chosen by Nehru. Private industry, hamstrung by the licence-permit raj, resorted to political and bureaucratic manipulation of the system. JRD was never drawn into it. He held to his principles when others, compromising theirs, raced ahead.

A little known contribution of JRD is the creation of the first software company in India and today the largest Indian outfit — Tata Consultancy Services. In an address on the Birth Centenary of JRD, Professor M. G. K. Menon, a former Director of TIFR and a good friend of JRD, said that way back in the 1960s, he (Menon) had mentioned to JRD about the possibility of India participating in the emerging field of software. "He (JRD) referred to this topic in the boardroom lunch discussion. To cut a long story short, the Tatas embarked on setting up TCS (in 1968) under the dynamic leadership of Mr F. C. Kohli. Today, TCS is a jewel in the crown of Tatas."

Though not directly connected with the Tatas and industry, it is JRD whose support to Dr. Homi Bhabha, and sharing his vision, that led to the setting up of the Tata Institute of Fundamental Research and, subsequently, the pursuit of atomic energy in India. Homi Bhabha called the TIFR "the cradle of atomic energy in India". M. G. K. Menon, who succeeded Homi Bhabha as Director of TIFR, observed: "Without support provided by Jeh, history would have been very different. Homi Bhabha may not have stayed on In India; TIFR may not have come into existence, as it is now. Jeh's was the hand that directed fate as it turned out to be."

JRD also contributed to starting the debate on family planning in 1951 and had he been heeded, as he should have been, many of the problems India faces today would have been mitigated even before they were born. If it is some consolation, a year before he died, JRD did receive the UN Population Award.

With Boeing's jets, JRD foresaw global tourism taking off, and though it took a few years to start, he encouraged the expansion of Indian Hotels which had then consisted of only one property —

the Taj Palace Hotel. Today, this landmark of Mumbai is the flagship of the largest chain of hotels in India.

JRD was also the first industrialist to move beyond the welfare of his own workers to that of the surrounding areas in which the Tata companies and factories operated. He did not want his companies to be islands of prosperity in a sea of poverty.

Great Institutions Established

The house of Tata took a leading role in setting up great institutions like Indian Institute of Science in Bangalore and Tata Institute of Fundamental Research in Mumbai. He believed that the lack of proper conditions and intelligent financial support hamper the development of science in India.

JRD Tata provided the necessary financial support to Dr. Hemi Habra to establish the Institute of Fundamental Research. The uniqueness of JRD is seen in yet another facet. He headed a group of engineering industries. His passion for building institutions for excellence was not limited to the field of technology. He was aware of the consequences of social science not keeping pace with growth of physical sciences. It was this deep insight which prompted to identify potential social scientists in several voluntary groups set up to help victims of various calamities and to establish Tata Institute of Social Sciences. Soon this institute acquired international standing and has contributed substantially to social sciences.

Cancer was, at that time, a dreadful and new disease. This disease could be treated only in advanced countries at enormous cost. Again JRD took interest in setting up the Tata Memorial Centre for Cancer Research Treatment for cancer comparable to that available in western countries is now available in India at affordable costs.

One of the most important aspects of his life was that he was a great and an expert pilot. One of his hobbies was flying. He established 'Air India' - the first company in Indian aviation industry. He was the first chairman of Air India. Thus JRD Tata was an amasing personality. The capability of JRD to convert hurdles into opportunities must stand out as unique role model for his countrymen.

The contribution of a great industrialist can be measured in terms both tangible and intangible. Tangible, as in the factories and plants he may have set up. Perhaps, more important, is his contribution to the spirit and thinking of the nation. J. R. D. Tata's contribution is on both counts.

JRD's life spanned almost the whole of the 20th century, from 1904 to 1993. He inherited 14 companies. When he stepped down as Chairman of the Tata Group, there were 95. Had he not been constrained by the licence-permit raj, there is no saying what he could not have done, not just for the Tatas, but for the country. When one of his associates had wondered if the Tata Group had expanded in the last couple of decades as much as some others. JRD firmly replied that had the Tatas adopted the means some others had, "we would have been twice as big as we are today. But we would not want it any other way."

Father of Civil Aviation

Air India is India's national flag carrier. Although air transport was born in India on February 18, 1911 when Henri Piquet, flying a Humber biplane, carried mail from Allahabad to Naini Junction, some six miles away, the scheduled services in India, in the real sense, began on October 15, 1932. It was on this day that JRD Tata, the father of Civil Aviation in India and founder of Air India, took off from Drigh Road Airport, Karachi, in a tiny, light single-engined de Havilland Puss Moth on his flight to Mumbai (then known as Bombay) via Ahmedabad.

He landed with his precious load of mail on a grass strip at Juhu. At Mumbai, Neville Vintcent, a former RAF pilot who had come to India from Britain three years earlier on a barn storming tour, during which he had surveyed a number of possible air routes, took over from JRD Tata and flew the Puss Moth to Chennai (then Madras) via Bellary.

For Population Control

Tata was among the first Indians to be drawn to the cause of population control when he realised the drag unchecked population growth could have on the country's developmental efforts. It was in 1951 when he came across statistics which revealed that the country had crossed the mark of 350 million people, Mr Tata sounded out Prime Minister Pandit Nehru on the issue and the latter ignored it.

JRD didn't wait for the government to act, but part funded Mrs. Avabai Wadia's efforts in starting the Family Planning Association of India. In 1970, he started the Family Planning Foundation jointly with the Ford foundation and was instrumental in conditioning the thinking of an entire generation, treating the issue as one of essential transformation of the society. For his crusading endeavours in the field, Tata was bestowed the United Nations Population Award in 1992.

JRD...think Big, but Check the Details

Quiet spoken, with piercing green-blue eyes, and aquiline nose and an aristocratic air, JRD remains a much revered figure within the Tata organisation and some what of an institution abroad. His October feat was a front page story in *The Times of India*, featured under a three column headline: "JRD re-enacts historic flight".

A casual dresser, he refrained from the ostentatious lifestyles of many Indian industrialists, preferring to live in a rented bungalow surrounded by skyscrapers in downtown Bombay.

JRD scoffed at the idea of being characterised as the Rockefeller of India. "I have never had an interest in the accumulation of wealth." He says. "I have always been more interested in what wealth can do for the betterment of society.

> "I suppose the big difference between the Tatas of India and the other great founders of trusts and foundations is that, while the Fords and the Rockefellers have remained very wealthy, the Tatas have retained very little individual wealth."

He reckoned that his personal wealth was probably just over $200,000, noting: "I am not even close to being a dollar millionaire, because whatever I inherited I put into a charity trust many, many years ago."

Though he rarely flied later, a sense of the young aviator's zeal for adventure lingered on in the ritual winter skiing holiday in the Swiss Alps. "I used to go skiing for three weeks but have cut it back to one week in the last three years." He said in a rare concession to the frailties of age. "When I turned 60, I found skiing a most strenuous sport."

Age had not changed his penchant for perfection, nor his habit of wanting to get involved in everything. "My standard has always been to aim for perfection, if you want to achieve excellence," he said.

"He's a great one for details, spending hours discussing the precise meaning of a word or looking up a date," said a Tata director. Others accused him of periodically scrutinising the second floor of Bombay House, where his office was located, to ensure that the pictures were hanging straight on the walls, the floors were scrubbed and the guards had all the buttons on their uniforms.

As for his round robin approach to making decisions. JRD believed that it all stemmed from when he become chairman of the Tata group at the age of 34. "I had to deal with executives who were older and more experienced than me," he said. He was firmly convinced that his ability to get consensus was one of his greatest strengths as a manager.

Others saw it differently. "He thinks around a decision too much," said a colleague. "He should go with his instincts. Invariably, they prove right. But he ends up with nothing, because he lets you, me and the lamppost all have their say and then tries to take account of all the opinions." Bounding up and down with pulsating energy from a chair in his huge, sparsely furnished office at Tata's headquarters in Bombay, he pinned the blame squarely on nearly four decades of ideological government policies aimed at holding back the development of large companies.

"Anti-monopolies legislation and a system of government licensing of new products were used to ensure that there would be no large concentrations of economic power in private hands," he said. "This prevented us from growing within our own sectors of industry. It also restricted our expansion into new industries."

Later, however, the climate for big business in India improved considerably. One reason for the transformation was that Prime Minister Indira Gandhi appeared to have concluded, after years of service to socialism, that "bigness" in the private sector was not necessarily bad.

With favourable business conditions auguring a new era of opportunity, JRD saw the urgent need for a more cohesive and unified group approach to expansion and diversification. Ratan's appointment was a first step in this direction.

One of Ratan's first acts after taking over as chairman of Tata Industries in October, 1981, was to call for a reassessment of Tata's business interests. The study, completed in a month, almost certainly recommended the rationalisation of several businesses. More important, it formulated a strategic 10 year plan designed to shift Tata's emphasis from capital-intensive basic and heavy industries to the more glamorous and rapid growth high-technology businesses that were so sorely lacking in the group's current make-up.

An essential part of the plan was to bring more synergy to group activities. Ratan pointed out that over the years the Tata companies had been allowed to become so parochial that there was no longer "a single directed objective of the group as a foremost endeavour".

Whether Ratan's plan would ever be implemented was open to a much speculation a the succession issue. The uncertainty was due to the peculiar equity and corporate power structure of the Tata empire. It really was a sort of corporate commonwealth that JRD ruled more by consent and persuasion than by the weight of the family's vested interests.

JRD and his relatives, in fact, had only minute equity holdings in the companies that made up the group. With limited financial resources, the Tata had always relied heavily on wide public participation to launch new businesses. Family shareholdings had been further diluted over the years by descendants endowing their wealth to trusts, a tradition started by the founder.

The Tata charitable and philanthropic trusts, which pioneered the principle of corporate participation in the development of the educational, social and scientific infrastructure of India at the turn of the century, received more than 80 per cent of Tata profits accruing to the parent company.

JRD was mindful of criticisms of Ratan's relative lack of experience and stature. He was also aware that Ratan did not command the allegiances from other top executives in the group that would be vital in preventing companies drifting away.

He admitted as much when conceding, "Ratan has the talent and now has been given the means to acquire the position of confidence that will show that he is fit to be a leader. I would like to continue the tradition of having a Tata lead this group. But I believe that the position has to be earned."

JRD clearly expected that the intense personal loyalty of Tata executives towards him would persuade them to go along with his wishes over his successor. If the level of loyalty among the ordinary workers was any thing to go by, it probably did.

Decades ago, several ministers of the Janata government began mooting the idea of nationalising Tisco. The union at the steel mill responded by passing a resolution warning that such a move "would lead to considerable discontent among the workers". The idea was quietly dropped.

This unsolicited act by the workers moved JRD. "The spirit of the workforce at Tisco is quite extraordinary." He said. "Such loyalty cannot be bought at any price."

To a large extent this loyalty was based on JRD's faithful adherence to the ideal of social responsibility set down by the founder, Jamsetji Nusserwanji Tata. Tisco for example, provided the sole livelihood for the 400,000 inhabitants of the city of Jamshedpur, which was named after the founder. For years, the company had made it a practice to defray the annual deficit (running at about $10 million) incurred by the city's educational, hospital and utility services. It also sponsored a wide variety of social and rural development projects in 125 surrounding villages.

5

Awards, Recognition and Achievements

JRD Tata was awarded the Legion d'honneur, by the French Government in 1954. In 1979, Tata was the recipient of the *Tony Jannus Award* for his distinguished contributions to commercial aviation. He also received the prestigious Guggenheim Medal for aviation in 1988. He was conferred India's highest civilian award Bharat Ratna in 1992 for his service to industry and nation building. In the same year, he was also bestowed with the United Nations Population Award for his crusading endeavors towards initiating and successfully implementing the family planning movement in India, much before it became an official government policy.

India's Highest Civilian Award Bharat Ratna

'Bharat Ratna' is the highest honour of the country. During the period from 1954 to 1992, it was conferred on 29 great persons. The first person to receive it was Dr. S. Radha Krishnan, a renowned philosopher and second President of India. Most of the persons, receiving this highest honour of the country are politicians. Then come the great authors and thinkers, philosophers, social workers, Engineers, Doctors, Devotees of Hindi, Artists and others. Nine persons were given this honour posthumous. Two foreigners also, received this top most honour of India.

A great magnet of Indian industries, JRD Tata, became a big personality in his life time. He conducted and directed successfully a number of industrial groups and companies for five decades Sri Tata, is not only a successful industrialist, but also a able administrator, enthusiastic player, courageous pilot and a popular orator. Thus, his field of action is very wide and extensive. His personality is many sided and influential. For his long services to the development of the industrial world of India, the Government of India, by conferring Bharat Ratna, on him, honoured not only a great Indian but also the symbol of the top most industrialist of the country.

After independence, a non-politician, a great industrialist was given the country's highest honour—Bharat Ratna, to JRD Tata. In furthering industrialisation of the country and establishing with the field of business, trade and industry, a clean working style, the contribution of JRD Tata has been unique and very remarkable. Besides this, he has the credit of finding a place for the Tata Group of Industries on the map of the world. With his long life a number of bear tales have been associate. The full name of Sri JRD Tata is Shri Jahangir Ratanji Dada Bhai Tata. He was born in Paris (France) on 29th July, 1904. His father, Sri Ratanji Dada Bhai Tata did export business in Paris. His mother Smt. Sufen was a French Lady. Jahangir had his school education in the Cathedral school in Bombay, he spent his holidays with his parents in Paris (France). During the first great war, he spent two years in Yakohama a city in Japan. After his school education, Jahangir jee went back to his parents in Paris.

In France, he was conscribed in the Army. He spent one year, the year of 1924, with the mounted regiment in Algeria. At that time. Jahangir's father Sri Ratanji tata had a mind to send him to Cambridge for higher education, but he ultimately decided to appoint him as assistant to John Peterson, the General Manager of Tata Steel Works. John Peterson was a Scott and was mad after work. He arranged an extra table for Jahangir in his office Jahangir worked with him for five years, and during these years, every paper marked for Peterson used to pass through Jahangir. Talking of that period, Jahangir says that he had to work for 75 hours a week, i.e.. *12½* hours per day.

After his father's death in 1926, JRD was appointed Director of Tata Sons. Before that, at the age of 15 years, JRD had a mind to be a pilot. In 1929, he was the first Indian to get a commercial licence. In the thirties, he started Tata Airlines. In 1932, he made the first commercial flight between Karachi and Bombay by one engine piper plane. This air service, in course of time, turned into Air India.

After the death of the chief of Tata Industries Group Sir Nauroji Sakalat wala, in 1932, Sri JRD Tata was made its chairman. He guided the Tata Group for more than forty years, and then handed over its leadership to comparatively young Ratan Tata Even then, JRD took deep interest in the working of the Tata Group. JRD had played great role in solving the dispute regarding a few appointments in TISKO during the last days. Under the leadership of JRD Tata Industrial Group started many Companies, viz. Chemicals, Electronics Engineering, Tubes, Voltas, Tata Services. Exports, Tata Industries Limited, etc. Besides this, he also established companies at Singapore and Malasia Tata Companies have been manufacturing steel for the last so many years. They manufacture light and heavy vehicles (Trucks), manufactures computers. They do other types of business as well, such as hoteling and printing. Good quality is the speciality of the Tata Companies. They have established new standard of quality in every branch.

By establishing many industries the Tata Group have provided employment to lakh of people and made them prosperous. No doubt, they earned mammoth wealth, but they made use of it in public interest and well-being the people of Tata Industrial Group consider Tata as incarnations of God. His qualities of business capability, industrial talent and sympathetic humanism are admired everywhere.

Some years back the magazine Life had brought out that part of this great industrialist knowledge of which very few people had. On him, a feature film was made for which they had appointed a female journalist who would watch his everyday activities and may take photographs of their every action at home. According to JRD Tata, she was a gentle girl who discharged her duties with full devotion. The aspects of his life which were exhibited in the magazine Life were—Tata as the president of the progressing industrial field of Tata, his managerial capacity and sharp intelligence.

Various Awards

Mr. JRD Tata was conferred on with *"Padma Vibhushan Award"* in the year 1957. In 1992 during his lifetime, he was awarded the highest Civilian Award of the Government of India, the *"Bharat Ratna"* Award. The Bharat Ratna award is rarely awarded to people during their lifetime.

ICAO Honour

Dr. Asaad Kotaite, president of the ICAO Council, conferred the Edward Warner Award on JRD Tata, the Indian aviation pioneer and longtime Chairman of Air-India on Oct. 2, 1986 at Montreal.

The award, consisting of a gold medal and a diploma, was presented to Mr. Tata in a ceremony during the 26th Session of the ICAO Assembly in the presence of high officials attending the Assembly and dignitaries from the Government of India.

Dr. Kotaite praised Mr. Tata's outstanding contribution as an aviator and industry leader as well as a father figure who has seen international aviation develop from its modest beginnings to its present dimensions.

'We are privileged to honour an outstanding figure. JRD Tata truly belongs among the great aviation pioneers who foresaw the potential of the aeroplane and capitalised on it when it was no more than a lightweight machine for daredevils,"

Dr. Kotaite said.

Jehangir Ratanji Dadabhoy Tata, a citizen of India, born in 1904, was the first person to qualify as a pilot in India in 1929. In 1932, with an operating fleet of two second-hand Puss Moths, he founded Tata Airlines, himself piloting the inaugural air mail service from Karachi to Bombay (a feat which he re-enacted fifty years later at the age of seventy-eight in an aircraft of similar type and vintage), out of these modest beginnings Air-India was born to grow into one of the world's major airlines. Mr. Tata remained all the while at the helm continuing to serve as Chairman when, in 1946, Air-India Ltd. was incorporated to take over Tata Airlines and when subsequently, in 1948, Air-India International was founded. He dedicated himself not only to establishing domestic air services in India but in developing new routes between India and Europe, India and South-East Asia and other parts of the world. To this day he continues to be a member of the Board of Air-India.

Mr. Tata's personal achievements, Dr. Kotaite noted, epitomise the gigantic strides of air transport in the last 50 years and the close association of the industry with the regulatory activities of ICAO in the various technical fields.

In promoting the development of aviation in India, Mr. Tata worked actively to build the aviation infrastructure in that country, particularly the provision of air traffic control and air traffic communication services. He was dedicated to the cause of international cooperation in the field of civil aviation and for twenty years was on the Executive Committee of the International Air Transport Association (IATA) serving also as Chairman in 1958-1959. His personal enthusiasm for flying and his faith in the potential of aviation is reflected in his role as the first president of the Aero Club of India.

Mr. Tata has received a number of high awards and honours in the course of his distinguished career. In November 1985 the Federation Aeronautique International conferred on him its highest honour, the Gold Air Medal.

Bestowed by the ICAO Council on behalf of the International Civil Aviation Organisation's 156 Member States, the Edward Warner Award is named after the first council president (1945-1957). A citizen of the United States, Dr. Warner guided ICAO through its earliest years, enlisting the cooperation of the nations to promote the safe and orderly development of international civil aviation. The Warner Awards were established by ICAO in 1958 for presentation to an individual or institution in recognition of outstanding contributions to the development of international civil aviation.

Achievements

Sri JRD Tata had several achievements to his credit. He had been involved in the achievements of Companies of Tata Group in one way or the other. Of some he had been the director, while of others the chairman or the president. He has been very closely associated with Indian Airlines and All India Sports Federation. He was in the General Assembly of limited Nations the representative of India in 1948. In 1974 he was declared honorary Air Vice Marshal by the I.A.F. He was honoured with at least three awards Durga Prasad Khetan Memorial Gold Medal 1970: August Award 1978 and Tonyjanes Award 1979. In 1983 on him was conferred Rank of Commander of Laison of Honour. He was adorned with honorary degrees D.Sc. by three universities of India, viz. Allahabad University in U.P.— 1947. D.Sc. Banaras Hindu University U.P.—1947. L.L.D. Bombay University Maharashtra—1981.

6

The Tributes

(Selected Articles on JRD Tata *by Admirers*)

A Legend Lives On (by Ratan Tata)

Mr. JRD Tata was a great visionary with tremendous personal charisma. For a person holding the position he did, he remained low-key, and lived relatively humbly throughout his life.

During the 53 years that he led the Tata group, he pioneered the group's involvement in the airline business, oversaw the early development of the group's activities in chemicals, commercial vehicles, computers and software services. In addition, he successfully led the group's growth in the areas of steel and other established business lines. Throughout his life, 'Jeh,' as we all knew him, gave much of his time and attention to various social causes to which he remained totally committed. These included family planning, gender equality and child welfare.

Jeh was a true nationalist. A proud citizen of India, with a strong desire to see India develop and shine, it was this strong national spirit that often led him to frustration when he felt that government action (or inaction) was shackling the free growth of India after its independence.

As Chairman of the Tata group for 53 years, Mr. Tata lived by the traditions and value system established by the founder, Mr. Jamsetji Tata, and these values have become deeply ingrained in the Tata group as one of the foundations on which the group has been built. Though Mr. JRD Tata is no more, the values, traditions and business ethics which he lived by will continue to be the driving force of the group. Mr. Tata made his mark on India during his lifetime, and his legend lives on after him.

JRD I Knew (by J.J. Bhabha)

JRD Tata's involvement in my life goes back more than 50 years. In 1929-30, I was posted at Jamshedpur with Tata Iron and Steel Company (Tisco) on a year's training in all departments of the steel works and the town. After a year I got my first appointment, as assistant chief town administrator, a post I held for a number of years. I had to work with two important officials. One was the town's deputy commissioner, L.K. Jha, then with the Indian Civil Service. The other was police superintendent Bill Stallard, an Englishman who was posted at Jamshedpur during the Second World War (he went back to England after the War). Both were close friends and we got on extremely well together in every way. At the outbreak of the War, I was already involved with the general administration at Jamshedpur and was concerned principally with operations relating to air-raid precautions.

At about that time, an unexpected problem cropped up. One evening, when my mother was having dinner with her invalid sister in the family dining room, a group of six Britishers burst into the room and asked for the servants to accompany them to the two upper floors of the house. Apparently, they had information about a clandestine radio transmitter in the premises. They rushed out of the house with the same discourteous haste with they had come in. My mother was so shaken by this incident that she telephoned Sir Ardeshir Dalal, Tisco's then managing director, requesting him to arrange for the transfer of my services from Jamshedpur to Mumbai (because my brother, Dr. Homi J Bhabha, could not be transferred from his high-altitude research work in Bangalore to Mumbai).

When Sir Ardeshir consulted the Tata Group's chairman, none other than JRD, he readily agreed to find a position for me in his office as a personal assistant. There was some background to his prompt agreement. A few years earlier, a communication had come from Jamshedpur seeking the head office's approval of the planned construction of a wall around the steel works. JRD had been sufficiently struck by the quality of the language used to find out who had drafted the letter. It was I. He must have made a mental note about wanting in his secretariat somebody who could write so well. Once I got involved with JRD's secretariat, I travelled with him whenever he went to Jamshedpur or Kolkata.

One such occasion was the chairman's visit to Jamshedpur in 1958, ahead of the Indian steel industry's golden jubilee celebration, which Prime Minister Jawaharlal Nehru had declared should be held at Jamshedpur. After careful consideration of various alternatives to mark this unique occasion, JRD decided that the most appropriate one would be to present the steel workers and other citizens of Jamshedpur with a park. A great deal of thought and planning, in which I was closely involved with JRD, resulted in the precise location and character of the 'Jubilee Park', with its terraced construction, fountains and flowering plants.

In his opening remarks at the function, Nehru, said, "I wanted to come not only because of the importance of these great steel works here and of the city of Jamshedpur, but even more because this place has become symbolic in some ways of the growth of Indian industry, starting from those days when Jamsetji Tata had the vision of developing the steel industry, and realising that steel was the base for any modern industrialisation of India."

He then added: "I have said that iron and steel are likely to play a vital role in human existence, but in the ultimate analysis I imagine that parks and flowers are more important than iron and steel. Flowers, parks and trees supply something which I imagine is of more basic importance to human beings and the human spirit than even iron and steel, and it was a very happy thought to commemorate the occasion of the jubilee of this great company by providing this beautiful park for all the workers and all the citizens of Jamshedpur."

No less important for me was JRD's involvement in the establishment and development of the National Centre for the Performing Arts (NCPA), Mumbai. At its inauguration by Prime Minister Indira Gandhi in December 1969 (observed to this day as 'founder's day' by the institution), JRD expressed his conviction that the NCPA would "play a powerful and unique role in the nation-building work under the dynamic leadership of my indefatigable and dedicated colleague, Jamshed Bhabha, who initially conceived the project, pursued it with formidable determination, and continues to be its moving spirit". Indira concluded her fine inaugural address with the following heartening words: "I wholeheartedly support the aims and objects of this institution. I think it is inspired by great vision and I sincerely hope that it will be sustained by a sense of dedication."

As a trustee of the Sir Dorabji Tata Trust, I had made the point that the Trust had funded several institutions of national importance, but these had all been in the areas of medicine and science and technology. No similar institution had been funded and nurtured for the arts and humanities, which form an important part of India's legacy. With the powerful support of JRD and Professor Rustum Choksi, then the Trust's managing trustee, a decision was taken to allocate an initial contribution of Rs 40 lakh on the condition stipulated by the Trust's then chairman, Sir Homi Mody — that a plot of 5 acres be found for the project in Mumbai.

The Maharashtra government initially said that the requisite area of 5 acres could not be found in the heart of Mumbai, but it agreed to my proposal for the reclamation by the Trust of an area of 5 acres from the sea. The government accorded its consent with two conditions: to ensure the requisite clearances for the construction of the planned 'west island freeway', and to secure official permission from its Water and Power Research Station in Pune.

This consent was so framed as to rule out any reclamation by the traditional method of solid-earth filling, which would divert the ocean's currents and cause erosion of the sands of Chowpatty, but in the form of a solid concrete platform of 5 acres to be constructed with piles in the sea. The formidable cost of such a platform ruled this option out. The government had, however, recorded its assent to the principle of reclamation, and I was, accordingly, able to secure its consent to carry out the reclamation at the end of Marine Drive (beyond the site of the Oberoi Hotel, then under construction).

It was at this stage that JRD played a valuable role in persuading the state minister concerned, Balasaheb Desai, to agree to add to the already sanctioned area of 5 acres an additional area of 3 acres, which had been earmarked by government for a Park. Finally, therefore, the total area allotted by the Maharashtra government for the NCPA amounted to the present total of 8 acres (approximately 32,000 square metres).

JRD's support to me continued to be expressed in many ways. I recall how, when I accompanied him to the state secretariat in Mumbai to meet the then chief minister, Shankarrao Chavan, I apologised for taking up his time when he had to attend to so many matters regarding the steel company. I shall never forget his reply: "No, Jamshed, you should not underestimate what the NCPA is doing. One day, perhaps, the NCPA's work may be more important for the country than the work of the steel company." These words of encouragement were memorable for me.

From Here to Eternity (Keshab Mahindra)

It all started with Jamsetji Tata. He laid down the standard for the Tatas, in terms of the pace the group set, the value system it abides by, and the sense of ethics that guides its entrepreneurial instincts. It would not be fair to comment on Jamsetji, but the concept of trusteeship that defines the Tata way of doing business comes from his convictions. This is very much in the philanthropic tradition of the Parsi community.

The Tata kind of mindset cannot be sired by a written code of conduct; it comes from deep-rooted belief. The Tata Finance example is an apt one. Not many companies would have handled this matter the way the Tatas did, openly and transparently. These days there's a lot of talk about corporate responsibility and accountability, about corporate governance. Actually, it's ethics and nothing else.

Jeh [JRD Tata] reflected this value system in abundance. He was a unique personality, never really interested in the nitty-gritty of running a company, occupied as he was with creating a wider idea about what the Tatas should do. Contrary to public opinion, Jeh was basically shy and reticent. But once you made friends with him he would be warm and candid.

Jeh could not suffer fools, but he had this extraordinary generosity of heart. I remember seeing him, during one of those Bombay bus strikes, stopping his car to give a lift to stranded commuters. Then there was this time I went over to his house. There was a hell of a racket going on and, when I asked the reason, he said the residence staff were watching television.

The abiding passion of Jeh's life was flight. Back in 1982, he was unwell in the run-up to the commemorative Bombay-Karachi flight [a re-enactment of JRD's pioneering airmail flight back in 1932]. Everybody tried to persuade him to opt out. I was dispatched to go and talk to him. He greeted me by saying, "Oh, you have arrived. They have sent you." I said I had come only to see him and he replied, "I know why you are here." I went back to Bombay House and I told the people there, "Don't stop him. You will kill him if you stop him. Make sure there is a co-pilot, a doctor and that there is a plane flying next to his." And that's what we did.

Jeh was a great nationalist (though he spoke English with a lousy French accent). He had an intense understanding of the country's problems (consider the interest he took in the population topic) and a wonderful zeal to help India's developmental efforts. Successive government placed plenty of trust in him, but Jawaharlal Nehru and Indira Gandhi never followed any of his ideas. That was pretty disheartening for Jeh. He was a close friend of Nehru's, but their relationship went a little sour when Jeh objected to the government putting up steel plants. And he was extremely disappointed when his airlines was nationalised.

He was a gentleman, no question about it, an incredible human being, and a great son of India. He cared a lot for people, but not necessarily on the golf course. I had the opportunity to play with him and — I have to say this — he was such a lousy golfer. He thought he knew everything about the game, and heaven help you if you had him for partner. He would after every stroke tell you what you were doing wrong. Then he'd get on that tee and hit 30 yards. I would go 150 yards and he'd say that wasn't the way to do it!

Naval Tata, unlike Jeh, was the kind of person who could get along with anyone and everyone. He had this tremendous capacity to gel with people from different walks of life. I watched him carefully when he was involved in labour relations and I got to know him and the way he worked over the last two years of his life (he forced me to take his position when he retired).

Naval was fantastic social company and he had this brilliant sense of humour. Of course, he was highly intelligent and well respected by labour. He was probably the only businessman that labour respected and had full confidence in. Part of this was due to his ability to get along with them, but it also had something to do with the fact that he was a superb listener.

Personalities aside, my association with the Tata Group stretches 43 years. I joined the boards of Tata Steel, Tata Chemicals and Indian Hotels in late 1960s and early '70s, and I continue to be on the boards of Tata Steel and Tata Chemicals. This experience gives a fair insight into the way the group has evolved.

Going back to the 1960s and '70s, despite their immense history, pedigree and credentials, the Tatas did not, I think, move fast enough, though they ran their companies efficiently and ethically enough. Mind you, there were serious problems then, in the '60s and '70s, because it was an entirely different ambience, a different environment. You couldn't do a damn thing without the government's consent.

Then came the mid 1980s — and look at the change that happened in the Tatas. Ratan Tata has to get the credit for this. I don't think we even realise the immense contribution he has made. Consider the expansion of a traditional company like Tata Steel and how far it has come in the last few years. Ditto with Tata Chemicals, Indian Hotels, the whole lot of them. I think it was Ratan who made these people feel that, hold it, it's great to have a Tata name, but you better perform.

Ratan had faith in his own vision. Everybody told him that [Tata Motors] would be a big flop but that's not how it has turned out. His telecom ventures may cost a fortune, but I think he is on the right track here too. These are things that people like the Tatas should be doing.

A lot of Tata money had to be spent in the last few years on consolidating the group's position. This had to be done because it's a different world from the one that Jeh operated in. He picked people he thought were competent and let them run their companies. In the process, he created what I call personal fiefdoms. He didn't mean to, but that's how life goes.

Ronald Reagan made a famous statement when he became the President of America. He said, "My job is not to run the government; I select and hire people to do that. My job is to lead the country." This is exactly what a company leader has to do. Leadership is a general sort of word. If you are the CEO of a company leadership means one thing. The definition changes dramatically when you are a group chairman.

It wasn't easy for Ratan, when he came in, to do it his way. His method of running companies was entirely different. He picked good people and gave them the authority to run the show but he kept a hold on them. And Ratan has got excellent people. That is a big difference and it is the basis of the transformation that has taken place in the Tata Group.

Appro JRD (by Sudha Murthy)

There are two photographs that hang on my office wall. Every day when I enter my office I look at them before starting my day. They are pictures of two old people, one of a gentleman in a blue suit and the other a black and white image of a man with dreamy eyes and a white beard.

People have asked me if the people in the photographs are related to me. Some have even asked me, "Is this black-and-white photo that of a Sufi saint or a religious guru?" I smile and reply "No, nor are they related to me. These people made an impact on my life. I am grateful to them." "Who are they?" "The man in the blue suit is Bharat Ratna JRD Tata and the black and white photo is of Jamsetji Tata." "But why do you have them in your office?" "You can call it gratitude."

Then, invariably, I have to tell the person the following story.

It was a long time ago. I was young and bright, bold and idealistic. I was in the final year of my master's course in computer science at the Indian Institute of Science [IISc] in Bangalore, then known as the Tata Institute. Life was full of fun and joy. I did not know what helplessness or injustice meant.

It was probably the April of 1974. Bangalore was getting warm and red gulmohars were blooming at the IISc campus. I was the only girl in my post-graduate department and was staying at the ladies hostel. Other girls were pursuing research in different departments of science. I was looking forward to going abroad to complete a doctorate in computer science. I had been offered scholarships from universities in US. I had not thought of taking up a job in India.

One day, while on the way to my hostel from our lecture hall complex, I saw an advertisement on the notice board. It was a standard job-requirement notice from the famous automobile company Telco [now Tata Motors]. It stated that the company required young, bright engineers, hard-working and with an excellent academic background, etc.

At the bottom was a small line: "Lady candidates need not apply." I read it and was very upset. For the first time in my life I was up against gender discrimination.

Though I was not keen on taking up a job, I saw this as a challenge. I had done extremely well in academics, better than most of my male peers. Little did I know then that in real life academic excellence is not enough to be successful.

After reading the notice I went fuming to my room. I decided to inform the topmost person in Telco's management about the injustice the company was perpetrating. I got a postcard and started to write, but there was a problem: I did not know who headed Telco. I thought it must be one of the Tatas. I knew JRD Tata was the head of the Tata Group; I had seen his pictures in newspapers (actually, Sumant Moolgaokar was the company's chairman then).

I took the card, addressed it to JRD and started writing. To this day I remember clearly what I wrote. "The great Tatas have always been pioneers. They are the people who started the basic infrastructure industries in India, such as iron and steel, chemicals, textiles and locomotives. They have cared for higher education in India since 1900 and they were responsible for the establishment of the Indian Institute of Science. Fortunately, I study there. But I am surprised how a company such as Telco is discriminating on the basis of gender."

I posted the letter and forgot about it. Less than 10 days later, I received a telegram stating that I had to appear for an interview at Telco's Pune facility at the company's expense.

I was taken aback by the telegram. My hostel mates told me I should use the opportunity to go to Pune free of cost — and buy them the famous Pune saris for cheap! I collected Rs 30 each from everyone who wanted a sari. When I look back, I feel like laughing at the reasons for my going, but back then they seemed good enough to make the trip.

It was my first visit to Pune and I immediately fell in love with the city. To this day it remains dear to me. I feel as much at home in Pune as I do in Hubli, my hometown. The place changed my life in so many ways.

As directed, I went to Telco's Pimpri office for the interview. There were six people on the panel and I realised then that this was serious business. "This is the girl who wrote to JRD," I heard somebody whisper as soon as I entered the room. By then I knew for sure that I would not get the job. That realisation abolished all fears from my mind, so I was rather cool while the interview was being conducted.

Even before the interview started, I reckoned the panel was biased, so I told them, rather impolitely, "I hope this is only a technical interview." They were taken aback by my rudeness, and even today I am ashamed about my attitude.

The panel asked me technical questions and I answered all of them. Then an elderly gentleman with an affectionate voice told me, "Do you know why we said lady candidates need not apply?

The reason is that we have never employed any lady on the shop floor. This is not a co-ed college; this is a factory. When it comes to academics, you are a first ranker throughout. We appreciate that, but people like you should work in research laboratories."

I was a young girl from small town Hubli. My world had been a limited place. I did not know the ways of large corporate houses and their difficulties, so I answered, "But you must start somewhere, otherwise no woman will ever be able to work in your factories."

Finally, after a long interview, I was told I had been successful. So this was what the future had in store for me. Never had I thought I would take up a job in Pune. That city changed my life in many ways. I met a shy young man from Karnataka there, we became good friends and we got married.

It was only after joining Telco that I realised who JRD was: the uncrowned king of Indian industry. Now I was scared, but I did not get to meet him till I was transferred to Bombay. One day I had to show some reports to Mr. Moolgaokar, our chairman, who we all knew as SM. I was in his office on the first floor of Bombay House [the Tata headquarters] when, suddenly, JRD walked in. That was the first time I saw 'appro JRD'. Appro means 'our' in Gujarati. That was the affectionate term by which people at Bombay House called him.

I was feeling very nervous, remembering my postcard episode. SM introduced me nicely, "Jeh (that's what his close associates called him), this young woman is an engineer and that too a post-graduate. She is the first woman to work on the Telco shop floor." JRD looked at me. I was praying he would not ask me any questions about my interview (or the postcard that preceded it). Thankfully, he didn't. Instead he remarked. "It is nice that girls are getting into engineering in our country. By the way, what is your name?" "When I joined Telco I was Sudha Kulkarni, Sir," I replied. "Now I am Sudha Murthy." He smiled that kindly smile and started a discussion with SM. As for me, I almost ran out of the room.

After that I used to see JRD on and off. He was the Tata Group chairman and I was merely an engineer. There was nothing that we had in common. I was in awe of him.

One day I was waiting for Murthy, my husband, to pick me up after office hours. To my surprise I saw JRD standing next to me. I did not know how to react. Yet again I started worrying about that postcard. Looking back, I realise JRD had forgotten about it. It must have been a small incident for him, but not so for me.

"Young lady, why are you here?" he asked. "Office time is over." I said, "Sir, I'm waiting for my husband to come and pick me up." JRD said, "It is getting dark and there's no one in the corridor. I'll wait with you till your husband comes." I was quite used to waiting for Murthy, but having JRD waiting alongside made me extremely uncomfortable.

I was nervous. Out of the corner of my eye I looked at him. He wore a simple white pant and shirt. He was old, yet his face was glowing. There wasn't any air of superiority about him. I was thinking, "Look at this person. He is a chairman, a well-respected man in our country and he is waiting for the sake of an ordinary employee."

Then I saw Murthy and I rushed out. JRD called and said, "Young lady, tell your husband never to make his wife wait again."

In 1982 I had to resign from my job at Telco. I was reluctant to go, but I really did not have a choice. I was coming down the steps of Bombay House after wrapping up my final settlement when I saw JRD coming up. He was absorbed in thought. I wanted to say goodbye to him so I stopped. He saw me and paused.

Gently, he said, "So what are you doing, Mrs. Kulkarni? (That was the way he always addressed me.) "Sir, I am leaving Telco." "Where are you going?" he asked. "Pune, sir. My husband is starting a company called Infosys and I'm shifting to Pune." "Oh! And what you will do when you are successful?" "Sir, I don't know whether we will be successful." "Never start with diffidence," he advised me. "Always start with confidence. When you are successful you must give back to society. Society gives us so much; we must reciprocate. I wish you all the best."

Then JRD continued walking up the stairs. I stood there for what seemed like a millennium. That was the last time I saw him alive.

Many years later I met Ratan Tata in the same Bombay office, occupying the chair JRD once did. I told him of my many sweet memories of working with Telco. Later, he wrote to me, "It was nice listening about Jeh from you. The sad part is that he's not alive to see you today."

I consider JRD a great man because, despite being an extremely busy person, he valued one postcard written by a young girl seeking justice. He must have received thousands of letters every day. He could have thrown mine away, but he didn't do that. He respected the intentions of that unknown girl, who had neither influence nor money, and gave her an opportunity in his company. He did not merely give her a job; he changed her life and mindset forever.

Close to 50 per cent of the students in today's engineering colleges are girls. And there are women on the shop floor in many industry segments. I see these changes and I think of JRD. If at all time stops and asks me what I want from life, I would say I wish JRD were alive today to see how the company we started has grown. He would have enjoyed it wholeheartedly.

My love and respect for the House of Tatas remains undiminished by the passage of time. I always looked up to JRD. I saw him as a role model for his simplicity, his generosity, his kindness and the care he took of his employees. Those blue eyes always reminded me of the sky; they had the same vastness and munificence.

One of a Kind (by Manek Dalal)

My association with JRD Tata goes back to many years, when I joined Tata Airlines [the original avatar of Air India]. I first met him at a party hosted by Jamshed Bhabha and his wife, Betty, at Mumbai's Willingdon Club. What struck me immediately about him was his willingness to and interest in taking to a junior employee such as me. He did this as if it were the most natural thing in the world, and not as the chairman of a company to one of his underlings.

I was impressed with the questions he asked and with his sharp mind. He expected prompt and intelligent responses (he could be scathing when confronted with shallowness). One of JRD's greatest qualities was this ability to treat everyone as an equal. He'd argue fiercely for what he thought was right, but he never gave the impression that you had to accept all that he said. He was keen to convince you he was right, but if you could persuade him otherwise he would accept your point of view.

I remember this incident when I was with Air India in London and we needed a new business premises. I had to move quickly to secure an expensive building in New Bond Street. I did not have time to wait for the sanction to come through from Bombay House [the Tata headquarters], so I paid what was called 'key money' (*pugree* in India). JRD happened to come to London a few days later and he was railing at me even as he was alighting from the plane. "I don't want to make side payments to people," he thundered. I asked him to see the proposition before letting loose and went on to explain how and why I did what I had to do. Big man that he was, he saw my side and immediately sent a telex back home: "Accept Dalal's proposition fully. Please put it up to the board and recommend that the chairman has suggested it."

This sense of fairness and decisive decision-making were characteristic of JRD. He could never suffer fools and pompous people; he was extremely intolerant of such types, but as a boss and as a human being he was quite remarkable. He could be impatient at times (he wasn't a saint in that respect), but he was a likeable person and a wonderful leader. He had a basic respect for human beings which was quite touching, and he was particularly sympathetic to the lower echelons of his staff.

JRD used to have this servant with several children and a wife. The man passed away and his wife and kids decided to go back to their relatives in Pakistan. JRD paid their airfare and, what's more, escorted them personally to Karachi. This was after arranging for their family to come from their village and pick them up at the airport. The junior staff — peons, liftmen and others — loved him; he would constantly be asking after them.

He was always curious about technology and the way things worked. I remember this episode from the time when a man called Sir Fredrick James was the managing director of the Tata Group's overseas arm in London. JRD had come calling and, on his way to the office, stopped by where the telephone operator sat. The lady's name was Mrs. Owen and she had this complicated switchboard in front of her. JRD promptly started trying to learn how she manoeuvred all those switches. He must have, in the process, messed up all the lines because Sir James was soon down in the lobby shouting furiously at Mrs. Owen for botching up his telephone. JRD was quick to the operator's rescue, saying, "It's all right, Jimmy, it was me."

JRD was a bit thrifty and he was never given to ostentatious displays of wealth. I recall going to his place for dinner in a Tata office car, which happened to be of American make. JRD used a home-grown Fiat those days, one that he himself drove. I joked that we couldn't have our chairman driving around so shabbily and he replied that he felt embarrassed to drive in those grand affairs. Fact is, he did have a bigger car — but that was mostly used to ferry his servants' children to the park and the beach.

Although JRD was chairman of an empire spread across several industries, it was the airline business — and aviation — that remained closest to his heart. His passion for flight was sparked when he was growing up in France and it stayed with him to his last days. Right to the end it still used to fascinate him that an aeroplane could carry 400-plus people, not to mention cargo and mail, and waft through the air at great speeds to far-flung destinations.

He was forever a flying man and he was the first Indian to become a licensed pilot. Here, too, his sporting nature and generosity of spirit marked him out. There was this prize instituted by the Aga Khan for the person who covered the Bombay-London stretch in the fastest time. JRD was pitted in this race against Aspi Engineer, who later headed the Indian Air Force. The two were flying in opposite directions and their paths happened to intersect in Cairo. Engineer was in trouble at that point with one of his aircraft's parts, and he did not have to resources to replace it. Realising that winning the prize meant more to his rival than himself, JRD gave him the spare part that he had. Engineer went on to claim the reward.

Tata Airlines (and Air India afterwards) was JRD's fondest love. The internationalism of the business was, I think, one reason why JRD felt a greater pull from it than he did from, say, the steel enterprise. This bias was so obvious that some senior Tata directors would jokingly criticise him for spending more time with Air India than he did on the entire Tata Group of companies.

JRD remained as chairman after Air India was nationalised and he continued to spend an enormous amount of time on it, though he got no money at all for it. He was very particular about details, sometimes ludicrously so. If the airhostesses displayed any unsightly bulges he would write a note asking them to be more particular about their fitness. He had this little black book in which he wrote all his comments every time he flew with the carrier. Beyond aviation, JRD liked adventure and he adored racing cars.

He was, obviously, one of India's leading entrepreneurs (the word wasn't even used those days). His go-ahead attitude separated him from lesser mortals and his vision was quite outstanding. He once told me he had won more recognition abroad than in India; this was before the government honoured with the Padma Vibhushan and the Bharat Ratna.

Jawaharlal Nehru admired JRD, but the leaders who followed did not have much time for his kind of person. They probably thought he was too western in his outlook. That's a pity because JRD had so much love for this country and its people. He had genuine affection for the poor, was extremely humane, and he was a truly good Indian.

Population control was almost a fetish for JRD. He thought India's destination would be defined by two factors: population and education (he always regretted not being able to go to Cambridge). He felt that the country's destiny lay in controlling its population and in ensuring its people were educated. He fervently believed that India had great intellectual talent.

Naval Tata was totally different from JRD. He had more patience than JRD and his leadership style, too, was different. If you were wrong about something, JRD would not hesitate to tick you off. Naval would be more kind. The one similarity between the two was their generosity.

Jamsetji Tata swam against the tide, not because he wanted to but because the tide was strongly against him. Indians faced a huge amount of prejudice then. It didn't suit British interests to have Indians progressing too fast in areas where the empire could be threatened economically. For somebody like him, coming from a colonised country and one considered backward, to even contemplate establishing a steel plant was out of the ordinary.

JRD: the Eternal Icon (by T.R. Doongaji)

As I set to pen this piece, I quite realise that there are many others, seniors and celebrities, who knew JRD Tata more closely than me and, so, would be more qualified to do the writing. All I can claim is that my good fortune had seen me positioned as a junior member of his secretariat in the late seventies. Again, so much has already been spoken and written about JRD in this centenary year of his birth that, at best, my effort cannot extend beyond reaffirming a few of his exemplary qualities. And, finally, there is no escaping the realisation that however extensive the effort, and however hard one may try, it would never be possible to constrict in words the 'spirit' that was JRD.

JRD's philosophy, and the ethos of the Group he symbolised, can best be described through lines, equally apt for Tatas, that I must borrow from an article I had come across some years ago, the title of which was "Business as a Spiritual Pursuit", which read: "(In Tatas) we have retained the fire of idealism and in its glow we have come to recognise that no wealth or power can be more valuable than our dignity; no loss or profit can be more critical than the loss of our credibility; no skills or qualifications can substitute the integrity of our character."

His unflinching and unwavering commitment to the highest principles and standards was the light that forever illuminated his path, inspired his speech and guided his actions. Surely there were those who did not necessarily agree with his views on issues such as the country's economic model, social concerns such as the growing population and business priorities and practices. And yet, even amongst such, I cannot think of one who could have ever doubted the nobility of his intent. No wonder then, JRD will always remain a symbol of integrity, of righteousness, of the highest ethical conduct and of credibility.

It amazes one to observe how successive Tata leadership has, for over a hundred and thirty years, zealously guarded, practised and propagated what internally in the Group is referred to as Tata values, the bedrock of the Tata edifice. It is this 'spiritual core' that differentiates Tatas from other business entities globally, as they all must struggle to compete and win in a material world.

JRD's commitment to perfection in whatever he said, did or wanted achieved, bordered on fanaticism. To borrow his own words, he was never satisfied with the second best, in any task, however small. Like Michelangelo, he believed that "trifles make for perfection for perfection is not a trifle." An inconsequential type in a note or letter would not get past him and back it would come, the word circled in turquoise blue ink (Chairman's ink as we called it) with the comment: "surely we know our spellings." Once, when complemented for my driving I enquired as to what made him approve of me he said "you did not rest your foot on the clutch pedal all the time." Nothing would escape his discerning eye. It would seem obvious then that the products and services of his companies had to be of the highest quality, the best in class; not ignoring, for a moment, the quality of corporate conduct that, in my view, remained always of paramount importance to him.

JRD had a deep, enquiring mind. He was curious; not only about things that mattered to business such as technology or finance; but also about places, people, music, medicine, literature, philosophy, religion, the arts and the sciences. He wanted to know just about everything. A lift in his car to children on their way to school was not just warmth and courtesy, which he had, in full measure; it was an opportunity to learn what they taught in school, an opportunity to catch a glimpse of the future. Building 'learning organisations' suddenly gained importance not long ago in the management lexicon. JRD, by himself, was a learning institution exploring ceaselessly, his thirst for knowledge never quenched. By any standards, therefore, he was truly 'educated'.

"Humility," said Bob Galvin, "does not mean that one thinks less of oneself, it means that one thinks of oneself less." If there could be one person that fits this description of humility, it would have to be JRD. He was humble in spite of the high pedestal on which he was perched and it was this quality that enabled him to constantly learn. He was far, really far, from being pompous. Unlike so many business leaders and executives who strive to remain in the media glare, he was not a man who cared to bask in the public eye. On one occasion when he entered a reputed clothing shop everyone just stopped going about their business unable to get their eyes off him. Realising what his (charismatic) entry had caused, he said loudly, but politely: "I have not escaped from the zoo. Why don't you ladies and gentlemen just ignore me. I am here to have an Indian style suit tailored for a function at which I am required to be present." That function was the one at which he was conferred the Bharat Ratna by President R. Venkataraman. "He touched power but remained untouched by it."

JRD was unusually warm and caring. Like Andrew Carnegie, he concentrated on "the ounce of gold" in his people and he did not focus on the tons of earth that must be mined to reach it. He said: "If I have any merit it is in getting on with individuals according to their ways and characteristics. At times it involves suppressing oneself. It is painful but necessary. To be a leader you have to lead human beings with affection." He inspired performance; he did not have to command it.

Leadership that depends on visibility alone survives for a given moment in time and tends to wither away with its passage. In the way in which he lived, through the strength of his character and the utter sincerity of his words and deeds, JRD touched and impacted not just minds but the soul of all people. He was a leader who neither craved or nor needed any visibility. His presence was pervasive; it could be felt, always, as it is even to this day. And, so, JRD lives on like a blossom perennially in bloom, its fragrance undiminished — the eternal icon.

The Man Behind the Icon (by S.A. Sabhavala)

There were three distinct phases of my life during which I was associated with JRD Tata. The first, between 1967 and '70, was when I was his executive assistant. The second was between 1970 and '75, when I was a director of Tata Industries in Delhi. The last phase was in Mumbai, when I returned from my stint in Delhi and became a director of Tata Sons, working, for part of my tenure, closely with JRD.

I remember him in these three distinct phases for what he gave me. As his executive assistant, I was amazed at the amount of time and energy he was willing to spend teaching me what he thought I should know. For instance, he taught me how to read a company's balance sheet. He got me interested in figures, something that, up until then, I did not like at all. Also, he taught me the real value of money and, most important of all, I learned that details are vital, even the most minute of them. For JRD, perfection was the key.

He was almost fanatical about cleanliness and tidiness in the office (I saw him, on occasion, instructing sweepers how to clean the carpet). While preparing a speech he would often get to a third draft, polishing the language, the structure of the language, the thought behind the language, until his staff was driven to distraction.

JRD wrote and spoke very well and I always thought that his first draft, his original thoughts as he put them down, were the best. I frequently complained to him that he spoiled things by diluting them, by making too many corrections and by probing too deep into his original thoughts, which by then would have lost some of its freshness. Many of his important speeches were sent out to his fellow directors for their comments. He would often want to incorporate some of these comments, thereby watering down what was a good, strong first speech. JRD was interested in doing things with his hands. No one who came to see him was safe from his inquisitiveness, particularly if you had a new watch on your wrist or a new piece of jewellery around your neck. He would want to take the stuff apart and then put it together. That may explain why he studied to become a mechanic (under the tutelage of Sumant Moolgaonkar at Telco). He even set up a workshop in his house to further this learning process.

Motherly Advice

We had picked up Mother Teresa in Jamshedpur. It was evening, the sun was setting and she was praying silently with beads in her hand. Now, JRD was a man who could never stop speaking. He kept talking to her, but she remained silent. I kept shushing him, saying she was praying. Then he asked her what the Tatas should do about the poverty that slum children had to live with. She turned to him and said, "Mr. Tata, you just do your job and get people employed. Leave the poverty to me." He shut up after that.

Aviation was, of course, JRD's greatest passion. He was also passionate about reading and writing, as well as children. He was interested in a wide variety of matters, and to each of them he strove to give time and energy in a way that was quite remarkable.

He was inquisitive about the people who worked for him; he wanted to know everything about them, particularly the manner in which they worked. I used to sit in a small room next to his office and quite often during the day I would find the interconnecting door open a little bit, with an eye looking in to see what I was doing. When I first came in, his peon told me never to cheat and hide papers that I had not worked on by putting them away in a drawer, because *saab* would come and open every drawer to see what work was pending.

During my time in Delhi I got to see the way JRD interacted with people. It was his genuine interest in people that gave him his charisma and, towards the end of his life, turned him into an iconic figure not only within the Tatas but across India.

He was very tolerant, always ready to accept a genuine mistake or a difficulty in understanding something he wanted you to do. What he would never accept was slackness of any kind. He was very quick to gauge whether you were working hard or not. JRD spent many hours in his office. The result was that his subordinate staff had to spend even longer hours there.

What JRD would have really liked to do was spend his life in aviation, but that was not to be. He was finishing his university education when his father suddenly died and he had to come back. Then came the chairmanship and that negated his passion for aviation. But Air India remained his first love; whatever extra time he had was devoted to the airline. Everybody in the Tatas used to complain about this, but there is nothing that they could do about it.

He had a tremendous knack with children, despite never having any to call his own. I remember the time I was in Delhi; whenever he came on his visits he would call my twin daughters over and spend hours with them. He would take them out, entertain them. The first time they went to a big hotel was with him. He would dilute their orange juice with a drop of gin and they would come back absolutely delighted. "Mama, we had gin today," they would proclaim.

He was marvellous with kids, those of colleagues, of friends and, at weekends in his home in Mumbai, those of the servants. Children were always around him. He never ceased to be amused by them, he never tired of them, and he was always patient with them.

JRD was quietly but intensely proud of India. What upset him most was the poverty, which he found almost degrading. He did what he could, of course, as chairman of the Tatas. All the street urchins near Bombay House and around his home at Cumballa Hill came to know him well — and he got to know each one of them. He sent many of them to school and he kept giving them clothes and toys.

The solution to the poverty problem, he believed, was education and, even more so, population control. He often quoted the Kerala example: reducing population growth through widespread education. His main thrust, his pet subject — outside the corporate world — was population control.

Every time he came to Delhi, whenever we called on a minister or the Prime Minister, he would before the end of the meeting invariably talk about the population issue. He would argue strongly that India wasn't doing enough on this count; he would plead with the people in power. He grew sad about this towards the end of his life, because he felt that very little was being done. But he remained proud of what had been accomplished in Jamshedpur, where in his lifetime the per capita population was brought below the all-India level.

JRD was an excellent time manger. He had his working life divided into almost ironclad compartments, and he would not deviate from these. If he had something to do every Monday morning at 10 am, he would do it Monday after Monday, no matter what came up. It was the same with his appointments. If he gave you an appointment, he would keep the time for you. He was also very strict about people trying to pass on work after a specified time. My orders as his executive assistant were never to accept anything at all, whoever it may have come from, after 5 pm.

JRD was always for progress. As he got older, he became increasingly conscious about choosing a successor. It took him a long time to appoint one, and he thought he had erred in delaying the decision. He felt that certain things had to remain constant: integrity, transparency, and the need for good governance. As for the rest, he was all for change, especially technological change. What annoyed JRD the most was lies. Untidiness or lack of cleanliness was another sore point, as was any form of unnecessary ostentatiousness. He lived austerely and he hated any form of extravagant expenditure.

JRD was an extraordinary man. He was extremely simple and very complex — at the same time. His great plus point was his simplicity of thought and action, reflected best in the way he lived. And, yet, he had an extremely sophisticated mind, and he enjoyed sophistication in all its forms. Anything crude and vulgar was abhorrent to him. This strange mixture attracted people to him. He was extremely polite. I remember flying with him on many occasions, me in the window seat and him near the aisle. People walking up and down would stop and talk to him, and he would respond as if he had known them all his life. And, inevitably, he would say: "Do come and see me when you are in Bombay." Needless to say, nine times out of ten the person would turn up. JRD would by then have forgotten all about the matter and it would be left to me to refresh his memory.

You always felt comfortable with him. He would go out of his way to put youngsters who came to see him at ease. When you came out of his room after, say, an interview, you felt like you had just met a friend or a family member. That was part of his greatness. It was instinctive.

Salute to a Great Man (by Prof. MGK Menon)

Here is a tribute made by an admirer of JRD Tata:

- Tomorrow is 29th July, the day on which JRD Tata was born in 1904. There will be events at a variety of places and in many institutions all over India to pay tribute to a man who was certainly amongst the greatest that India produced in the 20th century. Many in this audience knew him – some rather closely. As important as paying tributes to his great qualities, these will also be occasions to express a deep sense of gratitude for what he accomplished, and to analyse what made him an icon. He was truly a colossus who walked in our midst – but a gentle colossus at that. He was not only admired and respected but greatly loved. He was deeply humane.

- I am fully aware of the great honour and privilege done to me in being invited to give this talk. He was a generation older to me, but there was no difficulty whatsoever in my interacting closely with him; he was kind; I always felt good and uplifted after meeting him. He was a good listener, but asked penetrating questions. He was self-deprecating, and in many ways a person of humility, a quality which goes with greatness. This is, therefore, a unique occasion for me to pay my personal tribute to Mr. JRD Tata, whom I had addressed as Jeh for about three decades.

- There were many facets to Jeh's personality, interests, accomplishments and the legacy that he has left behind. As head of Tatas he had an undoubted position of leadership in business and industry of 20th century India. The diversity of activities under this umbrella in terms of areas, covering iron and steel, hydro and thermal power, aviation, chemicals, automotives, finance, fertilizers, agricultural and household products, construction, electronics and information technology and much else is truly amasing. Many represented wholly new initiatives when embarked upon, often involving advanced technologies. Jeh was constantly looking out for new leadership. He discovered and nurtured leadership; this was intrinsic to his philosophy. These leaders took new initiatives, opened up new industrial avenues and became household names in their time.

- But all was not 'a bed of roses'. He faced many ups and downs in all these various business enterprises. In dealing with these he never sacrificed integrity, which was always of the highest order - one of the great qualities that he possessed. He maintained the finest relations with labour. For him, business and industry was not a means for self aggrandisement but for national development. All these derived from Jamsetji Tata who for him was his role model.
- Apart from business and industry he was imbued with a great spirit of adventure, most significantly manifested by his foray into aviation: first personally and directly, and later, through an airline which all of us in India and many abroad learnt to love and use, when he led it. He loved speed, and enjoyed watching motor car races, particularly at Le Mans.
- He had a tremendous sense of curiosity, and an intuitive understanding concerning technical matters, whether it be in aviation, automobiles, energy, chemicals, information technology or steel.
- Each of the initiatives that he took would have justified his standing among the great. But Jeh could never be one to be restricted to one area or direction. He had an extraordinarily broad-ranging mind, with a keen intuitive feeling for the long range potential over a range of initiatives, and growing the people who could handle these.
- To cover his multifaceted personality and achievements would be truly impossible in one talk. It would make the coverage shallow and superficial, and would not do justice to him. Suffice it to say, he achieved greatness in his own right; and walked among the greatest that India was fortunate in producing in the 20th century. Perhaps India

was unique in many ways compared to anything that happened elsewhere in the world over this period in the leadership that was thrown up, that had a mix of long range vision, idealism, sacrifice, commitment and integrity and all the basic qualities that form the bedrock of all religions; Jeh represented all of this but always insisted that he was an ordinary human with whims, likes and dislikes, weakness, warts and all. This was India at its best; each leader was an icon. I do wonder why we do not have such role models today.

- In this talk I shall concentrate on an aspect not so well-known or talked about, which is the decisive contributions made by Jeh to the promotion and nurturing of science and higher education in India. In preparing this talk, I have spoken to many in the scientific community to find out what they knew about Jeh. They had only a dim awareness of him, as an icon. Only a few knew of any details of his actual contribution to the growth of science. I was amazed since they knew far more about much smaller personalities, who had contributed so trivially or superficially, but have received so much media publicity. This talk is an effort to put the record straight.

- A large part of what is in here is already covered in various publications concerning Jeh, or those related to him and the Tata Trusts. I therefore do not claim originality. My attempt is to bring out at one place his efforts relating to this one area, in an attempt to focus on his motivations, thought processes and insights on these matters, that few know about or appreciate, overawed as they are by the breadth and greatness of all else that he achieved.

- The Scientific Policy Resolution of the Govt. of India adopted on 4th March, 1958 which was placed before Parliament by Jawaharlal Nehru, and in the drafting of which Homi Bhabha had a significant role to play, opens with the statement:

"The key to national prosperity, apart from the spirit of the people, lies, in the modern age, in the effective combination of three factors, technology, raw materials and capital, of which the first is perhaps the most important, since the creation and adoption of new scientific techniques can, in fact, make up for a deficiency in natural resources, and reduce the demands on capital. But technology can only grow out of the study of science and its applications."

- Many great leaders of India in the 20th century have contributed to aspects that relate to "the spirit of the people" (which is key to any national development) in terms of political, social and human transformations; Jamsetji Tata and Jeh also made their contribution.

- Most leaders of business and industry have dealt with raw materials, capital and manufacturing, and Jeh was among the greatest in this regard. But he did more.

- With regard to the last sentence of the above statement, Homi Bhabha, in the last public address that he gave in January 1966 in Bombay, in an invited lecture to the International Council of Scientific Unions (ICSU), had said: "What the developed countries have and the underdeveloped lack is modern science and an economy based on modern technology". He was clear that it is not possible to have modern science on an imitative basis; and imitative technology tends to be sterile.

- Jeh was not a practising scientist, but he understood this philosophy and the importance of pure science in a more fundamental conceptual sense than any other of his contemporaries in business and industry as will be clearly seen from a quote from him later in this talk.

- I wish to give you one manifestation of the regard in which he was held by the scientific community in India. The Indian National Science Academy has a special arrangement under which: "persons who, in the opinion of the Council, have either rendered conspicuous service to the cause of science or whose election would be of a signal benefit to the Academy could be elected to the fellowship". In the history of the Academy since 1935, only four individuals have been made fellows under this clause. They are:

Jawaharlal Nehru, Indira Gandhi, JRD Tata, and Satish Dhawan. To me it is no surprise that Jeh would figure in this category, where no other businessman or industrialist has figured before.

- Jeh was the only person in his areas of business, aviation, industry, philanthropy, and related areas of economic development to be awarded a Bharat Ratna.
- *Those who Impacted on Jeh's Personality:* In his Foreword to the book 'Keynote' Jeh has remarked: "Those who made the greatest impact on me were naturally, political figures, starting with Gandhiji, who led the Freedom Struggle. Gandhiji, by far the greatest personality, and, to this day, the most extraordinary human being I have ever met, inspired in me, as in most people, a mixture of awe, admiration and affection combined with some scepticism about his economic philosophy. While I usually came back from meeting Gandhiji elated and inspired, but always a bit skeptical, and from talks with Jawaharlal fired with emotional zeal, but often confused and unconvinced, meetings with Vallabhbhai were joy, from where I returned with renewed confidence in the future of our country". Jeh has referred to Jawaharlal as "the heroic knight in armour who awakened in me some of the passion and fire that burnt within him." He was particularly fond of Jayaprakash Narayan for whom he developed an unbounded liking and admiration.
- However, he reserves his heartfelt admiration for Homi Bhabha: "Politicians were not the only distinguished people it was my good fortune to know and to be associated with.
- The most outstanding of the distinguished men I have known was, undoubtedly, Homi Bhabha. In addition to the unique intellectual gifts nature had bestowed on him, he was, in the mould of Jamsetji Tata, a visionary with the boldness, relentless energy and drive to convert his

vision into reality. Homi was one of those who made me believe that some men in human history are born with the stamp of predestination on them which leads them to accomplishments beyond ordinary human capabilities."

- But to me, from all that has been written in the various books on him, and my own interaction with him, his role model was undoubtedly Jamsetji Tata. He was inspired by him and made every effort to emulate him; in many situations, the touchstone by which he judged himself was, what Jamsetji Tata would have done in those circumstances.

- R.M. Lala has written in his book: "The Joy of Achievement" that more than once, when Jeh talked about reincarnation, he would say: "I told people I would like to come to India and part of me wants to return because India is such an interesting country". He goes on in the book to say that Jeh talked to Fr. Balaguer of his belief in reincarnation: "because I can't believe that a man is born to live for a second of a lifetime. I hope to be reborn in this world." "Fr. Balaguer observed: 'You may not necessarily be here". Somewhat shaken, JRD asked: 'You mean I will be in some other part of the universe?' Sometimes I wonder about the coincidence of dates: Jamsetji Tata passed away on 19th May 1904. JRD Tata was born two months later, on 29th of July, 1904.

- *Jeh's Views on Higher Education:* Jeh was far more concerned about higher education than most people realise. He, of course, was always keenly conscious of a missed opportunity of formal higher education in his own life. He has remarked that he would have gone on to be an engineer; but for personal family reasons he got inducted into the Tata Management at an early age.

- However, he had thought deeply about the issues relating to higher education. On this topic, two particular institutions clearly come to mind: the Indian Institute of Science, Bangalore and the National Institute of Advanced Studies, also in Bangalore; in both cases he expressed his thoughts explicitly.

- *Indian Institute of Science (IISc):* Jeh became president of the Court of the Indian Institute of Science in 1955 and his last address to the Court was in 1993, the year in which he died in November. He was thus president for 38 years, bringing a continuity to the spirit of management of the institution.
- His addresses at the IISc as president of the Court, and particularly on the occasion of the Golden Jubilee and Platinum Jubilee celebrations, bring out his conviction that the vision of Jamsetji Tata, which led to the setting up of IISc as an institution of higher learning, had turned out to be an inspired one. The years in which Jamsetji lived was a period of visionaries at a variety of places in the world, who charted new vistas for human progress. But what was remarkable was that such a man existed in India, not only as a visionary, but who was also highly successful in his enterprises in business and industry to create wealth, while fulfilling national objectives; further that wealth enabled him to pursue those visions, and to steadfastly ensure their implementation. That is what made him a philanthropist of the highest class in the world, but in much more unfavourable circumstances encountered in India.
- *Jamsetji Tata had Remarked:* "What advances a nation or community is not so much to prop up its weakest and the most helpless members, as to lift the best and most gifted so as to make them of the greatest service to the country. I prefer this constructive philanthropy which seeks to educate and develop the faculties of the best of our young men." It was invariably in this direction that Jeh's thoughts also went. And Jamsetji Tata's views, as also those of Jeh, were clear: ultimately science and engineering should not be compartmentalised activities by themselves in the system of higher education. There was need for considering the inclusion of humanities in the broadest sense.
- At the Platinum Jubilee celebrations of IISc, in his address as president of the Court, Jeh had remarked:

"...whether the Institute has lived up to the Founder's dream and fulfilled its intended role of leadership in the development of scientific research and education in the country. The answer to the question cannot but be a reasonably affirmative one. The Institute has not only been from the start, and remained throughout, a leading centre of higher research and training in science and technology but it has proved to be a fountainhead and cradle of scientific talent in the country from which has emerged a succession of men of outstanding technical skills, many of whom later manned and directed the national laboratories, Institutes of Technology, management institutes and other educational institutions established in the country..."

"A continuous change in every branch of knowledge has taken place throughout recorded history. In the past fifty years or so, the rate of change has accelerated in an unprecedented and almost explosive degree. Can research and teaching institutions in science and technology keep pace with such a galloping advance in knowledge without some change within their operating framework?"

- "I would like, in closing, to ask whether the time has not come to revive one of the original ideas Jamsetji had when he formulated his scheme for the Institute, namely the inclusion, in some form, of some of the subjects usually referred to as 'Humanities'.
- Jamsetji when mulling over his scheme for the Institute, thought of education not only as a means of raising the standards of living of his countrymen, but also their quality of life".
- *Jeh has Remarked:* "It has been said that education is what makes a man, what he is, the way he conducts himself through life, his interests, his values, his personality. The load of work imposed on young men and women pursuing advanced studies in our Institute is such that they have

little time or opportunity to expose themselves to literature, the arts, drama, poetry, music, history, philosophy, which, though unconnected with their study or research work, are essential elements in the make-up of a civilized, liberally educated person such as Jamsetji Tata had in mind."

- In his very first address, as president of the Court of the Institute in 1955, Jeh made an important point that science and scientific institutions in this country must always keep in mind: this was of cooperation with industry and industrialists. He has said: "I am more concerned with the efforts of the Institute to make itself felt, to give industrialists and governments the confidence that their problems can be effectively handled here."

- His thoughts were not only on general issues. He has said in the same address: "As recently emphasised by Dr. Bhabha, technical problems still to be overcome in the practical development and the application of atomic energy lie largely in the fields of metallurgy, chemistry and engineering. With its varied engineering resources, this Institute will be exceptionally qualified to play a leading part in this important work and I hope that in the planning of our future activities, some priority will be given to preparing ourselves for the opportunities which this new field of engineering offers".

- On a more specific issue he remarked: "Similarly, the development of the industrial gas turbine will, I believe, provide a great opportunity to the Institute for service to the country." He referred to the gas turbine in its initial application and development for aircraft propulsion and military purposes but went on to add.

  "The gas turbine, however, has also much to offer as a prime mover in other fields where it will in time usefully supplement and, in some cases, replace steam and diesel power"... "provide an exceptionally valuable addition to existing sources of power especially in the countryside and in small towns. The gas turbine has also great potentialities in the field of rail traction where, in time, it may well take the place of the steam locomotive."

- Jeh's horizons extended over the broad vision, policy issues as also the technical details of areas of opportunity.
- *National Institute of Advanced Studies (NIAS):* Jeh had a good feeling for the education system in France. He knew that mathematics was a key component, not just in its own right as a subject, but for creating an underpinning ability in an individual to think with an analytical approach and precision, which he felt was often lacking in India. In contrast, in India, mathematics was often a subject meant for the gifted in the field, or as an adjunct for use in other fields (including banking, commerce and finance), or regarded as a chore.
- Jeh was particularly impressed by the Grande Ecoles in France, the first of which was established by Napoleon. In particular, he discovered that they produced a very high class of output, from which was drawn the elite of the civil service in France dealing with areas as wide as administration, industry, mining and various educational and research institutions. Jeh had a study conducted on whether such an institution would be suitable for being put up in India; for this he put together a group of educationists from France and India. He thought this might be a suitable tribute to Jawaharlal Nehru and had raised substantial finances for the same. Since the Grande Ecoles insisted on a high level of mathematical knowledge for admission, there were many distinguished persons who felt that this would make it too restrictive and elitist in India. Jeh has remarked later that he should have proceeded with the project as a venture of the Tatas, like many others in higher education and science.
- But the idea was not one which he would abandon, and eighteen years later, he constituted another group to look at the requirements in the country, and the role of such an institution. I had the privilege of being a member of

this group which noted that many new types of institutions had come into existence, such as the IITs, the IIMs and the like.

- However, it was felt that there would still be a role for an institution which has since been created: the National Institute of Advanced Studies (NIAS) in Bangalore. It was planned as a research and training institute – but with training being restricted to shorter time periods and not necessarily the longer duration courses run in university-like institutions.
- It was meant to deal with more practical problems in Government, industry and society with mathematical rigour relating to policy-making and implementation as also options. It would take note of the many new developments that are rapidly occurring as a result of the rapid advances in science and technology. This was an institution set up wholly at the initiative and with the vision of Jeh.
- *Philanthropy: An Important Element for Higher Education and Science:* In the early history of humanity, activities such as higher education and scientific pursuits depended essentially on institutions supported largely by monarchy and oligarchy. However, since the 19th century, after the Industrial Revolution, the early pioneers who amassed wealth on a scale unimaginable at that time, through the discovery and effective utilisation of raw materials that form the backbone of industry and manufacturing such as oil, iron and steel, became the new patrons. It must be noted that these early pioneers had undoubted social commitment. A great deal has been written about this. I shall only provide some illustrations from elsewhere in the world concerning this matter; but few can parallel the history of the Tatas and the direction of their philanthropy in the circumstances in which they operated.
- One of the great philanthropists in this regard was John D. Rockefeller, who was born in July 1839; this was just three months after the birth of Jamsetji Tata, founder of the House of Tatas. When he retired from his business

activities essentially related to oil, in 1911, he was often called the richest man in the world. Twenty years before his retirement, had already decided to give away his money to worthy causes. His problem at that time was to define these causes. He was not interested in the large number of appeals for gifts. So he decided on a few major activities. He created the University of Chicago and financed it fully – but he refused to have his name attached to this creation. All in all, he gave 35 million dollars at that time to this University – one of the great universities of the world; and in science studded with the names of many who have won Nobel Prizes. These included our own Subramanyam Chandrasekhar and Enrico Fermi, who did the first experiments on criticality in neutron physics at that university in connection with the Manhattan (atomic bomb) project. It is a university of which any country would be proud. Thereafter, he created the Rockefeller Institute for Medical Research in 1901 in New York. It was housed initially in a loft of a building with a budget of 20000 dollars! Does that remind those from TIFR, about Homi Bhabha's philosophy about the work done in coastal gun battery barracks and an initial budget in 1945 of Rs.80,000/-. Since then, the Rockefeller Institute moved into permanent buildings on the East River, and was endowed with more than 60 million dollars. It has also been the home of many Nobel Prizes. John D Rockefeller then created a Trust, the Rockefeller Foundation, with an inscription on its crest which says: "well being of mankind throughout the world". India has ample cause to be grateful to this Foundation.

- The total amount disbursed over time by the Foundation goes to well over a billion dollars.
- It is interesting to note that one of the efforts of the Rockefeller Foundation, early in its history, was the creation of the Peking Union Medical College, which many called "Johns Hopkins of China". As far as I am aware, it was Dr. John Spies, head of the Cancer Service of this College who met Sir Nowroji Saklatwala on board an

ocean liner on the Pacific and convinced him of the concept that the Tata Memorial Hospital (TMH) had to be an institution way beyond the radium service initially contemplated by Sir Dorab Tata and the Govt. of Bombay. I have already dealt with TMH earlier in this talk.

- John D. Rockefeller was clear his approach to philanthropy: it had to directed to specific causes, normally of large magnitude, relating to education, science and medicine. Before him, Johns Hopkins, a Baltimore businessmen, had created a university named after him with a hospital and medical school; it has turned out to be one of the great Universities and medical institutions in the world. Again Andrew Carnegie, who made his money in steel, had embarked on a mission to give away an enormous personal fortune. In 1889, in an article entitled "Wealth" he had declared his intention "of dying poor" – a remarkable concept by any standards from a very rich man, and analogous to "Sanyas" that we have in Indian culture; except that, in the latter, only the individual personally adopts the path of renunciation. In fact, Carnegie wrote that it would be a disgrace for someone to die rich. In the uproar that followed his article, Carnegie wrote "Mr. Astor died, in my opinion, disgraced by leaving one hundred and fifty million dollars to one person."!

- I have referred just to three examples of Johns Hopkins, John D Rockefeller and Andrew Carnegie. These were not the only philanthropists of this type and class. There were many others including Stanford, Guggenheim and many others. They had all acquired wealth in the wake of the developments following the Industrial Revolution and the opening up of America.. There was a spirit of aggressiveness and acquisitiveness at that time, and no codes of ethics had been established relating to the accumulation of wealth.

- It was not, therefore, surprising that these wealthy individuals were often referred to as Robber Barons. But it must also be remembered that this enormous accumulated wealth went back to the nation (and to other nations) in ways of benefit to society: in support of higher education, of science, of art and scholarship. They set up universities, foundations, libraries and endowments. The final output was completely different from their public image of being called selfish, cruel and seeking wealth for self-aggrandisement. Indeed they invented the science and art of philanthropy for large scale public good, and mastered the difficult art of giving.

- I do not intend to expound on this topic at greater length. If you convert dollars to rupees, and also consider the objective for which these amounts were spent, (for science, higher education and medical services), you will see an exact analogy with what the Tatas did. From the concepts of Jamsetji Tata in conceiving of the Indian Institute of Science, through the philanthropy of Jamsetji, and of Sir Dorab and Sir Ratan Tata, and thereafter Jeh, in creating Trusts, and institutions nucleated by these Trusts, which were nurtured and grown to their present magnificence, you see the tradition of great men who regarded their wealth as held in trust for the people. But this culture was developed and nurtured by Jamsetji and his successors without any imitation of the earlier cited illustrations.
- It is extraordinary that Sir Dorab Tata gave all his wealth, down to the last pearl-studded tie pin, and the largest diamond in the world, the Jubilee Diamond, which was the possession of his wife the late Lady Meherbai Tata, to the Trust bearing his name.
- Jeh, in the Forward to the book by Frank Harris on Jamsetji Tata, has stated beautifully:

  "The wealth gathered by Jamsetji Tata and his sons in half a century of industrial pioneering formed but a minute fraction of the amount by which they enriched the nation. The whole of that wealth is held in trust for the people and used exclusively for their benefit. The cycle is thus complete; what came from the people has gone back to the people many times over."
- Jeh never forgot what Jamsetji had said:

"We do not claim to be more unselfish, more generous or more philanthropic than other people. But we think we started on sound and straightforward business principles, considering the interests of the shareholders our own, and the health and welfare of the employees the sure foundation of our success."

- He went on to remark about Jamsetji: ".... He had integrity. Not only money-related integrity. Jamsetji had integrity of thought and mind. The final attribute was his great humanity..."
- In total contrast today, one sees the very large accumulation of wealth by individuals, families and groups in ways that may correspond to the law of the land but not to the underlying spirit of these laws and ethical aspects of societal functioning – with no indication that the possessors regard this wealth as held in trust for the people; which was Gandhiji's basic philosophy. This has resulted in any number of family conflicts and disputes of various forms. There is often a scandalous, and often obscene, display of wealth by the rich. They are then the role models followed by others at various levels in society not so well off. Money has thus become, in its own right, the purpose in life.
- There is also great focus in the media on the wealth of individuals. These examples corrupt the generations that follow.
- What I have just stated might convey an impression that I am pessimistic about the future of the country – far from it. I know innumerable examples of professionals highly trained in various areas of science, engineering, medicine and the like who have done well in their careers and acquired significant wealth in the process. They use this for philanthropic purposes without much fanfare. This is happening because the advances in science and technology and a more open system for functioning without too many controls and restrictions, has enabled good people, who are educated and enlightened, to create wealth which they are using for worthwhile causes. Some of these

professionals are also going to the non-governmental sector and also helping charitable institutions in their work for society. Thus there is a positive ferment in society that has little to do with politics and bureaucracy. It has to do with good people who wish to do good in society.

- But I would still ask the creators of great wealth in the country: where are visions, the great initiatives and dreams for national development that someone like Jamsetji had, and to which his successors, particularly the subject of this talk, Jeh, contributed so abundantly and which were nurtured so carefully.

- *Computer Science and Technology:* There was a time when, on the occasion of Council meetings of TIFR, the Council as a whole or certainly some Members of it, particularly Jeh and Rustom Choksi, visited laboratories in the Institute when there was some particular new development, and also had lunch with the Faculty; sometimes the occasion for the visit was when some dignitary was being taken round the Institute. After one such visit, which was to the first computer designed and built in India, named TIFRAC, Jeh wanted to know more about the field. When Jeh talked to Homi about this, he suggested that Jeh should ask me to see him on this at Bombay House, which I did. Jeh started by referring to the enormous size of TIFRAC, and wanted to know what technology developments are taking place which could change the picture completely. I told him about the rapid developments in the field of microelectronics, first with the transistor and then with integrated circuits that had just been invented. This discussion was in early 1960s. Jeh rapidly concluded by saying that this would not be the right time for an industry or foundation to invest. Many years later, after I succeeded Homi as Director, TIFR and had been invited by Jeh for another lunch in the Board Room, he asked me to come a little earlier for a discussion. He had not given up the idea of Tatas moving into the computer field. (He kept ideas in his mind for a long time). I mentioned to him what I knew about global developments, and more particularly that there would be significant opportunities in hardware, relating to various subsystems, but not perhaps whole computers; and certainly in software. He referred to this topic in the Board Room Lunch Discussion. To cut a long story short, Tatas embarked on setting up TCS in 1968 under the dynamic leadership of F.C. Kohli. There was also the joint venture with Burroughs Corporation in the USA. In this connection I did visit Burroughs and others in the USA around that time. Today TCS is a jewel in the crown of the Tatas, and there are also several efforts relating to hardware in various Tata Companies.

- *Energy:* At a Board Room lunch of Tatas, Jeh once asked a general question whether there was anything that Tatas could do in the field of energy to meet national needs – other than what their industrial enterprises in hydro and thermal power were already engaged on. He posed the question to me first, since I was sitting next to him. I said that there was a great deal that needed to be done, particularly relating to the appropriate mix of energies (types, magnitudes, applications) and the strategies for their utilisation in different sectors. This would have to take into account circumstances in India that are totally different from the advanced countries, with a poorly developed rural hinterland where the cost of transmission and distribution would turn out to be exorbitant; this is where alternative energy supply systems, particularly decentralised and preferably renewable, could play an important role. I also added that energy, particularly of the conventional kind, was not an area where it would be wise to embark on major research and development, since it would be highly expensive; and there were many institutions already engaged in this. Decisive contributions were made by Darbari Seth and Nani Palkiwala in the discussion. Jeh asked them to pursue the matter further. Nani arranged for a dinner at his house, specifically for such a discussion, where I was invited. Darbari Seth offered to pick up the entire expenses connected with such an institution. The Tata Energy Research Institute (TERI) was born thereafter, and since then has established a name for itself in a unique manner in its fields of activity.

- I have given these two illustrations only to point out how Jeh had a mind that was constantly searching for new avenues that would benefit the country, and in which Tatas could play a role – as Jamsetji Tata had always wanted. There were other occasions and other discussions to discuss further new avenues of opportunity, but I shall not go into these.
- *Support for Homi Bhabha:* Homi Bhabha had done brilliant work in Cambridge England. He returned to India in 1939. The outbreak of the Second World War prevented him from returning to Cambridge which he would normally have done. The Sir Dorab Tata Trust created a position for him at the Indian Institute of Science, Bangalore, along with a Special Cosmic Ray Research Unit. He continued to do outstanding physics, but also thought deeply about the possibility of economic prosperity and social change for India based on science and technology. He felt the need for large numbers to be trained in the newly developing areas in mathematics and nuclear science. He spoke to Jeh about his wish to establish an Institute of Fundamental Research in India, and wrote a letter to him on this matter dated 19th August 1943. He was encouraged by Jeh who wrote back: " From what you say in your letter, it is evident that there is scope for rendering valuable service to the country and to the cause of scientific research in India. The advancement of science is one of the fundamental objects with which most of the Tata Trusts were founded".
- Homi wrote, on 12th March 1944, as advised by Jeh, a formal letter to Sir Sorab Saklatvala, Chairman of the Sir Dorab Tata Trust, in which he proposed the setting up of an institution which has since become the Tata Institute of Fundamental Research. This is a remarkably prophetic letter and contains many of the basic guidelines which defined his way of functioning throughout his life.

- It was in this letter that he said: "Moreover, when nuclear energy has been successfully applied for power production, in say a couple of decades from now, India will not have to look abroad for its experts but will find them ready at hand." This was his vision of abundant economic nuclear power, which he felt was so vital for the development of India. I would like you to remember that this was written by him sitting in Bangalore, in 1944; it was written more than a year before Hiroshima; the work on the atom bomb was being carried out with the greatest secrecy in the West; the only knowledge that Homi Bhabha had was that nuclear fission had been discovered. He predicted a time scale, and indeed in two decades, an agreement to bring nuclear power on stream to supply Maharashtra and Gujarat had come about. And today, India has a continuing stream of experts, which could be a major industrial strength and potential for growth as the need for nuclear power gets accepted world wide.
- Homi had remarked with great confidence: "The scheme I am now submitting to you is but an embryo from which I hope to build up, in the course of time, a school of physics comparable with the best anywhere".
- It was thus that, with the dynamic support of Jeh, the Tata Institute of Fundamental Research (TIFR) came into being in June 1945; it was initially located at the Indian Institute of Science at Bangalore.
- Exactly at that time, Jeh made an effort to get support for this venture from a friend who was a wealthy industrialist. He wrote to him: "I sincerely believe that this Institute can make a great contribution to the scientific knowledge of mankind.... You may perhaps feel that advanced physics, mathematics, astrophysics are particularly abstract subjects, research in which is unlikely to produce material or practical results within a reasonable period of time. I should, however, like to point out that most of the great practical advances in science, and, therefore, in industry, have had their origins in fundamental research, without

which they would have been impossible or would have been long delayed." Jeh would never have written such a letter if he was not personally and completely convinced. His conviction as expressed is important for the scientific community.

- When the new buildings of TIFR were inaugurated by Jawaharlal Nehru in 1962, (and by that time Homi had obtained for the Institute the fullest backing of Jawaharlal, whom he called 'Bhai'), Homi made his famous remark: "This Institute was the cradle of our atomic energy programme". He went on to say: "The support of such (fundamental) research, and of an institution where such research can be carried out effectively, is of great importance to society.... Paradoxically, it has an immediate use in that it helps to train and develop, in a manner in which no other mental discipline can, young men of the highest intellectual calibre in a society, into people who can think about and analyse problems with a freshness of outlook and originality which is not generally found. Such men are of the greatest value to society....". Homi Bhabha, Vikram Sarabhai, P.C. Mahalnobis are striking examples of this.

- All this came about because Jeh had intuitively understood that the importance of basic science lay in ways far beyond high quality papers, discoveries and new understanding relating to nature.

- I have had many discussions with Jeh on this matter in the years thereafter. This was particularly when I was Director, TIFR and he was Chairman of the Council of Management. We were embarking on programs of great importance to defence; these related to strategic electronics in the fields of computer science and microwave engineering. There were also other projects in applied science and technology development. While Jeh was happy that we were doing something of relevance to the country, he was equally concerned that we should not, in the process, dilute our thrust relating to fundamental research at the frontiers of science. I had to assure him that we would not. I also reminded him that Homi Bhabha had used TIFR for initiatives that would kick-start the atomic energy programme.

- Whilst Homi Bhabha's familial connections with the Tatas was important, to me the affinity between Homi and Jeh was much deeper. It arose out of a fundamental sense of respect each had for the other. Jeh has remarked: "It has been a source of great satisfaction to me that I was able to play a part, however small, in helping Homi Bhabha to launch a programme which led to his magnificent achievement in making India, in a mere two decades, virtually self-sufficient in nuclear science. Scientist, engineer, masterbuilder and administrator, steeped in the humanities, in art and music, Homi was a truly complete man."

- Equally few realise that Jeh was also gifted in more ways than being a great leader of business and industry. A pioneer in aviation, he was also very fond of poetry, both in French and English; he had catholic, and for me sometimes unusual tastes in what he liked. He enjoyed music and his sister Rodaboh has remarked on his sensitivity and proficiency in playing the piano as a child; he had an excellent ear for music. But he said later that moving around from place to place prevented him from pursuing his interest in music (on the piano) and there was also not the time available to practice regularly and rigorously. Jeh was not a great visitor of art museums of the world in contrast to Homi. But he deeply appreciated good art. In his support for the National Centre for the Performing Arts, a proposal that was put forward by Homi's brother, Jamshed, which was initially viewed with scepticism in the Sir Dorab Tata Trust, Jeh had argued "While we want to build a prosperous society, we do not want to be merely a materialistic consumer society". Equally, Jeh was one of the strongest supporters of Homi in the building of this auditorium in which this lecture is being held today, and visited TIFR often, just to go through the plans with Homi at site. I had the privilege of being with them on many occasions.

- In many areas there was strong personal rapport between Homi and Jeh. In a different context, that was also the case between Homi and Jawaharlal Nehru.
- Without the support provided by Jeh, history could have been very different. Homi Bhabha may not have stayed on in India; TIFR may not have come into existence as it is now. Jeh's was the hand that directed fate as it has turned out to be.
- In the memorial meeting for Homi on January 24, 1967, a year after he died, which was chaired by Jeh, I concluded my talk with the statement: "This Institute came into being because of the encouragement you gave to Homi Bhabha 24 years ago and has grown to its present stature with the dynamic support provided by you and Jawaharlal Nehru.
- Your presence in our midst today is indeed a source of strength to all of us and we are grateful to you for it".
- From the early beginnings of TIFR, Homi Bhabha went on to set up the Atomic Energy programme of India, with the Atomic Energy Commission (AEC) in 1948, the Department of Atomic Energy in 1954, and the establishment at Trombay now named after him in 1954. Apart from the initial objectives of generating capabilities that would lead to economic nuclear power, and all that this meant in terms of research, development and design of nuclear reactors and atomic power plants, and underlying areas of science and technology, there was also increasing emphasis on a variety of applications of atomic energy to agriculture, industry and medicine. In all of this effort Homi significantly leant on Jeh's wisdom and support. Once the programme got going Homi had Jeh as a Member of the AEC, in 1962. Jeh continued to be a Member of the AEC even after Homi's death. Jeh was a Member of the AEC for 26 years in all. Throughout his membership he was very active in the discussions. The

present Chairman of the AEC, Dr. Kakodkar, has informed me of the valuable contributions made by Jeh, particularly in the early years, to discuss matters such as the setting up of the Atomic Power Authority, as also the Nuclear Power Profile for the decade 1970 – 1980. Jeh was concerned about the long gestation period of 7-8 years for construction of nuclear power stations, and asked whether one could not get senior level expertise from abroad as available; he remembered Homi's friendship with the leaders in the field (Cockcroft, Perrin, Lewis, Emelyanov, Seaborg and others) that had been beneficial at the start of India's programme. I myself remember many active discussions with Jeh on matters relating to atomic energy: such as its role in national development; and the need for an independent regulatory authority which would instill public confidence and allay fears in society relating to safety.

- I shall now refer to another area of great relevance to society, which is also at the frontiers of modern medicine and of science, cancer, in which the Department of Atomic Energy has played an important role. Some of the pioneering thoughts in this came from Jeh.
- Lady Meherbai Tata died of leukaemia in 1931. Sir Dorab Tata, who had a basic desire to contribute to areas of human health decided to focus on the treatment of cancer.
- Originally, in consultation with the Government of Bombay, it was planned to establish a radium service in Bombay, with Sir Dorab Tata financing it. Just as happened to Jamsetji Tata in the case of the steel plant and the Indian Institute of Science, Sir Dorab Tata died in 1932 before the project could materialise. On the basis of later discussions, it was agreed to set up a hospital in which not only the radium service but all other methods of treatment would be available. By the late 1930s the concept of the hospital was finalised, and it was opened in 1941. In 1939 there is a comment by Jeh in which he emphasises the importance of ensuring the combination of medical service, education (training) and research. It was Jeh who

emphasised the importance of bringing in the finest expertise in the world initially, and this resulted in the linkage with the Memorial Sloan Kettering Hospital in New York. Two outstanding surgeons from there stayed at the hospital for several years and trained a new generation of brilliant surgeons. Jeh had emphasised that this is the only way technology can be transferred to our country, and furthermore, that the Tata Memorial Hospital should play a major role as catalyst for cancer treatment in India. He also envisaged, as early as 1948, that radiation treatment will become more sophisticated, with increasing knowledge in physics; his vision has proved to be correct, with the explosive advances in nuclear medicine for diagnosis and treatment. By 1957, it was clear that such a hospital could not be run by a Trust. The first effort was to get it taken over by the Ministry of Health of the Government of India, which could not undertake this task. It was at this moment, that the confluence of Jeh.

- The Sir Dorab Tata Trust, Homi Bhabha, Department of Atomic Energy and Jawaharlal Nehru came together – and as always, in the service of the nation. The Department of Atomic Energy decided to take over the hospital by analogy with the US Atomic Energy Commission running cancer research hospitals in the USA. The hospital has not looked back since, and has become the finest establishment for cancer research and treatment in this part of the world.

- Jeh's support for Homi Bhabha resulted not only in the setting up of TIFR, that in turn led to the birth of India's Atomic Energy Programme. Independently, Jeh had also supported Tata Memorial Hospital and Cancer Research; in course of time, that also became part of the stream supported through the Department of Atomic Energy (DAE).

- Another area that Homi Bhabha got DAE to take responsibility for was a laboratory created by Vikram Sarabhai, in Ahmedabad referred to as PRL (Physical Research Laboratory). Through close rapport between Homi Bhabha and Vikram Sarabhai from the days when they were both together at the Indian Institute of Science, Bangalore, funds for this laboratory were provided from the Govt. of India through the DAE under a quadripartite agreement, as given earlier to TIFR under a tripartite agreement. It was at the Physical Research Laboratory that Vikram envisioned the space programme which has been a remarkable success. Whilst the atomic energy programme was growing to maturity during the sixties, DAE supported the space programme which was in its infancy. In 1972 the two were separated; by then the space programme could stand on its own. Over the three decades gone by, the space programme has grown to maturity and proved highly successful.

- Little did Jeh realise the magnitude of what would grow from that initial support extended to Homi Bhabha in 1943 – 1944.

- On Vikram, Jeh has said:

"Few men that I have known called forth more admiration and affection than Vikram Sarabhai. I think of him and Homi Bhabha as exemplars of modern India. Vikram spoke often of new attitudes and new insights that make for a new operating culture in modern India. He felt that outworn patterns of thought are an obstacle to growth and development, that if the social and intellectual environment does not change sufficiently we shall continue to flounder despite the massive inputs of Plan after Plan. If we would apply ourselves to problems, then we must first apply ourselves to people. In his stress on the principle that scientific institutions should be built around the exceptional individual rather than by following the old practice of first creating laboratories and then searching for the best men to run them, Vikram emphasises his indebtedness to Homi Bhabha's own thinking and practice in this respect, and one is left once again to lament the loss to India of two such men in such a short period. In these critical years of our country's history when the future happiness and prosperity of its people, and perhaps their very survival as a nation, will depend so greatly on policies and decisions being founded on common sense rather than emotion, on scientific and rational considerations rather than political ones, on pragmatic and result-oriented thinking rather than ideology, India could ill afford the loss of men like Homi Bhabha or Vikram Sarabhai. Although they have gone, they have left us a rich intellectual heritage from which it is up to us to draw guidance and inspiration in the years to come."

- I have put these thoughts down as Jeh had himself expressed them, for he was one of the finest examples of implementing these in modern business and industry in India.
- Jeh's support for science was extremely important in coming at the right time, and given to the right person. As important as the programs themselves have been, the output in terms of a viable self-generating group of trained personnel, the scarcest commodity in a developing nation, imbued with a spirit of dedication in national endeavour, enthused to maintain highest standards of scientific integrity and setting standards of quality in all that they did has been as important.
- On this Jeh has said: "I believe that the greatest contribution Homi made to India's development into the modern state it is fast becoming, lies in training and bringing out to their full capability a host of young scientists and administrators who, today, lead so many of India's scientific and technical establishments".
- *Conclusion:* Lord Blackett, who was a frequent visitor to TIFR, and a great friend of Homi, and his contemporary at Cambridge in the 1930s, has said that a first class laboratory is one in which mediocre scientists can produce outstanding work. This is because of the interactive ambience and sense of excitement prevailing, which has been commented on beautifully by Jacques Monod the

French Nobel prize winning molecular biologist in relation to the California Institute of Technology. Much earlier, there is a story attributed to Lord Rutherford who headed the Cavendish Laboratory in its hey day. When there was an announcement of a Nobel Prize awarded to a scientist from the Cavendish Laboratory, the press asked Lord Rutherford "Sir, you seem to be riding the crest of a wave, with Nobel Prizes won almost every year by scientists of your laboratory. Pat came the reply "Damn it all, I created the wave, did'nt I".

- Thus, it was with Jeh. He was constantly looking for those with leadership qualities. He gave them opportunities and made great men out of them. K.S. Krishnan, a great Indian physicist, used to quote a Tamil proverb "Only the learned can recognise the learned".
- Jeh was truly learned though he never received a formal higher education. He was one of the greatest managers, with an uncanny approach to synthesis and bringing people together, and in creating a team and a family; but he never went through any formal management education.
- The founder of it all, Jamsetji Tata, was a person way ahead of his time in his thinking and vision. His ideas on the steel plant and the Indian Institute of Science were fulfilled in abundance after his death. But most important, Jamsetji Tata left behind him a culture and the start of a pedigree of the highest quality. His sons, Sir Dorab, and Sir Ratan, were indeed worthy successors not only in implementing his projects in business and industry but also concerning his visions on using wealth, as it should be used, for purposes of national development.
- Jeh was a modern man, imbued with everything that was great in the culture initiated by Jamsetji Tata. He kept the flame burning brightly, exhibiting not only leadership but all the needed human qualities, of idealism, compassion, caring, courtesy, kindness and most of all, integrity.
- I hope what I have said in this talk will demonstrate how much science and higher education owe to Jeh. We all

have cause to be grateful that such a man walked in our midst; many of us had the humble privilege of knowing him.

Wings for a Nation (by R.M. Lala)

It was in the first decade of the century. Two young boys spent their summer holidays at Hardelot, a beach resort near Boulogne in Northern France. One was the son of the legendary Louis Bleriot, the first man to fly across the English Channel in 1909. The other was the son of an Indian industrialist, R.D. Tata. As they played, the boys would occasionally see Bleriot's Chief Pilot Adolph Pegoud land a plane on the beach Pegoud was the first man to loop-the-loop in a plane. He was a hero, especially for Tata's young son Jehangir.

In such small beginnings lie the seed of history. The exploits of the Frenchman stirred the heart of the young Indian. At the age of 15 after taking a joy ride in a plane at Hardelot, Jehangir decided to become a pilot and if possible make a career in aviation. Young Jehangir had to wait nine years. He was 24 before a Flying Club opened in his home town Bombay, India — 5,000 miles away from that wind-swept beach in Northern France. Though not the first to register, he was the first Indian to pass out with 'No. 1' endorsed on his flying licence. And so it came to pass that India's first pilot was to pour most of his creative genius into building an airline for his country, giving his nation wings.

Those were years of adventure. In 1930, the Aga Khan announced a prize of £500 to the first Indian who would fly solo between England and India, starting at either end. Among the competitors was a young man called Manmohan Singh. His spirit was willing but his navigation was weak.

Twice he left England with a flourish to fly to India. Twice he lost his way over Europe and had to fly back to England to start all over again. Another hopeful from the England and was 18 year old Aspy Engineer. Still another to enter for fun, taking off from the Karachi end, was the now 26 year old Jehangir R.D. Tata. At Aboukir near Alexandria in Egypt, JRD ran into Aspy, who had left England a week earlier and who was stranded for want of spark plugs. JRD gave Aspy his spare spark plugs, and they took off in opposite directions. Aspy reached Karachi a few hours before JRD reached England, winning the prize. On the strength of his performance, Aspy was admitted into the Indian Air Force, which had just been created. Aspy Engineer was the second Indian to be Chief of the Air Staff. JRD, meanwhile, had another ambition and he did not have long to wait.

> "On an exciting October dawn in 1932, a Puss Moth and I soared joyfully from Karachi with our first precious load of mail, on an inaugural flight to Bombay. As we hummed towards our destination at a 'dazzling' hundred miles an hour, I breathed a silent prayer for the success of our venture and for the safety of those who worked for it. We were a small team in those days. We shared successes and failures, the joys and headaches, as together we built up the enterprise which later was to blossom into Air-India and Air-India International."

When JRD landed on the Juhu mud flats that October day in 1932, India's first air service was inaugurated. He does not take the credit for it. He gives it instead to a far-seeing Englishman — a former officer of the RAF called Nevill Vintcent, who a year earlier had come to India barnstorming the country giving joy rides. Nevill Vintcent offered JRD Tata a project to start an airline. The then Chairman of Tata Sons, Sir Dorab Tata, was not a bit enthusiastic about the proposition. But the initial investment was small — Rs. 200,000 — and he was persuaded by JRD's mentor and colleague John Peterson to give his approval.

> "We had no aids whatsoever on the ground or in the air," JRD recalls, "no radio, no navigational or landing guides of any kind. In fact we did not even have an aerodrome in Bombay. We used a mud flat at Juhu (fishing village-cum-beach resort near the city). The sea was below what we called our airfield, and during the monsoon the runway was below the sea! So we had to pack up each year, lock, stock and barrel — two planes, three pilots and three mechanics, and

> transfer ourselves to Poona (Pune) where we were allowed to use a *maidan* as an aerodrome, appropriately under the shadow of the Yeravada Jail!"

The annual report of the Directorate of Civil Aviation (DCA) of India for the year 1933-34 stated: "As an example how airmail service should be run, we commend the efficiency of Tata Services who on October 10, 1933, arriving at Karachi as usual to time, completed a year's working with 100 per cent punctuality... even during the most difficult monsoon months when rainstorms increased the perils of the Western Ghat portion of the route no mail from Madras or Bombay missed connection at Karachi nor was the mail delivered late on a single occasion at Madras... our esteemed Trans-Continental Airways, alias Imperial Airways, might send their staff on deputation to Tatas to see how it is done."

Karachi was chosen as the starting point because Imperial Airways terminated there with the mail from England and the route chosen by Tatas was Karachi-Bombay-Madras. Tatas requested the Government for a small subsidy for carrying the mail as was the normal practice in other countries. The subsidy asked for was small but the Government declined. Tatas reduced the figure to a bare minimum. Government still declined. So Tatas decided that they would just give the service to the country collecting the little stamp surcharge which the addressor put on the envelope to connect it with the Imperial Airways at Karachi. When asked why they did so, JRD replied, "Vintcent and I had faith in the future of aviation and believed that if we came in at the beginning of an era we had a better chance ultimately to achieve growth and leadership in the field."

The unfolding years were to justify that faith. In 1936 the all-up Empire Mail Service was launched by the British Government, under which all first class mail travelled by air without surcharge, and Tata Airlines' revenues soared. At the beginning the aeroplanes used were so small that the service was restricted to mail, but a single passenger was occasionally allowed to sit on top of the mail bags — usually with his heels higher than his head!

In 1936 larger aircraft, though still single-engined, were introduced. Tatas felt the need to give more sophisticated training to their pilots and hired an instructor from England to start a training centre for pilots. The Bombay-Delhi service was inaugurated in 1937. Then came the War and all services, including Tatas', were commandeered by the Government of India.

With their airline operations severely restricted and controlled, Nevill Vintcent and J. R. D. Tata looked for alternative avenues for their brimming enthusiasm and their growing expertise. A specially exciting opportunity, they felt, offered itself in the field of aircraft manufacture. Whereas the construction of metal aircraft would have involved an elaborately equipped factory, the De Havilland Mosquito, an outstanding twin-engined fighter-bomber made of wood, could, they felt, be put quickly into production in India. Tatas, therefore, submitted in 1942 a project to the British Government for the large-scale manufacture of Mosquito aircraft in a factory they would build for the purpose in Pune. The project was approved by the British Government and a new company, Tata Aircraft Limited, was formed to give it life. Land was acquired and a large factory building constructed. Had this plan come off, Tatas would have gone into aircraft production.

The British Government had second thoughts and decided instead that invasion gliders should be built under the project. This change was reluctantly accepted by Tatas as the work of building the factory, recruiting staff and organising manufacture had already gone too far to be abandoned. The project was revised accordingly.

Nevill Vintcent was a man of great physical courage and resourcefulness. More than once he flew to England for discussions with the British authorities. Usually flying by Imperial Airways long-range aircraft, he was flown by a sufficiently circuitous route to keep out of range of German fighters. Tragically, however, on one occasion Vintcent, as an ex-RAF officer, arranged to get a lift on an RAF Hudson bomber on the first leg of a flight from England to Gibraltar. The plane never reached Gibraltar and was reported to have been shot down off the coast of France. The loss of Vintcent was a grievous blow to Tatas and to JRD personally, for apart from being the able and moving spirit behind Tata Airlines and Tata Aircraft that he was, Vintcent and JRD were close friends. This tragic blow was followed by the cancellation of the project.

itself by the British, who in response to Tatas' own enquiries on the subject, discovered that invasion gliders made by Tata in Pune could not be used in the War because there were no aircraft to tow them! Thus came to a tragic end a project on which JRD had set his heart and which, if it had gone through, as originally planned, would probably have resulted in another invaluable addition to India's industry.

In 1946, Tata Air Lines, a Division of Tata Sons, went public and became a joint stock company. It was called Air-India Ltd. The age of passenger travel had arrived and there was to be plenty of competition. Even during wartime Tatas were working on a scheme to extend their services to London. In October 1947, in the turmoil of the post-partition period, Tatas proposed to the Indian Government a service to Europe. They placed an order for three Lockheed Constellations, on faith that this venture would be approved. It was a measure of their faith in the newly born independent India, then in the convulsions of the partition of the subcontinent.

Tatas proposed that the Indian Government take 49 per cent of the capital, Tatas 25 per cent and the rest be publicly subscribed. The Government had the right to buy a further two per cent from Tatas taking their share to 51 per cent giving them total control. This was the first ever proposal of a joint enterprise between the public and private sectors in the country. The proposal was made by JRD Tata at a most inopportune time, when communal strife raged in Delhi. To his astonishment, which still lingers, JRD got acceptance to his joint sector proposal from the Government within weeks. Many years later he asked a senior Cabinet Minister, Jagjivan Ram, why a decision could be made so speedily in those days when today it took the Government at least two years 'not to make a decision'. Mr. Ram replied, "We did not know any better then!"

The proposal provided for a new company to be called Air-India International. It was to be managed and provided with its staff, its maintenance and its services by Tatas' domestic airline Air-India. On June 8, 1948, Air-India International with its famous Maharaja, spread its wings to Europe. The fledgling airline soon established itself as one of the finest air carriers of the world.

Meanwhile India's domestic airlines were heading for a crisis. At the end of the War, planes were disposed of by the American Tenth Air Force in India at throwaway prices. For political reasons the Government sanctioned every airline applicant, and India soon found itself with eleven airlines while there was room for only two or three. As a result they all ran into rough weather for there were not enough traffic routes to allocate amongst them. Except Air-India all the airlines lost heavily. In 1953 the Government took a decision to nationalise the airlines proposing to merge them into a single State Corporation with JRD as Chairman. Mr. Tata advised that the domestic and the international airlines of India should be kept apart and two separate corporations be formed. The suggestion was accepted and he was invited to head the international airline, a task he accepted. For the next 25 years he was to be the Chairman of Air-India, and a Director on the Board of Indian Airlines.

The international airline business is ferociously competitive and JRD, Chairman of some of the largest companies in India, had to give more and more time to the running of Air-India. He carried this burden happily, for aviation was, and remains, his first love. He did everything he could to make Air-India as good as the best among the world's airlines. Its planes were lavishly decorated. He insisted that even if a plane was used for 20 years, it should always look as if it had come out from its factory — new, inside and outside. And it did. With Air-India, efficiently run, JRD saw no reason why all public undertakings could not also be run to the world's best standards and be profitable.

As Chairman, JRD believed in personalised attention. He was dubbed a perfectionist for he called upon his staff: "Always aim at perfection for only then will you achieve excellence." On every flight on which he travelled he kept detailed notes of his observations and would painstakingly take action on them on return to base. He gave India pride in its national airline. His 46 year aviation career spanned an era from the wood and fabric of the little two-seater Puss Moth to the gleaming 400 seater giant Boeing 747. He insisted that there should be no compromise on operating and maintenance standards or on service. One of the airline's publicity chiefs recalls how he once received a midnight phone call at his home from the Chairman suggesting how to improve the wording on a publicity hoarding. "We had to give so much of ourselves because he gave so much of himself," said this executive.

Air Marshal Nur Khan, former head of the Pakistan Air Force, and later Chairman of Pakistan International Airlines, when asked by an Indian magazine what he thought of his neighbour airline, Air-India, and its then Chairman JRD Tata, replied: "A great airline and JRD is an epic figure." In recognition of this epic figure's services to air transport, JRD was made the recipient in 1979 of the Tony Jannus Award, named after the founder pilot of the first scheduled airline in the world, which began in Tampa, Florida, in 1912. Amongst its recipients are the inventor of the jet engine Sir Frank Whittle; the developers of the Concorde SST, and the founders of the Douglas Aircraft Corporation, Pan-Am, the Eastern and the United Airlines. Other awards followed. In 1989, the Daniel Guggenheim Medal Award, first conferred on Orville Wright, was presented to JRD Tata.

The Great Legend

J. R. D. TATA, a doyen of Indian industry, a visionary, father of civil aviation in India, and, above all, an incredible human being, has left an indelible impression on the country's economic and social life.

He was at the helm of the largest industrial group in India for well over half a century and was also the head of one of the largest public sector undertakings, Air India International for over four decades.

JRD took over as Chairman of the Tata group at the young age of 34 in 1938 and guided its course till his death in 1993, though he relinquished Chairmanship in 1991. The fortunes of the group witnessed a spectacular growth during his tenurè lasting over half a century. The group's assets and turnover zoomed several fold under his stewardship. Over these long years, JRD was not only the head of the Tata group but was also seen as the captain of India Inc.

JRD was gifted with remarkable vision and foresight. He could spot the trends in business before they happened. Tata Consultancy Services, India's largest software and IT services company was a brainchild of JRD and his trusted aide Fakir Chand Kohli. It was born in the early 1970s and has grown to become the largest Indian company in its field with offices in several countries.

What is more important, despite his extremely busy schedule, he found time for various social causes including promoting family planning, gender equality and child welfare.

He played a crucial role in the setting up of the Tata Institute of Fundamental Research and India's first cancer hospital, the Tata Memorial Hospital for Cancer Research and Treatment, apart from playing an important part in the creation of the National Centre for Performing Arts in Mumbai and the National Institute of Advanced Studies in Bangalore.

At 40, he set up a multipurpose trust, the JRD Tata Trust, by donating many of his valuable shares in Tata Sons Ltd and other Tata companies.

Among his concerns was the plight of disadvantaged women and he established a trust of his own called the JRD Tata and Thelma J. Tata trust to improve their lot. The nation's highest civilian honour, Bharat Ratna, was conferred on him in 1992, the only industrialist to receive the honour so far. July 29, 2004 was JRD's birth centenary day. JRD not only changed the lives of all those who had come in touch with him but also contributed a great deal to the economic and social life of India.

Delivering the inaugural address at the JRD Tata Centenary celebration in New Delhi on August 24, the Prime Minister, Dr. Manmohan Singh, referred to JRD's great contribution to the formulation of 'Bombay Plan' of 1944. He had played an exceedingly important role, along with G. D. Birla, Purshottamdas Thakurdas, Ardeshir Dalal, and John Mathai, in the formulation of this long-term plan for the country's economic development after the Second World War. "When we read it today, nearly 60 years later, we see how relevant many of the central propositions of the Bombay Plan remain," Dr. Singh added.

India's Most Enterprising Entrepreneur

Mr. Jamsetji Tata, the founder of the "Tata Sons" which later became the "Tata Group" is the uncle of Mr. JRD Tata. Mr. Jamsetji Tata is known as the "father of Indian Industries". Mr. JRD Tata joined "Tata Sons" as an apprentice in 1925.

In the year 1938, Mr. JRD Tata was elected as the Chairman of "Tata Sons" with 14 enterprises. In the year 1988, after 50 years, when Mr.JRD Tata retired from the Tata Group of Companies, there were 95 enterprises in the Tata Group.

During the last half of the twentieth century "Tata Group" entered several new unconventional businesses and produced/ handled a vast range of products and services like:

> airlines, hotels, air conditioning, trucks locomotives, tea, soda ash, lipsticks, cologne, other heavy chemicals to pharmaceuticals and financial services.

Due to the innovative ideas and implementation of the same, the Tata-Group made everything and do everything.

One of Tata's earliest achievements was to cajole ten rival cement companies, to merge and form the 'Associated Cement Companies', run by the Tata-Group.

JRD strengthened existing businesses such as:

> steel, power and hotels.

As an industrialist, Mr.JRD Tata is credited with placing the "Tata Group " the International map. As an aviator and pioneer flier, he brought commercial aviation to India.

As a patron of the arts, he was revered by India's artists, sculptors and performing artists; under Mr.JRD Tata's tutelage, the Tata-Group became the biggest buyers, promoters and supporters of the art world in India.

And as a philanthropist, he was respected for keeping alive and building up the tremendously active 'Tata charitable trusts'.

He had the honour of being India's first pilot; was Chairman of Tata & Sons for 50 years; launched Air India International as India's first international airline; received Bharat Ratna in 1992.

JRD Tata was one of the most enterprising Indian entrepreneurs. He was a pioneer aviator and built one of the largest industrial houses of India.

JRD Tata was born on July 29, 1904 in Paris. His mother was a French, while his father was Parsi. JRD's full name was Jehangir Ratanji Dadabhoy Tata and he was popularly known as Jeh to his friends. JRD's father Ratanji Dadabhoy Tata and Sri Jamsetji Tata shared their greatness from the same great-great-grandfather, Ervad Jamsheed Tata, a priest of Navsari.

JRD Tata was the second of four children. He was educated in France, Japan and England before being drafted into the French army for a mandatory one-year period. JRD wanted to extend his service in the forces but destiny had something else in store for him. By leaving the French army JRD's life was saved because shortly thereafter, the regiment in which he served was totally wiped out during an expedition in Morocco.

JRD Tata joined Tata & Sons as an unpaid apprentice in 1925. He has great interest in flying. On February 10, 1929, JRD became the first Indian to pass the pilot's examination. With this distinctive honour of being India's first pilot, he was instrumental in giving wings to India by building Tata Airlines, which ultimately became Air India. His passion for flying was fulfilled with the formation of the Tata Aviation Service in 1932.

In 1938, at the age of 34, JRD was elected Chairman of Tata Sons making him the head of the largest industrial group in India. He started with 14 enterprises under his leadership and half a century later on July 26, 1988, when he left, Tata & Sons was a conglomerate of 95 enterprises which they either started or in which they had controlling interest.

JRD was the trustee of Sir Dorabji Tata Trust from its inception in 1932, which remained under his wings for over half a century. Under his guidance, this Trust established Asia's first cancer hospital, the Tata Memorial Centre for Cancer, Research and Treatment, Bombay, 1941. It also founded the Tata Institute of Social Sciences, 1936 (TISS), the Tata Institute of Fundamental Research, 1945 (TIFR), and the National Centre for Performing Arts.

In 1948, JRD Tata launched Air India International as India's first international airline. In 1953, the Indian Government appointed JRD as Chairman of Air-India and a director on the Board of Indian Airlines-a position JRD retained for 25 years. For his crowning achievements in Aviation, JRD was bestowed with the title of Honorary Air Commodore of India.

In 1956, JRD Tata initiated a programme of closer "employee association with management" to give workers a stronger voice in the affairs of the company. He firmly believed in employee welfare and espoused the principles of an eight-hour working day, free medical aid, workers' provident scheme, and workmen's accident compensation schemes, which were later, adopted as statutory requirements in India.

JRD Tata cared greatly for his workers. In 1979, Tata Steel instituted a new practice; a worker is deemed to be "at work" from the moment he leaves home for work till he returns home from work. The company is financially liable to the worker if any mishap takes place on the way to and from work. Tata Steel Township was also selected as a UN Global Compact City because of the quality of life, conditions of sanitation, roads and welfare that were offered by Tata Steel.

JRD Tata received a number of awards. He received the Padma Vibhushan in 1957 on the eve of silver jubilee of Air India. He also received the Guggenheim Medal for aviation in 1988. In 1992, because of his selfless humanitarian endeavors, JRD Tata was awarded India's highest civilian honour, the Bharat Ratna-one of the rarest instances in which this award was granted during a person's lifetime. In the same year, JRD Tata was also bestowed with the United Nations Population Award for his crusading endeavors towards initiating and successfully implementing the family planning movement in India, much before it became an official government policy.

Spirit of the Skies

It is a measure of the man and the life he lived that long before his demise, Jehangir Ratanji Dadabhoy Tata came to represent an exalted idea of Indianness: progressive, benevolent, ethical and compassionate. It did not really matter that the country itself failed this utopian test. JRD, as he was known to commoner and king, had by then transcended the frailties of his milieu.

As an adolescent, JRD loved France and flying more than anything else. By the time he stepped into the autumn of his existence, he had devoted some 50 years to heading and defining a unique business conglomerate, and just as long to championing the interests of India and her myriad people. The evolution, from a thoughtful if self-indulgent young man to a pan-Indian icon revered even by those who knew little about business, contains the essence of the JRD story.

Being one of the last of the great patriarchs of Indian industry contributed, no doubt, to the moulding of his legend, but to call JRD an industrialist is akin to saying Mahatma Gandhi was a freedom fighter. He considered his leadership of the Tata group and his dedication to the cause of India as complementary, and he brought to the two undertakings a rare dignity and sense of purpose.

It is said of JRD that he spoke French better than English and both better than any Indian language. That did not preclude him from forging a special bond with Indians of all ages and backgrounds. Kalpana Chawla, the Indian-born astronaut who perished in the Columbia space shuttle disaster, cited JRD and his pioneering airmail flights as her inspiration for taking up aeronautics. He touched the lives of countless others, rich and poor, manager and worker, as he became the embodiment of the principles and philosophy of the House of Tata.

Nobody could have guessed this is how destiny would unfold when JRD was born, in Paris in 1904, to R.D. Tata, a business partner and relative of Jamsetji Tata, and his French wife Sooni. JRD, the second of four children, was educated in France, Japan and England before being drafted into the French army for a mandatory one year period. JRD wanted to extend his stint in the forces (to avail of a chance to attend a renowned horse-riding school), but his father would have none of it. Leaving the French army saved JRD his life, because shortly thereafter the regiment he served in was wiped out while on an expedition in Morocco.

JRD then set his mind on securing an engineering degree from Cambridge, but R.D. Tata summoned his son back to India (JRD would forever regret not being able to attend university). He soon found himself on the threshold of a business career in a country he was far from familiar with. This was a young man aware of his obligations to the family he belonged to. In a letter to his father on his 21st birthday in 1925, JRD wrote, "One more year has fallen on my shoulders. I have been looking back and also deep inside myself with the merciless eye of conscience, and have been trying to find out whether during this last year I have gained in experience or wisdom. I haven't found out much yet!"

JRD entered the Tatas as an unpaid apprentice in December 1925. His mentor in business was John Peterson, a Scotsman who had joined the group after serving in the Indian Civil Service. At 22, soon after his father passed away, JRD was on the board of Tata Sons, the group's flagship company. In 1929, aged 25, he surrendered his French citizenship to embrace the country that would become the central motif of his life.

The first of JRD's big adventures in business was born of his childhood fascination for flying. He had grown up in France watching the famous aviator Louis Bleriot's early flights, and had taken a joyride in an airplane as a 15 year old. In 1929, JRD became one of the first Indians to be granted a commercial pilot's licence. A year later, a proposal landed at the Tata headquarters to start an airmail service that would connect Bombay, Ahmedabad and Karachi. JRD needed no prompting, but it would take Peterson to convince Dorabji Tata, then chairman of the Tatas, to let the young ace have his way.

In 1932 Tata Aviation Service, the forerunner to Tata Airlines and Air India, took to the skies. The first flight in the history of Indian aviation lifted off from Drigh Road in Karachi with JRD at the controls of a Puss Moth. JRD nourished and nurtured his airline baby through to 1953, when the government of Jawaharlal Nehru nationalised Air India. It was a decision JRD had fought against with all his heart.

Nehru and JRD shared an unusual relationship. They had been friends for long and there was plenty of mutual respect, but they differed significantly on the economic policies India needed to follow. JRD was not a political animal and he never could come to terms with the nature of the socialistic beast then ruling the roost (he once joked, many years after Nehru's passing, that the Chinese steward the Taj Group of Hotels had brought in from abroad earned more money than him). JRD was an articulate and persistent votary of economic liberalisation long before it was finally implemented in India.

The Air India saga certainly hurt JRD, but he wasn't the kind to bear a grudge. Nehru insisted that he continue to head the national carrier and that's what JRD did, right up to 1977, when another act of government forced him out. Indira Gandhi, when she came back to power, reinstated JRD to the chairmanship, but by then he no longer had the appetite for the responsibility.

Air India was never just a job for JRD; it was a labour of love. Tata executives would always be complaining — in private, undoubtedly — that their chairman spent more time worrying about the airliner than he did running all of the Tata group. JRD's ardour for and commitment to Air India was what made it, at least while he was at the helm, a world-class carrier. Wrote Anthony Simpson in his book *Empires of the Sky*: "The smooth working of Air India seemed almost opposite to the Indian tradition on the ground... [JRD] could effectively insulate Air India from the domestic obligation to make jobs and dispense favours."

The qualities that JRD brought to the running of Air India were as much in evidence in his steering of the Tata group. The 'permit raj' era created a difficult, if not hostile, environment for ethical entrepreneurship. The socialist dogma of the time insisted that capitalism was a creature that had to be rigidly controlled, to be tolerated but never trusted. JRD and the Tata group were certainly stymied by the political tenets and orthodoxy of the period.

When JRD was elevated to the top post in the Tata Group in 1938, taking over as chairman from Sir Nowroji Saklatvala, he was the youngest member of the Tata Sons board. Over the next 50 odd years of his stewardship the group expanded into chemicals, automobiles, tea and information technology. Breaking with the

Indian business practice of having members of one's own family run different operations, JRD pushed to bring in professionals. He turned the Tata group into a business federation where entrepreneurial talent and expertise were encouraged to flower.

In later years, this system began to fray at its edges. Detractors contend that it degenerated, as satraps and fiefdoms emerged to challenge the core structure of the Tatas. If it can be held against JRD that he failed to comprehend the dangers of handing away too much control in the operation of individual Tata companies, it must also be acknowledged that he took the lead in consolidating the group when matters came to a head. JRD was brave enough to run the gauntlet and he was man enough to face the fusillade that came in its wake.

Conducting the affairs of a business empire as panoptic and complicated as that of the Tatas would by itself have been a prodigious task, but JRD had plenty more to offer. He played a critical role in increasing India's scientific, medical and artistic quotient. The Tata Institute of Fundamental Research, the Tata Memorial Hospital, the Tata Institute of Social Sciences, the National Institute of Advanced Sciences and the National Centre for the Performing Arts, each an exemplar of excellence in its field, were projects that would not have come to fruition without JRD's steadfast support.

In India the term 'national interest' means all sorts of things to all kinds of people. To JRD, it meant advancing the country's scientific and economic capacities. He had strong views on what would help India and what would hinder its gigantic struggle to eradicate poverty. Though he did his share of it, casual charity did not hold any charms for him. His inclination to put his own money where his beliefs were resulted in the setting up, in 1944, of the multipurpose JRD Tata Trust. A few years later he sold more of his shares and an apartment in Bombay to establish the JRD and Thelma Tata Trust, which works to improve the lot of India's disadvantaged women.

A pet theme with JRD was India's "desperate race between population and production". Here, too, he disagreed with Nehru, who thought "population is our strength". JRD spent a considerable amount of time and resources in figuring out and propagating methods to control the country's population growth. To this end, he helped start what eventually became the International Institute of Population Studies. In 1992, JRD received the United Nations Population Award, late recognition for a lifelong obsession.

Despite his very public persona, JRD was a shy and reticent man. He never hankered after honours but was showered with them, to much bemusement on his part. On being told that the Indian government was thinking about giving him the Bharat Ratna, the country's highest civilian award, he is reported to have said: "Why me? I don't deserve it. The Bharat Ratna is usually given to people who are dead or it is given to politicians. I am not prepared to oblige the government on the former and I am not the latter."

Self-effacing, modest, wistful and endearing are a few of the adjectives used to describe JRD. It wasn't all peaches and cream, though. JRD could not suffer fools and he was scathing when confronted with pomposity or pretension. There was always about him a dapper and cosmopolitan air, with a dry wit thrown in to lighten the load of legend. When a friend began a letter to JRD with the 'Dear Jay' salutation, he wrote back: "I have looked up the dictionary and find that a Jay is 'a noisy, chattering European bird of brilliant plumage' and, figuratively, 'an impertinent chatterer or simpleton'. For future reference, please note that my name is spelt 'Jeh', in abbreviation of 'Jehangir'. Any resemblance between me and the bird is purely coincidental."

He and his wife, Thelma, whom he married after a Paris romance in 1930, did not have any children, but JRD always appeared most comfortable with kids. With adults, a more problematic lot, he displayed a generosity of spirit which held that, whether in business or in life, it was people who mattered. When JRD breathed his last, in a Geneva hospital on November 29, 1993, it could be truly said that an epoch had ended. A noble bit of India — and Indianness — was gone forever.

The Father of the Civil Aviation of India

Mr. JRD Tata was very much interested in flying. In 1929 he became the first Indian to obtain a 'Pilot License'. Mr. JRD Tata's interest in flying enabled him to start "Tata Airlines" which later became "Air India". In 1948, Mr. JRD Tata launched 'Air India International' as India's first international airline. In 1953, the Indian Government appointed Mr. JRD Tata as Chairman of Air-India and a director on the Board of Indian Airlines-a position Mr. JRD Tata retained for 25 years. For his crowning achievements in Aviation, Mr. JRD Tata was bestowed with the title of 'Honorary Air Commodore of India'. He was known as the 'father of India's Civil Aviation'.

The Trustee of "Tata Trust:

> In 1932 'Sir Dorabji Tata Trust' was founded and Mr. JRD Tata was its trustee for more than 50 years.

The Tata—Trust established Asia's first cancer hospital, the 'Tata Memorial Centre for Cancer Research and Treatment' at Bombay in the year 1941.

The Story of Steel (from Tata Steel Website)

The Beginning

The modern iron and steel industry in India owes its origin to the grand vision and perseverance of Jamsetji Nusserwanji Tata. The Tata Iron and Steel Company Limited (Tata Steel) was registered in Bombay on 26th August 1907. The construction of the steel plant was then taken up in earnest with the first stake being driven in February 1908. R.G. Wells, an American with steel plant construction experience took over as the General Manager in 1909. Success came when the first blast furnace was blown in on 2nd December 1911, and the first ingot rolled on 16th February 1912.

The company was originally constructed for a capacity of 160,000 tonnes of pig iron, 100,000 tones of ingot steel, 70,000 tones of rails, beams and shapes, and 20,000 tonnes of bars, hoops and rods. The plant essentially consisted of a battery of 180 non-recovery coke ovens and 30 by-product ovens with a sulphuric acid plant, two blast furnaces (each of 350 tonnes per day capacity), one 300 tonne hot metal mixer, four open hearth furnaces of 50 tonne capacity each, one steam engine driven 40 inch reversing blooming mill, one 28 inch reversing combination rail and structural mill with reheating furnaces, and one 16- inch and two 10 inch rolling mills. Besides, the steel works had a power house, auxiliary facilities and a well-equipped laboratory. The cost of the plant as erected came to around Rs. 23 million.

The War Years

Soon after the outbreak of the First World War in 1914, the plant was geared to meet the priority needs of the government. It worked on a 24 hour schedule, and sold its product to the government at a fraction of the price prevailing in the open market. Two more open hearth furnaces of 60 tonnes capacity each were added to make more steel. Tatas supplied 1500 miles of rails and 300,000 tonnes of steel to the allies' war effort. During this period, Tata steel embarked on an expansion of the works. The greater extension programme was taken up in 1917 to raise the steel production to 500,000 tonnes. This phase saw the then latest Duplex process of steel making being introduced along with an electric driven blooming mill.

The programme was delayed due to the war and could be completed only in 1924. As against the original estimate of Rs. 67.6 million, the final cost came to Rs. 196 million.

The company progressively added new units such as the third Duplex furnace in 1929, two new roughing and finishing mills in 1933, and a new blast furnace along with coke ovens in 1935. Simultaneously, mining leases were renewed or obtained afresh and attention was given to ancillaries and, a capacity of 800,000 tonnes of saleable Steel was attained by 1939. At that time, Tata Steel came to be regarded as the largest Steel plant in the British Empire and also the cheapest exporter of pig iron in the world (the latter reminiscent of the state in 1999).

During the years of the Second World War between 1939 and 1945, Tata Steel contributed in a big way towards supplying war materials. This was a result of successful experimentation and innovation with existing resources. At the instance of the Government, in 1941, Tata Steel put up a wheel, tyre and axle plant to meet the requirements of the railways; in 1942 a mill to manufacture 1,000 tonnes per month of armour plates for defence carriers was added; a benzol recovery plant for producing toluene needed for the manufacture of explosives was put up in 1943; special quality sheets of alloy Steel and of high silicon were made in 1944-45 along with Steel for the famous "Tatanagar" tanks.

Subsequently, Tata Steel was looking for new areas of diversification and for modernising the works.

Expansion to Two Million Tonnes

The Steel target of six million tonnes of ingot Steel per annum in India set for the second five year plan included expansion of the existing Steel plants. Tata Steel was permitted to go in for an expansion to two million tonnes of ingot Steel per annum. Tata Steel's expansion programme, the largest project in the private sector, was started in 1955 and completed by December 1958.

The rated daily capacity of the five blast furnaces in existence prior to TMP was 4200 tonnes. Blast furnace F, with a rated capacity of 1650 tonnes per day, provided sufficient hot metal for the two million tonne programme.

By providing sintered ore, blast furnace production increased by 10 per cent to an annual output of 1,870,000 tonnes. Blast furnace F was completed and put in operation on October 10, 1958. One of the largest and most modern furnaces in the world, it was designed for high top-pressure operation and the use of sinter in the burden. The blowing-in ceremony of blast furnace was regarded as the official christening of TMP.

A huge Steel Melting shop no. 3 (closed down in 1999) comprising two 800 tonne hot metal mixers, three 32 tonne Bessemer converters and seven 200 tonne open-hearth furnaces (with the possibility of adding an eighth furnace) was the corner stone of steel making under TMP.

A new rolling mill complex was constructed consisting of soaking pits, Blooming Mill No. 2 and a sheet Bar and Billet mill (this was closed in early 1999). Between the two mills, the primary capacity was nearly three million tones of ingots per annum. The continuous sheet bar and billet mill No. 2 was the main mill for semi-finished products for feeding the sheet mills, tin bars for the tinplate company and gothics for the manufacture of seamless tubes.

The Medium and Light Structural mill, which was also installed along with the other mills, was capable of rolling diversified products in wide ranges and was designed to roll 350,000 tonnes of blooms per annum. The products manufactured were to be mainly beams, channels, angles, junior beams and parallel flange beams-the last two for the first time in country. The revamping of the rail and structural mill (closed down in 1989), sheet bar and billet mill No. 1 (closed down in 1998) and the merchant mill were also undertaken. A new merchant mill No. 2 was commissioned in 1962. The additional service facilities included water supply arrangement, power supply and distribution to meet the total maximum demand of 125,000 KW and railway track facilities. The two million tonne programme was completed on schedule and involved no major delay.

Period between 1960-80

During the decade of the sixties, consideration was given to the expansion of Tata Steel in the private sector. In July 1961, Tata Steel obtained an industrial license for setting up alloy steel

Sinter plant: A new 1.37 mtpa sinter plant (SP2) to raise the total sinter production to 2.5 mtpa and thereby, increase sinter in blast furnaces to around 65 per cent.

Coke ovens: A coke oven battery with 54 ovens using stamp charging technology to make coke of internationally acceptable quality was established. Stamp charging has given following advantages:

- Superior coke strength after reaction (CSR) compared with top charged coke, as well as higher bulk density.
- Higher yield of sized coke for the blast furnaces.
- Improved blast furnace productivity because of usage of coke with better room temperature and high temperature properties.

Waste recovery: 1 mtpa Waste recycling plant to recover metallics from the plant was established.

Ancillary Technologies: The main technology improvement in phase II was the introduction of coal injection in blast furnaces.

The limited reserves of coking coal in India have always spurred Indian iron makers to strive for lower coke rates. Tata Steel commissioned a coal injection unit in 1991 for its F blast furnace. The system developed by Kloeckner Sstahl Technik (KST) was adopted on the success of coal injection in F blast furnace; the technology was extended to G blast furnace as a part of modernisation phase III and thereafter, also incorporated in D blast furnace.

Modernisation Phase III

The success of modernisation phases I and II and the need to enter the flat product market, provided the necessary impetus to embark on the crucial third phase of modernisation. Keeping in view the international and domestic Steel scenario, it was felt necessary for Tata Steel to set up an internationally competitive flat products complex. Apart from a one million tonne hot strip mill, a new one million tonne G blast furnace was also installed. The landmarks during this phase were:

Ironmaking: To augment steel making capacity, a corresponding increase in hot metal production was necessary. Hence, a highly automated blast furnace of 1 mtpa capacity, called the G blast furnace, was commissioned in November 1992.

Steel making: A new LD shop 2 with two 130t capacity LD vessels, with one out of two operating at any given moment, was commissioned.

New Cold Rolling Mill at Tata Steel

In addition to modernisation, Tata Steel has defined its vision for the next millennium and has embarked on an unprecedented expansion in flat products. As a first step, taking into account the doubling of the capacity of the HSM, a 1.2 million tonnes cold rolling complex has been commissioned in Jamshedpur towards the middle of the year 2000. Some of the salient features of this new development are highlighted.

Facilities in the Cold Rolling Complex

Internationally, the technology of cold rolling has developed to an extremely sophisticated level. This progress has been augmented by the work on technology by equipment suppliers around the world, focused on further improving the processes to produce better products, thereby propelling cold rolled strips to higher levels of quality and cost competitiveness.

The major facilities include a pickling-cum-tandem cold rolling mill, an annealing facility, and galvanising lines.

Steel making and Casting

Major developments in the steel making and casting area includes the following:

- Switchover from duplex and open hearth steel making to the oxygen process.
- Adopting optimum KD vessel configuration (to accommodate the high slag volume as a result of high silicon and phosphorus in hot metal) and use of bottom inert gas agitation.
- Strategy to make low phosphorus Steel.
- Improvement of vessel lining life from 160-180 heats to over 1000 heats
- Adoption of continuous casting through billet and slab casters.

Tata Steel Today

As a result of innovations and technological upgradation, Tata Steel, has become a well-run ultra modern plant - one of the best in the world. Fundamental changes in some metallurgical parameters have brought about this remarkable transformation. Necessity became the mother of invention and numerous innovations invoked improvement. The metallurgical changes introduced were essentially centered around:

- Reducing alumina level in sinter from 4.4 to 2.5 per cent.
- Improving in coke quality
- Making changes in the fluxes used in sintermaking essentially to decrease the alkali input.
- Adopting the optimum LD vessel configuration and blowing conditions to accommodate the high slag volume

required to deal with high silicon and phosphorus in Indian hot metal.

- Increasing the yield during LD steel making
- Introducing continuous casting (CC) instead of ingot casting to increase the net yield.

All these factors have made Tata Steel internationally cost competitive. In terms of hot metal costs, Tata Steel is amongst the lowest in the world and has a clear advantage over other major integrated producers. The cost of conversion from hot metal to a finished product such as hot rolled coils where Tata Steel has not been very competitive so far would be taken care of in the near future as investments already made to achieve the results foreseen. High ash in coke, poor room temperature and high temperature strengths of coke, high alumina in the iron oxide feed, high silicon in hot metal, low yields during steel making, low yield of finished products, high energy consumption, high manpower, etc. have been the weaknesses not only of Tata Steel but of the Indian Steel industry as a whole.

Appropriate steps taken by the Company have already resulted in better yield lower energy consumption, lower silicon in hot metal, lower lime consumption in steel making, higher vessel life, etc., all of which augur well for the Steel Company in future.

Tata Steel in the New Millennium

Tata Steel is all set to establish itself as the supplier of choice by delighting all its customers with its products and services. The Organisation is envisaged to become the most cost competitive Steel plant to serve the community and the nation. Where Tata Steel would venture, others will follow. The 21st century will certainly see a new Tata Steel an integrated Steel plant in India with truly world class facilities along with a will to win amongst a committed and streamlined workforce.

7

Selected Letters

JRD Tata Letters (Collection by S.D. Naik)

The publication of *JRD Tata Letters*, compiled and edited by Mr. Arvind Mambro is, undoubtedly, a unique and wonderful tribute to the memory of this great son of India.

This first compilation of 300 letters out of some 40,000 JRD wrote in his lifetime, reveal various fascinating facets of his personality, his relationships with people, the projects he was involved in, his views on various issues, his kindness, forthrightness and sense of humour, his concerns as a citizen, the values he lived by, and his personal interests.

The range and depth of his interests and concerns are reflected in the huge cross-section of people these letters are addressed to: family members, his colleagues in Tata, business associates, ministers and bureaucrats, friends in India and abroad, as well as to others who were not known to him. He took every letter even from strangers seriously.

Mrs. Sudha Narayan Murthy, who was a student at the Indian Institute of Science, Bangalore in 1974 saw an advertisement for the post of an engineer in Telco (now Tata Engineering) with a line at the bottom: "Lady candidates need not apply." In a fit of anger she shot off a postcard to JRD expressing surprise at the discrimination from a such progressive group as Tata and forgot all about it. She fondly recalls: "Within ten days, I received a telegram stating that I had to appear for an interview at Telco, Pune at their expense." She got the job. She writes: "I consider JRD a great man because, in spite of being an extremely busy person, he valued one post card written by a young girl, who was asking for justice and questioning him.

He must have received thousands of letters every day. He could have thrown mine in a dustbin. But he didn't do that. He respected the intentions of that unknown girl, who had neither influence nor money, and gave her an opportunity to work in his company. He did not merely give her a job, but also changed her life and mindset forever."

Divided into seven sections, the collection contains letters to eminent political and economic personalities, scientists and artists of his time including Mahatma Gandhi, Jayaprakash Narayan, Jawaharlal Nehru, C. Rajgopalachari, Sardar Patel, Indira Gandhi, Morarji Desai, Rajiv Gandhi, Henry Kissinger, G. D. Birla, Shri Ram, David Rockefeller, J. K. Galbraith, Homi Bhabha and Yehudi Menuhin — people who have played a prominent role in contemporary world history.

The collection also includes JRD's correspondence with his parents, shedding light on the intimate and distinctive relationship that they shared.

Some of the letters addressed to political leaders and leading economists on the country's economic policy turned out to be prophetic. JRD was an ardent advocate of free enterprise and had a vision of a healthy partnership between public and private sectors, each concentrating on those fields for which it was best suited. He was against draconian controls on all activities of private sector companies that acted as a major constraint on the country's economic growth and prosperity.

In a letter to Jayaprakash Narayan, in January 1955, who was then a convinced Marxist, he wrote: "I must confess that I do not share your understanding of the capitalist system or its place in history.... I believe that in most part of the world the system of free enterprise, far from dying, will be given a new lease of life in recognition of its ability and willingness to serve the community well and also from a revulsion against the unpleasant reality — as distinct from the myth of state socialism."

This was 35 years before the collapse of Berlin wall and the disintegration of the Soviet Union. A decade later, even conservative China began opening its doors. India took much longer to do away with the licence-permit raj and launch the process of liberalisation and globalisation.

In a letter to Dr. V. K. R. V. Rao in November 1964, in response to his invitation to participate in a Round Table discussion on Economic Growth and Social Justice, JRD expressed anguish over the innumerable restrictive laws and ordinances, endless and all-pervasive controls and an ever proliferating bureaucracy to administer them. "As a result, instead of prosperity combined with social justice, we have today acute shortages and inflation coupled with rampant tax evasion and black markets," he pointed out.

At the same time, he did not spare the private industrialists and businessmen who indulged in unethical business practices.

He frankly admitted that the Indian private industry's poor, or in places downright bad, public image was due far more to the depredations and unethical practices of some its members than to its deficiencies in the use of its resources.

Apart from being efficient producers, he wanted private companies to shoulder some social responsibilities, particularly towards the welfare of the communities in the midst of which they were established.

Family planning and population problem remained his life-long concern. As early as in January 1959 he had written to Nehru expressing concern over the problem as he felt that it presented the most serious obstacle in the country to rapid economic and social progress.

He also wrote on the subject, among others, to Dr. Sushila Nayar (Gandhian social worker and Union Health Minister 1962-67) in July 1964; Dr. Karan Singh in October 1974; and Rajiv Gandhi in April 1988. He received the UN Population award in 1992.

Many of the letters included in this volume, to political leaders and policy-makers reflect his life-long concern over the wrong policies of the Government over the years that turned out to be the roadblocks on the path of country's rapid economic development and poverty alleviation. In a letter to P. N. Haksar (Principal Secretary to the Prime Minister 1972-73) dated September 26, 1984, JRD wrote: "I began my 55 year career as an angry young man because I couldn't stomach the foreign domination of our country. I end it as an angry old man, certainly not because I didn't grow wealthy or powerful; not even because Tatas were prevented from serving the country and enriching its economy to the full extent of their capacity and will, but because it simply breaks my heart to see the continuing miserable fate of the vast majority of our people, for much of which I blame the 35 years of ill-conceived economic policies of our Government."

8

The Tata Group

Introduction

The Tata Group is a multinational company based in Mumbai, India. In terms of market capitalisation and revenues, Tata Group is the largest private corporate group in India and has been recognised as one of the most respected companies in the world. It has interests in steel, automobiles, information technology, communication, power, tea and hospitality. The Tata Group has operations in more than 85 countries across six continents and its companies export products and services to 80 nations. The Tata Group comprises 114 companies and subsidiaries in seven business sectors 27 of which are publicly listed. 65.8 per cent of the ownership of Tata Group is held in charitable trusts. Companies which form a major part of the group include Tata Steel, Corus Steel, Tata Motors, Tata Consultancy Services, Tata Technologies, Tata Tea, Titan Industries, Tata Power, Tata Communications, Tata Teleservices and the Taj Hotels.

TATA Companies

TATA Motors

Tata Motors Limited is a multinational corporation headquartered in Mumbai, India. Part of the Tata Group, it was formerly known as TELCO (TATA Engineering and Locomotive Company). Tata Motors has a consolidated revenue of USD 16 billion after the acquisition of British automotive brands Jaguar and Land Rover in 2008. Established in 1945, when the company began manufacturing locomotives, the company manufactured its first commercial vehicle in 1954 in a collaboration with Daimler-Benz AG, which ended in 1969. Tata Motors is a dual-listed company traded on both the Bombay Stock Exchange, as well as on the New York Stock Exchange. Tata Motors in 2005, was ranked among the top 10 corporations in India with an annual revenue exceeding INR 320 billion.

It is India's largest company in the automobile and commercial vehicle sector with upwards of 70 per cent cumulative Market share in the Domestic Commercial vehicle segment, and a mid sized player on the world market with 0.81 per cent market share in 2007 according to OICA data. The OICA ranked it as the 19th largest automaker, based on figures for 2007 and the second largest manufacturer of commercial vehicles in the world. The company is the world's fourth largest truck manufacturer, and the world's second largest bus manufacturer. In India, Tata ranks as the leader in every commercial vehicle segment, and is in the top 3 makers of passenger cars. Tata Motors is also the designer and manufacturer of the iconic Tata Nano, which at INR 100,000 or approximately USD 2300, is the cheapest car in the world.

Tata Motors has auto manufacturing and assembly plants in Jamshedpur, Pantnagar, Lucknow, Ahmadabad and Pune in India, as well as in Argentina, South Africa and Thailand.

JRD Tata Founder of Tata Motors (1938-1993)

JRD Tata, a man who has grown into a legend touched the lives of countless people, rich and poor, manager and worker, as he became the embodiment of the principles and philosophy of the House of Tatas.

He led the Tata Group for 55 years. During that period, as a financial daily put it, 'The Tata group's crowning achievement was the making of Tata Engineering & Locomotive Company, a giant that has earned a reputation for investing in men as much as in machines, in nurturing and developing creativity instead of simply buying technology from abroad, in making products appropriate for India and yet good enough for the international markets."

JRD's principles and vision laid the foundation for Tata Motors' growth. His style of management was to pick the best person for the job at hand and let him have the latitude to carry out the job. He was never for micro-management. It was he who zeroed in on Sumant Moolgaokar, the engineering genius who successfully steered our Company for many years.

He was a visionary whose thinking was far ahead of his time. The dream of a passenger car developed in India was born in his time and remained an enduring vision through the years. This provided support to many activities in Tata Motors, which were necessary to see the dream become a reality, e.g., establishment of a full-fledged R&D department at Pune, in-house development of gear box technology, entry into passenger car market and so on.

JRD firmly believed in employee welfare and espoused the principles of an eight-hour working day, free medical aid, workers' provident scheme, workmen's accident compensation schemes, which were later adopted as statutory requirements in the country. In 1956, he initiated a programme of closer "employee association with management" to give workers a stronger voice in the affairs of the Company.

He believed that the social responsibilities of industrial enterprises should extend even beyond serving people, to the environment. He commented on building the lake near the site of the Tata Motors, Pune plant, 'We did not have to create a lake to produce a truck, but we did.' His emphasis on values, on ethics, on investing in education, research, science, technology, health care and in improving the quality of life of ordinary people was a forerunner of the more recent concepts of "corporate social responsibility".

His every visit to the Tata Motors plant was characterised by a keen interest not only in machines and manufacturing processes but also in the employees. He was at home with any age group and his infectious enthusiasm and warmth as also his courtesy, philanthropy and humanity were legendary even in his lifetime.

JRD Tata was awarded the country's highest civilian honour, the Bharat Ratna, in 1992 — one of the rare instances when the award was granted during a person's lifetime. And, on his death, the Indian Parliament was adjourned in his memory, an action that spoke much more than any words could have done.

Tata Motors - Providing the Wheels for India's Growth

This quote reflects the philosophy of Tata Motors. A pioneering spirit, the pursuit of excellence and the will to succeed in the face of challenges are the pillars on which the foundation of Tata Motors rests. Maintaining high standards of excellence; raising the bar with each new product while meeting and persevering to exceed customer expectations, have been the guiding principles driving Tata Motors in its pursuit of automotive excellence over the past five decades. From the first Tata truck that rolled out in 1954 to the present day, Tata Motors has been on a journey of constant evolution and growth.

In a message to employees at the inception of Tata Motors (then Tata Engineering and Locomotive Co.) in 1945, Mr. JRD Tata had said, "Undertaking the manufacture of boilers first, then locomotives and eventually engineering machinery is an important step forward in the country's march towards industrial self-sufficiency." The founders of Tata Motors also envisioned that in the post-independence era, the socioeconomic and political developments taking place would mean the movement of men and material across the nation. To meet the huge transportation needs and taking the opportunity to be a part of nation building; Tata Motors collaborated with Daimler Benz of Germany in 1954 to manufacture trucks. The two parted ways in 1969 and the Company's vehicles got a new name - from Tata Mercedes Benz Trucks, they were now Tata trucks.

Mr. Sumant Moolgaokar, Chairman, Tata Motors (1972-1988) had said, "Profits should come from productivity and not by raising prices in a favourable market. Our greatest asset is customer affection." This has remained the Company's credo throughout.

But the story of Tata Motors is not just about trucks and buses. Realising the opportunity for entering a new segment, Tata Motors launched two passenger vehicles - the sports vehicle, Tata Sierra in 1991 and the Tata Estate in 1992. The first fully indigenously developed small car - Tata Indica followed soon after. A car that rewrote the rules of the Indian car industry and propelled India into a select group of nations that manufactures its own car.

Tata Motors, with its full range of commercial and passenger vehicles, is all about meeting India's needs. With trucks that move men and material in places where even roads are non-existent; Tata Motors helps India's armed forces guard the nation's borders. It ensures that little children reach school safely in their Tata school buses.

Equally important to Tata Motors is its belief that it has a special responsibility to the community in which it operates. This has formed the guideline for its community development programme that strives to improve the quality of life of the people.

Having won the hearts of millions of Indians, Tata Motors is set to tap opportunities in global markets. With the Company's recent acquisition of Daewoo Commercial Vehicle Co., South Korea, and its foray into international markets, Tata Motors is geared for its cruise on the world track. On a relentless quest for excellence, Tata Motors looks forward to new challenges.

TATA Power

Started as the Tata Hydroelectric Power Supply Company in 1911, it is an amalgamation of two entities: Tata Hydroelectric Power Supply Company and Andhra Valley Power Supply Company (1916).

Today Tata Power Company Limited is India's largest private sector electricity generating company with an installed generation capacity of over 2670 MW. The Company is a pioneer in the Indian power sector. Tata Power has a presence in thermal, hydro, solar and wind areas of power generation, transmission and retail. The founders of Tata Power pioneered the generation of electricity in India with the commissioning of India's first large hydroelectric project in 1915 in Bhivpuri and Khopoli, Karjat.

The thermal power stations of the company are located at Trombay in Mumbai, Jojobera in Jharkhand and Belgaum in Karnataka. The hydro stations are located in the Western Ghats of Maharashtra and the wind farm in Ahmednagar.

TATA Tea

Tata Tea Limited, also known as Tata-Tetley, is the world's second largest manufacturer and distributor of tea. Owned by India's Tata Group, the Tata Tea Limited markets tea under the major brands Tata Tea, Tetley, Good Earth Teas and JEM'A. While Tata Tea is the largest tea brand in India, Tetley is the largest tea company in the United Kingdom and Canada and the second largest in the United States by volume and JEM'A is Czech Republic's leading tea company. Tata Tea manufactures 70 million kilograms of tea in India, controls 54 tea estates, packaging factories and employs around 59,000 people. The company owns 51 tea estates in India and Sri Lanka, especially in Assam, West Bengal in eastern India and Kerala in the south. The company is the largest manufacturer of Assam tea and Darjeeling tea and the second largest manufacturer of Ceylon tea.

TATA Communication

Tata Communications Limited, formerly known as Videsh Sanchar Nigam Limited or VSNL, is India's largest telecommunication company in international long distance, enterprise data and internet services.

Part of the Tata Group, Tata Communications is based in Mumbai and has operations in over 80 cities spread across 40 countries. Through its subsidiary Tyco Global Network, it is also one of the world's largest submarine cable bandwidth providers and has the world's largest network of submarine cables. Other subsidiaries of Tata Communications include VSNL International Canada, formerly known as Tele globe while it is the majority shareholder of Neotel, South Africa's second national operator (SNO) for fixed line telecommunication services.

In 1986, VSNL was formed as a Government of India-owned company. In 2000, Tata Group acquired controlling stake in VSNL which was later expanded to 46 per cent. In February 2008, VSNL was renamed as Tata Communications Limited.

Taj Hotels, Resorts and Palaces

Taj Hotels Resorts and Palaces is a worldwide chain of luxury hotels and resorts. The Indian Hotels Company Limited and its subsidiaries are collectively known as Taj Hotels Resorts and Palaces. A part of the Tata Group, one of India's largest business conglomerate, Taj Hotels Resorts and Palaces comprises 76 hotels, 7 palaces, 6 private islands and 12 resorts and spas, spanning 52 destinations in 12 countries across 5 continents. Besides India, Taj Hotels Resorts and Palaces are located in the United States of America, United Kingdom, Africa, the Middle East, Maldives, Mauritius, Malaysia, Bhutan, Sri Lanka and Australia.

Jamsetji Nusserwanji Tata, founder of the Tata Group, opened the Taj Mahal Palace & Tower, the first Taj property, on December 16, 1903. He was inspired to open the grand luxury hotel after an incident involving cultural unfairness at the Watson's Hotel in Mumbai, where he was refused entry as the hotel did not permit Indians. Hotels which accepted only European guests were common across British India. Jamsetji Tata travelled to London, Paris, Berlin and Düsseldorf to get the best materials and pieces of art, furniture and interior artifacts for his hotel. Due to its prime location, traditional architecture and massive size, this hotel soon gained the status of the most iconic hotel in Mumbai.

Titan Industries

Titan watch division was started in 1987. At launch it was the third watch company in India after HMT and Allwyn. Titan formed a joint venture with Timex, which lasted until 1998, and setup a strong distribution network across India. As of 2005, Titan watches account for a 25 per cent share of the total Indian market and are also sold in about 40 countries through marketing subsidiaries based in London, Aden, Dubai and Singapore. Titan watches are sold in India through retail chains controlled by Titan Industries.

Titan Industries has claimed to have manufactured the world's slimmest wrist watch - Titan Edge. Produced indigenously after four years of research and development, the Titan Edge has a total slimness of just 3.5 mm and a wafer thin movement of 1.15 mm. Apart from the Titan Edge, Titan also offers Steel, Regalia, Raga, Fastrack, Technology, Nebula, Bandhan, Sonata, Octane Tamil Nadu.

Fastrack is a popular brand among youth in India. Fastrack watches come in a variety of styles, shapes and colours.

Tanishq is currently the most prominent jewellery brand of India, and it pioneered the concept of branded jewellery and ornaments in India. The name Tanishq has been formed by combining "Ta" (the first two letters of Tata) and "Nishk or Nishkh" (meaning gold coin or necklace in Sanskrit).

Tanishq is India's largest jewellery brand with a wide range of jewellery in 22 Kt pure gold studded with diamonds or coloured gems. It is the fastest growing jewellery brand in India.

TATA Teleservices

Tata Teleservices Limited (TTSL) is a part of the Tata Group of companies based in Navi Mumbai, an Indian conglomerate. It operates under the brand name Tata Indicom in various telecom circles of India. In Nov. 2008, Japanese telecom giant NTT Docomo picked up a 26 per cent equity stake in Tata Teleservices for about Rs. 13,070 crore ($2.7 billion) or an enterprise value of Rs. 50,269 crore ($10.38 billion). In Feb. 2008, TTSL announced that it would provide CDMA mobile services targeted towards the youth, in association with the Virgin Group on a Franchise model basis.

Tata Teleservices Provides mobile services under 3 Brand names:

- Tata Indicom (CDMA Mobile operator),
- Tata DoCoMo (GSM Mobile operator),
- Virgin Mobile (CDMA& GSM Mobile operator).

Tata Teleservices spearheads the Group's presence in the telecom sector. Incorporated in 1996, Tata Teleservices was the first to launch CDMA mobile services in India with the Andhra Pradesh circle.

The company acquired Hughes Telecom (India) Limited [now renamed Tata Teleservices (Maharashtra) Limited] in December 2002. With a total investment of Rs. 19,924 Crore, Tata Teleservices has created a Pan India presence spread across 20 circles that includes Andhra Pradesh, Chennai, Gujarat, J&K, Karnataka, Delhi, Maharashtra, Mumbai, North East, Tamil Nadu, Orissa, Bihar, Rajasthan, Punjab, Haryana, Himachal Pradesh, Uttar Pradesh

(E), Uttar Pradesh (W), Kerala, Kolkata, Madhya Pradesh and West Bengal.

TATA Chemicals

Tata Chemicals has the largest single soda ash production capacity plant in India. Since 2006 Tata Chemicals has owned Brunner Mond, a United Kingdom-based chemical company with operations in Kenya and the Netherlands.

Advinus Therapeutics, headquartered in Bangalore, India, a Contract research organisation focused on drug discovery and development for Pharmaceutical, Agro and Biotech industries.

TATA Steel

Tata Steel formerly known as TISCO and Tata Iron and Steel Company Limited, is the world's sixth largest steel company, with an annual crude steel capacity of 31 million tones. It is the largest private sector steel company in India in terms of domestic production. Ranked 258th on Fortune Global 500, it is based in Jamshedpur, Jharkhand, India. It is part of Tata Group of companies. Tata Steel is also India's second-largest and second-most profitable company in private sector with consolidated revenues of Rs. 1,32,110 crore and net profit of over Rs. 12,350 crore during the year ended March 31, 2008. Its main plant is located in Jamshedpur, Jharkhand, with its recent acquisitions, the company has become a multinational with operations in various countries. The Jamshedpur plant contains the DCS supplied by Honeywell. The registered office of Tata Steel is in Mumbai. The company was also recognised as the world's best steel producer by World Steel Dynamics in 2005. [The company is listed on Bombay Stock Exchange and National Stock Exchange of India, and employs about 82,700 people (as of 2007).

Strategy Management at Tata Steel

The growth of a company is invariably determined not just by its strategy, but on how it responds to the challenges it encounters. Over the decades, Tata Steel has successfully countered several challenges that have come its way with innovative responses and continuous improvement which have enabled it to remain stable and even convert some of these challenges into opportunities.

It is this culture of endurance that has accorded Tata Steel the insight and focus to deal with the current economic environment. Drawing from its inner strength and beliefs, Tata Steel responded by launching several initiatives across all its operations in various geographies that are helping the Group achieve sustainable growth even in the current times. It is also this very culture that will propel Tata Steel to continue on its growth trajectory in the years to come.

Tata Steel, formerly known as TISCO and Tata Iron and Steel Company Limited, is the world's sixth largest steel company, with an annual crude steel capacity of 31 million tons. It is the second largest private sector steel company in India in terms of domestic production. Ranked 315th on Fortune Global 500, it is based in Jamshedpur, Jharkhand, India. It is part of Tata Group of companies. Tata Steel is also India's second-largest and second-most profitable company in private sector with consolidated revenues of Rs. 1,32,110 crore and net profit of over Rs. 12,350 crore during the year ended March 31, 2008.

Its main plant is located in Jamshedpur, Jharkhand, with its recent acquisitions; the company has become a multinational with balanced global presence in over 50 developed European and fast growing Asian markets, with manufacturing units in 26 countries operations in various countries. The Jamshedpur plant contains the DCS supplied by Honeywell. The registered office of Tata Steel is in Mumbai. The company was also recognised as the world's best steel producer by World Steel Dynamics in 2005. The company is listed on Bombay Stock Exchange and National Stock Exchange of India, and employs about 82,700 people.

Tata Steel's Jamshedpur (India) Works has a crude steel production capacity of 6.8 MTPA which is slated to increase to 10 MTPA by 2010. The Company also has proposed three Greenfield steel projects in the states of Jharkhand, Orissa and Chhattisgarh in India with additional capacity of 23 MTPA and a Greenfield project in Vietnam.

Through investments in Corus, Millennium Steel (renamed Tata Steel Thailand) and Nat Steel Holdings, Singapore, Tata Steel has created a manufacturing and marketing network in Europe, South East Asia and the pacificrim countries.

Tata Steel, through its joint venture with Tata Blue Scope Steel Limited, has also entered the steel building and construction applications market.

The iron ore mines and collieries in India give the Company a distinct advantage in raw material sourcing. Tata Steel is also striving towards raw materials security through joint ventures in Thailand, Australia, Mozambique, Ivory Coast (West Africa) and Oman. Tata Steel has signed an agreement with Steel Authority of India Limited to establish a 50:50 joint venture company for coal mining in India. Also, Tata Steel has bought 19.9 per cent stake in New Millennium Capital Corporation, Canada for iron ore mining.

On 2nd April, 2007, the Company completed the acquisition of Corus Group plc, Steel Company headquartered at UK for an Enterprise Value of USD 14.7 billion. Post the acquisition of Corus, Tata Steel Group is now the world's 6th largest steel company with current steel deliveries of 32 million tons. Set up as Asia's first integrated steel plant and India's largest integrated private sector steel company, a century ago, it is now the world's second most geographically diversified steel producer, with operations in 24 countries and commercial presence in over 50 countries. The Jamshedpur operations in India is increasing its capacity from 5 mtpa to 10 mtpa by end 2010 and the Company has also signed MoUs to set up four greenfield steel projects in the states of Jharkhand, Orissa and Chhattisgarh in India and one in Vietnam.

History

The Swadeshi Movement encouraged Jamsetji Tata to set up Asia's first ever privately owned integrated iron and steel plant. His interest in iron making was triggered in 1882 when he came across an official report on the Chanda district which identified large deposits of high-quality iron ore but also noted a lack of suitable coal in the region. His idea of endowing his country with its own iron and steel industry gained support within the government and in 1907, when the Swadeshi Movement was at its height, the Tata Iron and Steel Company Ltd. was incorporated.

The Tatas raised the finance to build the steel plant within India– a significant milestone in Indian economic history. They proved a point to the then British government that an Indian company had the vision and the wherewithal to build an industry from the ground up and had the know-how to apply international standards to meet local needs. The setting up of the Tata Iron and Steel Company Ltd. gave Indian industry a voice paving the way for many a future enterprise.

Tata Steel introduced an 8 hour work day as early as in 1912 when only a 12 hour work day was the legal requirement in Britain. It introduced leave-with-pay in 1920, a practice that became legally binding upon employers in India only in 1945. Similarly, Tata Steel started a Provident Fund for its employees as early as in 1920, which became a law for all employers under the Provident Fund Act only in 1952. Tata Steel's furnaces have never been disrupted on account of a labour strike and this is an enviable record.

Time-Line

- *1907:* Tata Steel was established by Parsi businessman Jamsetji Tata in 1907
- *1924:* Manufacture of Steel by Duplex Process commenced.
- 1935: Production of high-tensile steel commenced.
- *1940:* The new 100 Tonne Blast Furnace started operation.
- *1961:* An industrial license is obtained by Tata Steel for an Alloy-Steel project in July.
- *1963:* The government approves in principle expansion by One Million tons during the 4th Plan.
- *1965:* The Steel Ministry agrees to expansion to 4 Million Ingot tons with a Strip Mill.
- *1974:* Amalgamation with West Bokaro Limited for coal mine operations.
- *1979:* Five-year Rural Development programme for upliftment of the villagers near Jamshedpur takenup.
- *1981:* In 1981, Ratan was named Chairman of Tata Industries; the Group's other holding company, where he

became responsible for transforming it into the Group's strategy think-tank and a promoter of new ventures in high-technology businesses.

- *1985:* JRD Tata becomes Chairman Emeritus after guiding Tata Steel as Chairman for 46 years. Russi Mody takes over as new Chairman. Merger of the Indian tube company with Tata Steel.
- *1986:* Started an export cell which coordinated the Company's growing exports.
- *1991:* In 1991, Mr. Ratan N. Tata took over as group chairman from JRD Tata, pushing out the old guard and ushering in younger managers. Since then, he has been instrumental in reshaping the fortunes of the Tata Group, which today has the largest market capitalisation of any business house on the Indian Stock Market. Dr. J.J. Irani becomes Managing Director.
- *1993:* The new One million ton capacity "G" Blast Furnace was commissioned.
- *1997:* The Company sold the 67.5 MW Power Plants, under construction at Jojobera, put under its earlier Modernisations Programme-Phase III, to Tata Electric Companies for a total consideration of Rs. 300 crore. Received Prime Minister's trophy for the Best Integrated Steel Plant for the year 1995-96. Dr. J.J. Irani was conferred an Honorary Knighthood by the Queen of Great Britain.
- *2000:* Mr. Tata was honoured by the Government of India with the Padma Bhushan on 26th January 2000, on the occasion of the 50th Republic Day of India.
- *2000:* Company was recognised as the world's lowest-cost producer of steel.
- *2005:* The company was also recognised as the world's best steel producer by World Steel Dynamics.
- *2007:* On January 31 2007 Tata Steel won their bid for Corus after offering 608p per share, valuing Corus at £6.7 bn ($11.3bn); as a result and pending acceptance and

completion of the takeover, the joining of the two will create the fifth largest steel company in the world.

Vision and Mission

The vision of a company provides managers with unity of direction that transcends a well-conceived vision of an organisation comprises two main components. The first component is Core Ideology and second is Envisioned Future. Core Ideology defines "what an organisation stands for, and why they exist" that never changes and sets forth envisioned future that defines "what an organisation aspires to become to achieve to create" that demands significant change and progress.

Vision Statement of Tata Steel

> "We aspire to be the global steel industry benchmark for Value Creation and Corporate Citizenship"

We make the difference through:

- Our people, by fostering team work, nurturing talent, enhancing leadership capability and acting with pace, pride and passion.
- Our offer, by becoming the supplier of choice, delivering premium products and services, and creating value with our customers.
- Our innovative approach, by developing leading edge solutions in technology, processes and products.
- Our conduct, by providing a safe working place, respecting the environment, caring for our communities and demonstrating high ethical standards.

Elucidation: A Vision of an organisation should reflect the concerns of other stakeholders such as shareholders, customers, the local community and society in order to be effective. The vision statement of Tata Steel also stresses on people concerns. The vision statement of Tata Steel is describing that "We aspires to become the global steel industry benchmark" which gives the view of Tata Steel`s future direction and course of business activity.

TATA Steel lays stress on their core ideology in vision statement by taking People, Suppliers and Ethics into account. It also emphasises on their innovative approach for cost leadership and differentiation in their products and process. The vision statement of Tata Steel provides managers with unity of direction that transcends individuals, parochial and transitory needs.

Mission Statement

A vision becomes tangible when it is expressed in the form of a mission statement. Such a statement verbalises the beliefs of the managers and the directions in which the manager seeks to lead the organisation. Mission is defined as a fundamental and enduring purpose of an organisation that sets it apart from the organisation in the similar business.

Mission Statement of Tata Steel:

- Achieve sustainable, profitable growth in steel and related businesses.
- Create differential value for our customers through innovative offerings.
- Continuous improvement of business processes and technologies.
- Foster partnership with key stakeholders.
- Enhance employees' competencies to create a high performing and innovative organisation. Be a responsible corporate citizen and enhance the quality of life of employees and key community.

Elucidation: Tata Steel's mission embodies the business philosophy of strategic decision-makers like to achieve sustainable and profitable growth, it reflects the firm's self-concept like being the high performer and innovative organisation.

A well designed mission statement of an organisation should talk about the customer needs, the company activities, technologies and competencies. In the same way mission statement of the Tata Steel describes to create differential value for the customers with the help of continuous improvement in their business process and technology.

Policies

Quality Policy: Tata Steel is committed to creating value for all our stakeholders by continually improving our systems and processes through innovation, involving all our employees. This policy shall form the basis of establishing and reviewing the Quality Objectives and shall be communicated across the organisation. The policy will be reviewed to align with business direction and to comply with all the requirements of the Quality Management Standard.

Corporate Social Responsibility Policy: Tata Steel believes that the primary purpose of a business is to improve the quality of life of people. So it is committed to improve the quality of the life of the people in the areas where it operates.

Environmental, Occupational Health and Safety Policy: Tata Steel reaffirms its commitment to provide safe working place and clean environment to its employees and other stakeholders as an integral part of its business philosophy and values under which it will continually enhance its Environmental, Occupational Health and Safety (EHS) performance in its activities, products and services through a structured EHS management framework.

Research Policy: Tata Steel nurtures and encourages innovative research in a creative ambience to ensure that the competitive advantage in its overall business is retained and surpassed. Towards this goal, the Company commits itself to providing all necessary resources and facilities for use by motivated researchers of the highest calibre.

Core Values

The TATA Group has always sought to be a value – driven organisation. These values continue to direct the Group's growth and businesses. The five core values underpinning the way TATA does business are:

- *Integrity:* They believe in conducting their business fairly, with honesty and transparency. Everything they do must stand the test of public scrutiny.
- *Respect for Individuals:* They show care, respect, compassion and humanity for employees and customers around the

world, and always work for the benefit of the communities they serve.

- *Excellence:* Constantly striving to achieve the highest possible standards in their day to day work and in the quality of the goods and services they provide.
- *Unity:* They believe in working cohesively with their employees across the group and with customers and partners around the world, building strong relationship based on tolerance, understanding and mutual cooperation.
- *Responsibility:* Their endeavour to continue to be responsible, sensitive to the countries, communities and environments in which they operate, and always ensuring that what comes from people goes back to the people many times over.

Company Strategy

With the global increase in opportunities and demand of steel, TATA steel has planned to become 2nd largest by 2012, by expanding the production. Financial prudence remains the hallmark of any strategy that Tata Steel adopts that's why it reduces the capital expenditure plan by 40 per cent. By keeping stiff control on financial risk TATA steal remain committed to its long-term strategy and will continue to allocate capital towards its existing operations and new projects that are of strategic importance.

In February 2008, the Tata Steel Group launched a new Vision with the aim of setting a world benchmark in Value Creation and Corporate Citizenship. With regard to Value Creation, the Tata Steel Group set itself a target of increasing the return on invested capital of its existing assets to 30 per cent by 2012-13 and to generate selective growth. In order to meet this target, the Group has developed a twofold strategy:

- In order to increase the quality of earnings of its existing assets, the Group will pursue hospitalisation of its European assets, restructure low profitability assets and continue to derive benefits through continuous improvement and synergies across the Group.

- In order to generate selective growth, the Group will pursue capacity expansions and securing access to raw materials. The Group is increasing its capacity in India, through expansion of its current operations in Jamshedpur and through the construction of a greenfield site in Orissa, and assessment of raw material investment opportunities as and when they arise. Corporate citizenship involves providing a safe working place, respecting the environment, caring for its communities and demonstrating high ethical standards. The Group wants to be a part of the climate change solution and has set a target to reduce its CO_2 emission from the current 2.07 tonnes of CO_2 per tonne of liquid steel to 1.5 tonnes of CO_2 per tonne of liquid steel by 2012 through process improvements, breakthrough technologies and development of new products and services. More specifically, the emission target is planned to be achieved through:
- Large investments including BOS gas recovery and back pressure valves at Port Talbot and a new ladle furnace at IJmuiden.
- Burden optimisation, e.g. through switching to pellet feed, increased scrap ratio, reduced slag volume and increased coal injection.
- Smaller investments and housekeeping actions, e.g. yield improvements, lighting efficiency and variable speed drives across all entities.

During the year, the Group has continued to execute its long-term strategy and the tactical planning for development of new markets is well under way. South East Asia is one of the key growth regions and the Group is focused on developing a greenfield expansion in Vietnam and optimising operations in both Nat Steel and Tata Steel Thailand. In the construction sector, the Group is exploring options to develop strong positions in India and in South East Asia through leveraging its European expertise. The Group also continued to explore raw material opportunities to improve the cost competitiveness of its European and South East Asian operations.

Growth Strategy

Company's long term strategy is to continue to pursue capacity expansion in India through Greenfield projects as well including Orissa, Jharkhand and Chhattisgarh projects. Therefore the Indian growth strategy remains a fundamental part of the long term strategy of the Tata Steel Group.

The strategic levers of the Group have remained the same over the last few years. The current global economic scenario has only rephased some of these strategies in terms of timing and speed. The four levers are:

- Making the European operations competitive by hastening the speed of the "Weathering the Storm" and "Fit for the Future" programme.
- Quick completion of the expansion plans in India. The 3 mtpa project will be commissioned by 2011 and will add significant value to the Group. Further expansion in India through the Greenfield project in Orissa and Chhattisgarh are ongoing and their commencing will depend on ground realities and iron ore allocation.
- Investment in raw material assets to provide better raw material security especially to our European operations.
- Vigorous pursuit of continuous improvement across all our operations.

Despite the current slowdown in consolidation within the global steel industry, mergers and acquisitions remain a critically important business strategy for most corporates. Steel analysts are expecting a new wave of consolidation to take place in the next three years. Global giants are refocusing on positive markets by applying their resources to the core business where they are most needed. This creates opportunities to gain market share from competitors who diversify and split their focus. Acquisitions and strategic alliances are also critical to strengthen, refocus and position companies for increased growth and profitability. The Tata Steel Group is strongly pursuing its long-term strategy of acquiring and developing mining projects for its raw material security for iron ore and coking coal. The Group has been concentrating on the geographies that are logistically favourable with respect to its plants in Europe and Asia.

Raw Material Strategy: One of the major problems faced in the steel sector is the availability of raw material. Tata Steel in India is an integrated player, for the majority of its raw material requirements. However, raw material self-sufficiency for the consolidated entity is at 25 per cent post the Corus acquisition. It has been the stated objective of the company to increase self-sufficiency of raw materials to 50 per cent in the medium to long term. Therefore company is acquiring new virgin sites with significant resource potential and stocks or in terms of smaller existing ventures which can be quickly aligned to the requirements in Europe. Riversdale Energy Mining Limited, holds an inferred reserve of around 4 billion tons in one tenement, in Mozambique.

Financing and Liquidity Strategy: For the global financial crisis, the company responded very quickly on many fronts and financing was certainly one of them. Recognising the uncertain financing environment and the fragile state of the global banking industry, company has focussed on both internal and external levers. Primary importance is placed on conserving liquidity through reduced spend management and sharp reduction in working capital levels. Also focus is given on improvement in the productivity levels and reduction in overheads. On capital expenditure, company has reprioritised on the most value creating and critical projects and reworked the capital planning strategy. On the external front, long term capital are raised which acts as a liquidity buffer in the current circumstance. The above actions ensured that the Tata Steel Group had adequate liquidity and also financial flexibility for growth and exigencies.

Present Strategic Issues:

- Global Leader/presence both in means of Quality and Quantity.
- Security and procurement of raw materials.
- Entering the new markets.
- Eliminating the RED colour from balance sheet.

- Struggle to digest the big ticket global acquisitions.
- Leadership crisis within the company.

Strategic Focus: The strategic focus of the Company has been to increase the steel making capacity in excess of 50 million tons by 2015 through organic and inorganic growth. The key enablers identified to achieve the strategic goal and to build a sustainable value centric culture are:

- Being the employer of choice
- Oneness with the society
- Leadership and talent management
- Adaptability to changes in the external environment
- Security of raw materials
- Research and development and technological up gradation.
- Branding
- Financial prudence through capital stewardship and performance management.

Strategic Business Units: Apart from the main Steel Division, Tata Steel's operations are grouped under the following Strategic

Business Units:

- *Bearings Division:* Manufactures ball bearings, double row self-aligning bearings, magneto bearings, clutch release bearings and tapered roller bearings for two wheelers, fans, water pumps, etc.
- *Ferro Alloys and Minerals Division:* Operates chrome mines and has units for making ferro chrome and ferro manganese. It is one of the largest players in the global ferro chrome market.
- *Agrico Division:* Tata Agrico is the first organised manufacturer in India of hand tools and implements for application in agriculture.
- *Tata Growth Shop (TGS):* Has designed, developed, manufactured, erected and commissioned thousands of tonnes of equipment ranging from overhead cranes to

high precision components, including a rocket launch pad for the Indian Space and Research Organisation.

- *Tubes Division:* The biggest steel tube manufacturer with the largest market share in India, it aspires to strengthen its market presence by expanding and modernising its commercial and precision tube manufacturing capacity.
- *Wire Division:* A pioneer in the manufacture of steel wires in India, it produces coated and uncoated wires, branded as Tata Wiron. The division also operates a wholly owned subsidiary in Sri Lanka.

Joint Ventures, Mergers and Acquisitions:

- *Corus:* Europe's second largest steel maker with operations in the UK and mainland Europe and over 40,000 employees worldwide. It's long and strip products cater to the construction, automotive, packaging, and engineering and other markets worldwide. Corus's takeover was the one of the biggest merger in steel industry for which TATA was paying 608 pence per share which is seven times of is original value.
- *Tinplate Company of India Limited (TCIL):* With a market share of over 35 per cent, it is the industry leader in India.
- *Tayo Rolls Limited:* India's leading roll manufacturer and supplier, the company produces rolls which find application in integrated steel plants.
- *Tata Ryerson Limited (TRYL):* TRYL is in the business of steel processing and distribution.
- *Tata Refractories Limited (TRL):* It produces High Alumina, Basic, Dolomite, Silica and Monolithic Refractories and offers design, procurement and relining applications services.
- *Tata Sponge Iron Limited (TSIL):* TSIL is the first Indian sponge iron plant based on Tata Steel's Direct Reduction Technology.
- *Tata Metaliks:* Amongst the top wealth creating companies (EVA+) in the country, Tata Metaliks is engaged in the business of manufacturing and selling foundry grade pig iron.

- *Tata Pigments Limited:* TPL's range of products includes oxides of iron, dry cement paint, exterior emulsion paint and distemper.
- *Jamshedpur Injection Powder Limited (Jamipol):* JAMIPOL manufactures carbide de-sulphurising compounds which are used for de-sulphurising hot metal for the production of low-sulphur, high-quality steel.
- *TM International Logistics Limited (TMILL):* TMILL provides material handling and port operation services at Haldia and Paradip Ports.
- *Mjunction Services Limited:* Mjunction, operating at the cutting edge of Information Technology, is a 50:50 venture of SAIL and Tata Steel. It is India's largest *e*-Commerce company and the world's largest *e*-Market place for steel.
- *TRF Limited:* TRF, one of India's leading companies in the business of design, manufacture, supply, installation and commissioning of engineered-to-order equipment and systems in the areas of bulk material handling, processing, reclaiming and blending.
- *Jamshedpur Utility and Service Company Limited (JUSCO):* Re-engineered out of Tata Steel's town services, JUSCO is a wholly owned subsidiary of Tata Steel and is the country's first enterprise that provides municipal and civic services for townships.
- *The Indian Steel and Wire Products Limited (ISWP):* Recently acquired by Tata Steel, ISWP has two units - a wire unit comprising wire drawing mills, wire rod mills and a fastener division.
- *Tata Blue Scope Steel Limited:* A joint venture with Blue Scope Steel Limited, Australia, Tata Blue Scope Steel Limited offers a comprehensive range of branded steel products for building and construction applications.
- *Dhamra Port Company, Orissa:* A JV between Larsen & Toubro Ltd. and Tata Steel Ltd., the company will build a deep-draft (18 mtr) all weather port on the east coast of India.

- *Hooghly Met Coke & Power Co.:* A joint venture with West Bengal Industrial Development Corporation Ltd., HMC & PC envisages an annual met coke production capacity of 1.2 million tons and 90 MW of electric power.
- *Lanka Special Steel Limited:* The only unit in Sri Lanka manufacturing galvanised wires.
- *Sila Eastern Company Limited:* Established to develop limestone mines in Thailand, mainly for the captive use of Tata Steel.
- *Nat Steel Holdings (NSH):* A leading supplier of premium steel products for the construction industry. Nat Steel Holdings became a 100 per cent subsidiary of Tata Steel in February 2004.
- *Tata Steel Thailand:* The Company is the dominant steel producer in Thailand. The company has the capacity to produce 1.7 million tons of steel for the construction industry per year.
- *Tata Steel KZN:* Proposes to set up high carbon ferrochrome plant in South Africa.
- *Tata NYK:* A joint venture with Nippon Yusen Kabushiki Kaisha (NYK Line) for setting up a shipping company to cater to dry bulk and break bulk cargo.

Metal Junction:

Technology Strategy: A technology strategy is concerned with a firm's approach towards the development and use of the technology. This strategy plays a key role in developing an overall competitive strategy and hence needs to be consistent with the other value activities of an organisation. So in the same way TATA Steel also made a technological strategy by making use of E –portal with the collaboration of SAIL. So TATA Steel forged new business strategies using the Web, i.e. metaljunction.com, a 50:50 joint venture of Tata Steel and Steel Authority of India Ltd.

This is a dotcom story with a difference. TATA Steel made a "transformational change through process innovation." www.metaljunction.com, which accounts for over 14 million tonnes of saleable steel annually.

Benefits: First Mover Advantage: It was in the mid 2000 that both Tata Steel and SAIL realised that trading on the internet will happen and will be there to stay. Both companies decided to get together, form a task force and put in place a mechanism whereby we could leverage on the Internet not just for mutual benefit but for the benefit of the entire steel industry as well, to begin with. So in this way it was TATA Steel who got the first mover advantage in India.

Competitive Advantage: Metal junction is now the largest *e*-marketplace for steel in the world, having sold over 4 million tonnes of steel for its clients and currently selling at an average rate of 150,000 tonnes per month. No other Steel maker in India could really reach this level of sale.

Enhancement in Value Chain: With the use of technology an organisation is able to enhance value in its value chain. There are two channels *e*-procurement and *e*-sales. Metaljunction.com has truly succeeded in leveraging the power of the internet to re-engineer, simplify and streamline processes across the entire steel value chain. Earlier strength has been on selling steel and procuring inputs required by the steel industry, it has initiated the process of augmenting its service offerings and adding new products, such as minerals and ferro alloys, to its portfolio.

Cost Leadership: At present, both Tata Steel and SAIL out source their selling and purchase needs to metaljunction.com which, in turn, leverages on the internet to facilitate "procurement at smart rates and sales at highest possible rates." This is done on a case-to-case basis and in lieu of a commission that is based on the value of the transaction.

Sustainability of the technology: The company, metaljunction.com pvt. ltd., was incorporated in February 2001, the next one year was spent in brainstorming sessions and hectic parleys on what kind of working and revenue generating model should be adopted. The company's top brass went to Europe and the US to study and learn from similar initiatives there. In the US and Europe, company went to existing players in the market and endeavoured to learn of their experiences and tried to find out the reasons why some of the companies succeeded and the reasons behind the failures of some others.

While the initial thinking veered round making metaljunction.com a virtual marketplace where others could come to buy and sell, a very distinct business model was finally arrived at. Company eventually evolved into a procurement services provider and a selling services provider for promoter companies, who are their clients now. Separate sourcing and selling teams with appropriate domain knowledge oversee the entire exercise.

More on Offer: Besides *e*-sourcing and *e*-selling, company has started offering services pertaining to asset sales and facilitating the financing of clients' channel partners, and new services such as logistics management will be rolled out shortly.

New domestic clients are being roped in even as the plans in the long term are to expand the company's footprint to South-East Asia, Europe, China and South Africa.

The buyer community of 5400 plus buyers comprising traders, fabricators, re-rollers and end-users have placed their confidence on metal junction because of the operational efficiency, transparency and equal access that the platform provides metaljunction's clients have experienced significant benefits on migrating to online selling. Immediately on migration, from their traditional sale process, to the metaljunction online process, their price realisations increased by up to 23 per cent.

Future Outlook

Currently, the global steel industry is going through unprecedented times. The steel demand is strong with over 6 per cent growth year on year over the last seven years – unseen in the last several decades, primarily driven by robust growth in China, India, South East Asia, Middle East, Russia and Brazil. The iron ore and coking coal prices are at a record high both due to insufficient capacity creation for these and the heavy consolidation of minerals companies. Oil prices and ocean freight rates are at an all time high. The combined effect of all these have driven steel prices to a level higher than ever before. Though there is increasing pressure on margins of steel companies due to very high input costs.

The new scenario – both external, due to high raw material and freight costs and internal, called for a new Vision, strategies and action plans. The Company has cocreated a shared Vision with its employees of becoming a global benchmark in Value Creation and Corporate Citizenship. Company has set goals for 2012 in terms of Returns on Invested Capital, Safety, Carbon dioxide emissions and of becoming the employer of choice in the industry. The integration with Corus is proceeding smoothly and is yielding better than the predicted results. Continuous improvement projects are being given focus in all companies' sites and businesses. Greenfield projects in India are progressing, though somewhat slower than planned. Company's effort to enhance their raw material security has yielded positive results in Ivory Coast for iron ore, in Mozambique for coal and in Oman for limestone. There is greater emphasis on safety. They have well laid out plans to reduce CO_2 emissions to benchmark levels.

The Tata Steel Group will pursue strategic growth through capacity expansions and securing access to raw materials. The Group is expanding its capacity in India through the expansion of its operations in Jamshedpur to 10 million tons per annum and through the construction of a 6 million tons per annum greenfield' site in Orissa. Other Greenfield opportunities in India and across Asia are being assessed. The Group is also looking at further integration upstream in raw materials with an ambition to achieve 100 per cent self-sufficiency in India and around 50 per cent self-sufficiency in Europe over time. Agreements for the exploration of iron ore in the Ivory Coast, coal in Mozambique and limestone in Oman have already been signed and opportunities are under review in India to support the Indian Greenfield projects; and in Africa and South America, primarily to support its European steel making assets.

Climate change is probably the biggest challenge ever to confront the steel industry. In response to this challenge, the Tata Steel Group will be part of the solution and is committed to minimising the environmental impact of its operations and its products. It has a goal to reduce its CO_2 footprint by at least 20 per cent by 2020 compared to 1990. To meet this objective, the Group will, for example, continue to improve its current processes, invest in breakthrough technologies and develop new products and services that reduce the environmental impact over the product life cycle. To improve its processes, priority is given to energy conservation schemes; in technology breakthrough such as Ultra Low Carbon Steel making and in other innovative projects where the Group has proprietary technology.

Application of Business Strategy Models to TATA Steel

SWOT Analysis: SWOT analysis is done for a company, to find out its overall Strengths, Weaknesses, Threats and opportunities leading to gauging the competitive potential of the company. The SWOT Analysis enables a company to recognise its market standing and adopt strategies accordingly. Here SWOT analysis of ICICI bank is made to understand the positioning of the bank better:

Strengths: Tata Steel's Indian operations are self-sufficient in the case of its major raw material iron ore through its captive mines.

Very advanced Research and Development wing which is carrying out researches and experiments in the areas of raw materials, blast furnace productivity, steel making, product development, process improvement, etc. Several thrust area projects were taken up.

Tata had a strong retail and distribution network in India and SE Asia. Tata was a major supplier to the Indian auto industry and the demand for value added steel products was growing in this market.

The Company is on its way to reach a crude steel capacity of 10 million tonnes per annum by FY 2011. The first phase of reaching the crude steel capacity of 6.8 million tonnes per annum, Brownfield projects, is nearing completion

The Company has in place adequate internal control systems and procedures commensurate with the size and nature of its business. The effectiveness of the internal controls is continuously monitored by the Corporate Audit Division of the Company. Corporate Audit's main objective is to provide to the Audit Committee and the Board of Directors, an independent, objective and reasonable assurance of the adequacy and effectiveness of the organisation's risk management, control and governance processes Corporate Audit also assesses opportunities for improvement in business processes, systems and controls and may provide recommendations, designed to add value to the organisation. It also follows up on the implementation of corrective actions and improvements in business processes after review by the Audit Committee and Senior Management.

Tata Steel has been on a path of accelerated growth with foray into several geographies and markets through aggressive mergers and acquisitions.

Tata Steel now is in the process of implementing a structured approach in risk management called Enterprise Risk Management (ERM). The key objectives of the Company through ERM are:

- To enshrine the process of ERM as a usual Business Process and integrate into all decision-making and planning processes.
- To ensure that all levels of Management identify and monitor risks through a properly defined framework.
- To provide periodic information and updates to the Board and the Shareholders on the significant risks and the ways of mitigating the same.

Tata Steel addresses the risk of cyclicality of the Steel industry by marinating rich product mix and higher value added products whose volatility is lower. Moreover, the industry itself has been undergoing some structural changes with Consolidations. These changes are expected to bring in greater stability to prices.

Tata Steel with its modernisation plans has ensured that it deploys the best technologies to ensure quality, cost-efficiency and environment-friendly processes. Through acquisition of Corus and with new Greenfield ventures, Tata Steel has ensured that it has diversified the concentration risk in single technology of Iron and Steel making.

Weakness:

- *Endemic Deficiencies:* These are inherent in the quality and availability of some of the essential raw materials available in India, e.g., high ash content of indigenous coking coal adversely affecting the productive efficiency of iron-making and is generally imported. Advantages of high Fe content of indigenous ore are often neutralised by high basicity index. Besides, certain key ingredients of steel making, e.g., nickel, Ferro-molybdenum are also unavailable indigenously.

- India is deficient in raw materials required by the steel industry. Iron ore deposits are finite and there are problems in mining sufficient amounts of it. India's hard coal deposits are of low quality and the prices of coking and non-coking coal are ever increasing
- Raw materials for steel production are rapidly depleting and are non-renewable; company has to come up with sustainable methods in steel production.
- Steel production in India is also hampered by power shortages.
- Insufficient freight capacity and transport infrastructure impediments to hamper the growth of Indian steel industry.
- *Low Labour Productivity:* In India the advantages of cheap labour get offset by low labour productivity; e.g., at comparable capacities labour productivity of SAIL and TISCO are 75 t/manyear and 100t/manyear, for POSCO, Korea and NIPPON, Japan the values are 1345 t/man year and 980 t/manyear.
- *High Cost of Basic Inputs and Services:* High administered price of essential inputs like electricity puts Indian steel industry at a disadvantage; about 45 per cent of the input costs can be attributed to the administered costs of coal, fuel and electricity, e.g., cost of electricity is 3 cents in the USA as compared to 10 cents in India; and freight cost from Jamshedpur to Mumbai is $50/tonne compared to only $34 from Rotterdam to Mumbai.

Opportunities:

- The biggest opportunity before Indian steel sector is that there is enormous scope for increasing consumption of steel in almost all sectors in India.

- Unexplored Rural Market: The Indian rural sector remains fairly unexposed to their multifaceted use of steel. The rural market was identified as a potential area of significant steel consumption way back in the year 1976 itself. However, forceful steps were not taken to penetrate this segment. Enhancing applications in rural areas assumes a much greater significance now for increasing per capital consumption of steel. The usage of steel in cost effective manner is possible in the area of housing, fencing, structures and other possible applications where steel can substitute other materials which not only could bring about advantages to users but is also desirable for conservation of forest resources.

- Excellent potential exist for enhancing steel consumption in other sectors such as automobiles, packaging, engineering industries, irrigation and water supply in India. New steel products developed to improve performance simplify manufacturing, installation and reliability is needed to enhance steel consumption in these sectors.

- It is estimated that world steel consumption will double in next 25 years. Quality improvement of Indian steel combined with its low cost advantages will definitely help in substantial gain in export market.

- The Tata Steel Group is leveraging the Group's collective Research and Development experience in the Group's various geographies to further enhance the Group's performance and also the integration process.

- Corus acquisition bring in a tremendous technological advantage by access to best practices in global steel industry.

- Global M&A brought in following synergies.

- Greater productivity leading to increased output and market size.

- Greater economies of scale leading to cost reduction through combined buying.

- Cross fertilization of Research and Development capabilities and operational best practices, leading to greater innovation and operational efficiencies.

- Booming infrastructure has opened up high demand for steel worldwide.

Threats:

- In the developed world, industries have been facing rising environmental costs due to the increased concerns on Global Warming. It is, therefore, a challenge and responsibility for the Steel industry to be the trustee in conservation of nature for future generations.
- It is recognised that the steel and aluminium industries are significant contributors to man-made greenhouse gas emissions as the manufacture of steel produces carbon dioxide (CO_2), and the manufacture of primary aluminium generates both CO_2 and per fluorocarbons (PFCs).
- High raw material input cost and scarcity of non-renewable raw materials are a threat to the industry. (e.g.: Coal, limestone, etc.)
- Threat of Substitutes: Plastics and composites pose a threat to Indian steel in one of its biggest markets automotive manufacture. For the automobile industry, the other material at present with the potential to upstage steel is aluminium. However, at present the high cost of electricity for extraction and purification of aluminium in India weighs against viable use of aluminium for the automobile industry. Steel has already been replaced in some large volume applications large diameter water pipes (RCC pipes), small diameter pipes (PVC pipes).

Porter's Five Forces Model

Backed by robust volumes as well as realisations, steel Industry has registered a phenomenal growth across the world over the past few years. The situation in the domestic industry was no exception. In fact, it enjoyed a double digit growth rate backed by a robust growing economy. However, the current liquidity crisis seems to have created medium term hiccups. In this case we have analysed the domestic steel sector through Michael Porter's five force model so as to understand the competitiveness of the sector as well as pointed out the initiatives taken by Tat

Steel to safeguard its position from all the five forces of threats, namely:

- Threats of new entrants: the willingness and ability of firms to enter a particular industry depends on the barriers to entry. Such barriers include; capital requirements, economies of scale, government policy and product differentiation.
- Intensity of rivalry among existing competitors
- The bargaining power of suppliers
- The threat of substitute products
- The bargaining power of buyers
- Entry barriers: High
- Capital Requirement: Steel industry is a capital intensive business. It is estimated that to set up 1 mtpa capacity of integrated steel plant, it requires between Rs 25 bn to Rs 30 bn depending upon the location of the plant and technology used.

Tata Steel has already made sufficient efforts to safeguard itself in this regard. It has a line-up of Greenfield projects which it plans to establish not only in domestic markets (Jharkhand, Orissa and Chhattisgarh) but also internationally (Bangladesh, Iran and Vietnam). Besides, it has already completed its expansion capacity of its existing plant from 5 mtpa to 6.8 mtpa at Jamshedpur with an investment of Rs. 5,000 crore, while it is in the process of expanding the capacity from 6.8 mtpa to 10 mtpa with an estimated investment of Rs 15,000 crore. The company has invested Rs 8,000 crore out it and it expects to achieve 10 mtpa capacity by 2011-12. It would prove to be very difficult for any new entrant to come up with such huge investment outlays.

- *Economies of Scale:* As far as the sector forces go, scale of operation does matter. Benefits of economies of scale are derived in the form of lower costs, R& D expenses and better bargaining power while sourcing raw materials. Tata Steel being an integrated steel company has its own mines for key raw materials such as iron ore and coal and this protects them for the potential threat for new entrants to a significant extent. Tata Steel owns raw material assets such as coal and limestone mines through joint ventures or completely, with the assets spread across countries such as Australia, Oman and Mozambique.

- *Government Policy:* The government has a favourable policy for steel manufacturers. However, there are certain discrepancies involved in allocation of iron ore mines and land acquisitions. Furthermore, the regulatory clearances and other issues are some of the major problems for the new entrants.

Tata Steel being a century old company under the flagship Tata Sons which is known for its Corporate Social Responsibility already enjoys a respectable position in front of the Indian Government. The Jharkhand government on May, 24th 2009, has granted a prospecting licence (PL) to Tata Steel for the Ankua iron ore mines. A senior company official said that Tata Steel has been allocated 1,800 hectares for prospecting in the Ankua area. Another 10,000 acres of land will be allocated to them for their project in Ranchi.

- *Product Differentiation:* Steel has very low barriers in terms of product differentiation as it doesn't fall into the luxury or speciality goods and thus does not have any substantial price difference. However, Tata Steel still enjoy a premium for their products because of its quality and its brand value created more than 100 years back. Tata Steel has introduced brands like Tata Steelium (the world's first branded Cold Rolled Steel), Tata Shaktee (Galvanised Corrugated Sheets), Tata Tiscon (re-bars), Tata Bearings, Tata Agrico (hand tools and implements), Tata Wiron (galvanised wire products), Tata Pipes (pipes for construction) and Tata Structura (contemporary construction material). Apart from these product brands, the company also has in its folds a service brand called "steel junction".

- Currently two Global Steel majors namely Arcelor- Mittal, which is the world's largest I and POSCO, are posed to be the biggest threat as they plan to enter the Indian Steel Industry very soon.

Competition: High:

- The steel industry is truly global in terms of competition with large producing countries like China significantly influencing global prices through aggressive exports.
- Steel, being a commodity it is, branding is not common and there is little differentiation between competing products.
- The Four major domestic rivals are SAIL, JSW, ISPAT & ESSAR STEEL. Rest are all smallish mills which together accounts for 30 per cent of the total market share. The market shares of the 5 major players in the Indian Steel Industry are:

Competition Analysis:

- Concentration Ratio
- In Economics the concentration ratio of an industry is used as an indicator of the relative size of firms in relation to the industry as a whole. This may also assist in determining the market form of the industry. One commonly used concentration ratio is the four-firm concentration ratio, which consists of the market share, as a percentage, of the four largest firms in the industry. In general, the N-firm concentration ratio is the percentage of market output generated by the N-largest firms in the industry
- The four firm concentration ratio of the Iron and Steel Industry is 71 per cent. This implies that there is oligopoly in the industry as it is dominated my few major players. Major percentage of market output is generated by the 4 largest firms in the industry.
- All the major domestic competitors like SAIL, ESSAR, JSW, JSPL have announced massive expansion plans recently:
- SAIL has announced that it will achieve production capacity of 40 Million Tons by 2020.

- JSW plans to expand its production to 32 Million Tons by 2020.
- Other players such as JSPL, ESSAR have similar production expansion plans which will contribute in overall achievement of 200 Million Tons steel production by the year 2020.

Bargaining Power of Suppliers: High

- The bargaining power of suppliers is low for the fully integrated steel plants as they have their own mines of key raw material like iron ore coal for example Tata Steel. However, those who are non-integrated or semi-integrated has to depend on suppliers. An example could be SAIL, which imports coking coal.
- Since domestic raw material sources are insufficient to supply the Indian steel industry, a considerable amount of raw materials has to be imported. For example, iron ore deposits are finite and there are problems in mining sufficient amounts of it. India's hard coal deposits are of low quality. For this reason hard coal imports have increased in the last five years by a total of 40 per cent to nearly 30 million tons. Almost half of this is coking coal (the remainder is power station coal). India is the world's sixth biggest coal importer. The rising output of electric steel is also leading to a sharp increase in demand for steel scrap. Some 3.5 million tons of scrap have already been imported in 2006, compared with just 1 million tons in 2000. In the coming years imports are likely to continue to increase thanks to capacity increases.
- Globally, the Top three mining giants BHP Billiton, CVRD and Rio Tinto supply nearly two-thirds of the processed iron ore to steel mills and command very high bargaining power. In India too, NMDC is a major supplier to stand alone and non–integrated steel mills.
- In order to safeguard itself from the high bargaining power of the buyers, Tata Steel has forayed much earlier into the strategy of 'Backward Integration'. "Ownership of raw materials and a continuous improvement in production

have been the key to Tata Steel's profitability. In fact we've believed in owning raw materials for the past 100 years," said managing director B. Muthuraman while elaborating on the century-old company's performance.

- Tata Steel and state-owned SAIL have largely been able to withstand raw material price fluctuations due to captive iron ore mines. Tata Steel is also one of the least cost markers of steel in the world. Other private steel companies, hit by steep iron ore and coal prices, have passed on the hikes to the customers, prompting the government to clamp down on price increases to control inflation.
- The company is dependent on imports for a major portion of its raw material — iron ore and coking coal — requirements. Tata Steel is self-sufficient to the extent of 25 per cent for iron ore needs. With supplies coming in from its mines at New Millennium Corporation in Canada and potentially from the Ivory Coast over a longer term, its iron ore security would gradually increase to around 62 per cent by 2015. Overall, raw material security would reach 50 per cent by 2015 and go up to about 60 per cent by 2018.
- It is also evaluating several other mineral projects in Brazil and Australia
- Progressing towards the goal of achieving logistics control, Tata NYK Shipping Pte Ltd, the Singapore-based joint venture (50:50) between Tata Steel and Nippon Yusen Kabushiki Kaisha (NYK Line), a Japanese shipping major has entered into a long-term charter for eight supramax/ panamax vessels and orders have been placed for building two new supramax vessels. The joint venture was floated to handle ocean transportation of bulk cargoes such as coal, iron ore, limestone as well as finished steel, both imports and exports, not only for Tata Steel but also for others including other Tata Group companies.
- To achieve coal security by way of imports, the company has formed a joint venture with an Australian company

for producing coal in Mozambique, acquired strategic interest of 5 per cent with 20 per cent off take-rights in the coal mining project in Australia in partnership with several other foreign companies and formed a 50:50 joint venture with Steel Authority of India Ltd (SAIL).

- For limestone, Tata Steel has entered into a joint venture with the Al Bahja Group of Oman for a 70 per cent stake. The joint venture will undertake mining of limestone in the Uyun region in Salalah province of Oman.

  By undertaking such long term strategies to increase its raw material security, Tata Steel is making it difficult for the suppliers of raw material to bargain exorbitant prices.

Threat of Substitutes: Low

- Plastics and composites pose a threat to Indian steel in one of its biggest markets — automotive manufacture. For the automobile industry, the other material at present with the potential to upstage steel is aluminium. Perhaps the most attractive alternative to stainless is aluminium. Stainless producers themselves are offering their customers a range of alternatives in an effort to prevent business being lost to non-ferrous or carbon steel materials. Such options include lower-nickel duplex grades and ferritic types. In the meantime, nickel's fluctuations will continue to create problems for the stainless industry worldwide.
- However, at present in India the high cost of electricity for extraction and purification of aluminium weighs against viable use of aluminium for the automobile industry. Steel has already been replaced in some large volume applications: railway sleepers (RCC sleepers), large diameter water pipes (RCC pipes), small diameter pipes (PVC pipes), and domestic water tanks (PVC tanks). The substitution is more prevalent in the manufacture of automobiles and consumer durables.

Bargaining power of Consumers: Mixed: Some of the major steel consumption sectors like automobiles, oil and gas, shipping, consumer durables and power generation enjoy high bargaining power and get favourable deals.

However, small and retail consumers who are scattered and consume a significant part do not enjoy these benefits.

"Slept" Analysis of Tata Steel

Economic:

- The Financial market in the last 12 months has been volatile triggered by the subprime mortgage crisis in the US. This has adversely affected the liquidity and the risk perception of the international capital markets. Inflation has increased around the World boosted by mainly increase in food and energy prices. The real effective exchange rate for the US dollar has declined since mid 2007 as foreign investment in US bonds and equities has been dampened by reduced confidence in both the liquidity of and the returns on such assets, weakening of US growth prospects and interest rate cuts. The main counterpart to the decline of the dollar has been appreciation of the euro, the yen, and other floating currencies such as the Canadian dollar and some emerging economy currencies. Corus acquisition is being financed by a substantial amount of debt. This puts pressure on the Company's bottom line, and should the business environment deteriorate, the necessity to service this debt could restrain Tata Steel in its future investment and capacity expansion plans. In addition it could also limit the Company's inorganic growth options.
- Due To Subprime Crisis in USA a subsequent tremor all along the world, especially in developed market in Western Europe make the vulnerable position of Corus even more riskier. UK, Germany, Netherlands the main market for Corus products are facing the fear for recession on negative growth.
- The steel industry is highly cyclical, receptive to general economic conditions and reliant on the condition of a number of other industries, including the automotive, appliance, construction and energy industries. If these industries experience a downturn, Tata Steel too would take a hit, thus negatively impacting its rating.

- Corus follows the policy of entering into long term supply contracts with raw materials vendors. Thus there can be a huge time gap between variation in prices under purchase contracts and the time when Corus can make a corresponding price change under its sales contacts with its consumers. Moreover, Corus may not be able to pass on the increased raw materials costs to its customers. Such developments would lead to a down side in our rating.
- Steel production processes are energy dependent and price movements in the energy market would accordingly affect Tata Steel's bottom line.
- Tata Steel became 6th biggest Steel Producer in the World after acquiring Corus, but the cost of the integration goes much more beyond the financial aspect. There are other factors which will add to overall integration costs such as:
  - — Cross Cultural Integration
  - — Employer-Employee Relationship

Political:

- Tata committed a huge amount of investment in politically unstable country like Bangladesh, Iran, Mozambique and Thailand. The entire process of setting up plan is getting delayed in question of gas supply (in Bangladesh), Iron ore mine lease in Iran is escalating the Project cost.
- Increased infrastructure spending by the Government of India and development of roads could generate significant savings in freight and transportation cost, making Indian steel companies and other industries globally competitive.

Impact of Liberalisation: The economic reforms initiated by the government in 1991 have added new dimensions to the industrial growth in general, and steel industry in particular. Some of the important features due to liberalisation are:

- Licensing requirement for capacity creation has been abolished.
- Steel industry has been removed from the list of industries reserved for the state sector.

- Automatic approval granted for foreign equity investment in steel has been increased up to 74 per cent.
- Price and distribution controls were removed from January 1992.
- Restrictions on external trade, both in import and export, have been removed.
- Import tariff reduced from 105 per cent in 1992/93, to 30 per cent in 1996-97.
- Other policy measures like convertibility of rupee on trade account, permission to mobilise resources from overseas financial markets, and rationalisation of existing tax structure.
- The Government plays a key role in the economics of TATA Steel. It has a role as a resource allocator (the mining policies of the Government), as Competitor (the public sector steel companies) and as Regulator. In volatile times the regulatory risk rises with measures like reduction in import duties, levy of export duties and withdrawal of DEPB benefits, threats of price curbs, etc. Tata Steel counters this risk by being a role model corporate citizen and playing an important role in contributing to the Nation building. Tata Steel is the second largest steel producer in terms of Geographical spread of its facilities.

Social:

- Tata Steel Ltd has been awarded the Golden Peacock Global Award for Corporate Social Responsibility (CSR) for the year 2009. The award looks for continual commitment by business to ethical behaviour, to economic development and to improving the quality of life of employees and their families, as well as to engagement with local communities and society at large.
- From policies on corporate accountability, drugs and alcohol, and HIV prevention, to a Code of Conduct that extends to its stakeholders, ethics and responsibility are interwoven in the daily course of Tata Steel's business. CSR is an integral component of Tata Steel's business

strategy, and constitutes one of the company's key enterprise processes. Tata Steel aims to create a favourable social environment in its areas of operation by improving health, education and economic well-being, as well as nurturing young talent in sports. The Company's CSR philosophy is put into practice not only in the city of Jamshedpur, but also in its neighbouring districts, as well as in more than 800 villages in the states of Jharkhand, Orissa and Chhattisgarh.

- Some of the Tata Welfare programmes elements are prenatal and postnatal care, child health and immunisation, free IUDs and sterilisation, sterilisation "camps" for city residents conducted by top Bombay gynecologists and incentive payments of Rs. 5000 in addition to the government payment for sterilisation acceptors. Tata holds motivation meetings during worker management councils, trains rural opinion leaders as family planning motivators, and innovated peer motivation for youths as well as discussion sessions for young married women with their mothers-in-law.
- Hundreds of people born with cleft lips or cleft palates have been operated on, for free, through 'Operation Muskaan' a project initiated by steel giant Tata Steel. It's a small operation that has made a huge difference to people's lives.
- TATA being socially responsible is the deployment of Company's mobile medical unit (Hospital on Wheels) and treating more than 145600 habitats in urban slums and remote rural areas.

Legal: Tata steel requires huge chunk of land. Sudden spree of big corporate houses for grabbing land makes the situation even more competitive. In this regard it can be compared with Singur drama as mentioned by some top Tata executives.

Police firing in Kalinga Nagar in Orissa and subsequent death of protesters make the situation complex.

- Unstable Jharkhand government and Tribal protester at an increase worsening the situation.

- Representatives of environmental activist group Green peace stormed into the AGM in the guise of shareholders of Tata Steel, got on to the podium and alleged that the proposed port at Dhamra on the Orissa coast will kill the migratory Olive Ridley Turtles.

Tata, the world over is respected for its ethical practices, CSR (Corporate Social Responsibility) not just for the name sake but in true sense. It is very difficult to find any issues in TATA's hundred year old history regarding unethical practices or behaviour. But of late the Company is suffering from Land Acquisition problem in Singur, West Bengal. Although it's not a problem directly related to "TATA STEEL" but the dilution in brand "TATA" has a significant effect on the share prices of Tata Steel.

BCG Product Portfolio Matrix

Tata Steel has stable market growth but has a relatively high market share so it comes under cash cow.

This implies it is generating enough revenue that can be pooled into "stars" and "question mark".

Indian Steel Industry

Steel industry reforms – particularly in 1991 and 1992 – have led to strong and sustainable growth in India's steel industry. Since its independence, India has experienced steady growth in the steel industry, successive governments that have supported the industry and pushed for its robust development. Further illustrating this plan is the fact that a number of steel plants were established in India, with technological assistance and investments by foreign countries. In 1991, a substantial number of economic reforms were introduced by the Indian government. These reforms boosted the development process of a number of industries – the steel industry in India in particular – which has subsequently developed quite rapidly. The 1991 reforms allowed for no licenses to be required for capacity creation, except for some locations.

India continually posts phenomenal growth records in steel production. In 1992, India produced 14.33 million tons of finished carbon steels and 1.59 million tons of pig iron. In 2008, India produced nearly 46.575 million tons of finished steels and 4.393 million tons of pig iron.

Powered by an increased demand for steel from neighbouring China, which has been clocking a 15 per cent sectoral growth annually on account of construction projects in preparation for the Olympics, the steel industry in India has grown by about 10 per cent in the past two years, compared with the global growth rate of about 6 per cent a year.

The country's production of crude steel in 2005-06 stood at 42.1 million tons, reflecting an increase of 7.1 per cent over the previous fiscal. On the other hand, the consumption of steel during the year was pegged at 41.43 million tons, a massive growth of 13.88 per cent when compared with the 2004-05 figures. Currently, India is the largest sponge iron producer in the world and ranks seventh among steel producing countries.

Global Steel Industry

The biggest boom in history of steel industry is that of the 1950s and 1960s, when the steel industry was driven by the post-war boom in the developed world. Whereas the current boom is being led by growth in the developing world, particularly China, India and Brazil. China is clearly the engine that has driven steel consumption in the Asian region.. Steel prices, primarily buoyed by the Chinese boom, hit their peak between 2002 and 2004. This ensured high profits from investments in steel. Despite the moves towards consolidation, steel capacities are still fragmented. The gap between Arcelor-Mittal and Nippon Steel, the second biggest producer, highlights this. Nippon produced 32 million tons of steel in 2005 less than one-third that of the industry leader. More significantly, although the Tata-Corus combine will be placed at number five in the global steel pecking order.

The point about consolidation is that it is only happening at the top. The top 10 companies produce about 25 per cent of the global steel output. The rest of the steel — about 75 per cent of the global capacity is still widely dispersed over 62 countries around the world, in plants with much smaller capacities. Industry sources say that consolidation needs to happen at the bottom end of the steel market.

In the year 2004, the global steel production has made a record level by crossing the 1000 million tons. Among the top producers in the steel production, China ranked 1 in the world. Production of steel in the 25 European Union countries was at 16.3 mmt in

January 2005. Production in Italy increased by 11.5 per cent in comparison to the same month in 2004. Italy produced 2.5 mmt of crude steel in January 2005. Austria produced 646,000 metric tons. In Russia it increased by 4.0 per cent to reach at 5.5 mmt in January. Incase of the North America region particularly in Mexico it was 1.5 mmt of crude steel in January 2005, up by 8.0 per cent compared to the same month in 2004.

Tata Airlines

Tata Airlines, a division of Tata Sons Ltd. (now Tata Group) was founded by J. R. D. Tata in 1932 as Tata Sons. It was started as a mail service over the route Karachi to Bombay and on south to Madras.

The Beginning

On 15th October 1932, J. R. D. Tata himself flew a single-engined De Havilland Puss Moth carrying air mail (postal mail of Imperial Airways) from Karachi's Drigh Road Aerodrome to Bombay's Juhu Airstrip via Ahmedabad. The aircraft continued to Madras via Bellary piloted by former Royal Air Force pilot Nevill Vintcent. Tata Airlines initially consisted of one Puss Moth aircraft, one Leopard Moth, one palm-thatched shed, one whole time pilot assisted by Tata and Vintcent, one part-time engineer and two apprentice-mechanics.

Initial service included weekly airmail service with a Puss Moth aircraft between Karachi and Madras via Ahmedabad and Bombay, covering over 1,300 miles. In its very first year of operation, Tata Airlines flew 160,000 miles, carrying 155 passengers and 10.71 ton of mail. In the next few years, Tata Airlines continued to rely for its revenue on the mail contract with the Government of India for carriage of surcharged mail, including a considerable quantity of overseas mail brought to Karachi by Imperial Airways. The same year, Tata Airlines launched its longest domestic flight - Mumbai to Trivandrum with a six-seater Miles Merlin.

Re-christened

In 1938 it was re-christened as Tata Air Services and later same year was renamed as Tata Air Lines. By this time Delhi and Colombo were also serviced.

Post World War II

Following the end of World War II (when Calcutta was added to the network), regular commercial service was restored in India and Tata Airlines became a public limited company on 29 July 1946 under the name Air India.

Change in Guard

In March 1948, after the Independence of India, 49 per cent of the airline was acquired by the Government of India, with an option to purchase an additional 2 per cent. In return, the airline was granted status to operate international services from India as the designated flag carrier under the name Air India International.

Nationalisation

In 1953 all airlines of India including *Air India* and *Indian National Airways* were nationalised to form Indian Airlines Corporation.

Time Line of Air India 1932 – 1940

1932

Month	*Date*	*Event*
July	-	The Aviation Department of Tata Sons Ltd. established.
October	15	Tata Sons Ltd. operated the first Karachi/Ahmedabad/Bombay/Bellary/Madras mail service to connect with Imperial Airways' London/Karachi services. The first service carried mail which had left London on October 8. The first was operated by a De Havilland Puss Moth VT-ADN flown by Mr. J R D Tata from Karachi to Bombay and by Mr. Nevill Vintcent from Bombay to Madras. The first service arrived at Madras on October 16 and the first westbound flight left Madras on October 17.

Contd...

Month	***Date***	***Event***
		1933
-	-	In the first full year of operations, Tata Airlines flew 1, 60,000 miles, carried 155 passengers and 10.71 tonnes of mail.
		1934
-	-	The de Havilland Fox Moth DH-83, a four-seater biplane, acquired.
		1935
January	4	The Karachi/Bombay/Madras service was rerouted via Hyderabad instead of Bellary. Frequency increased to twice-weekly.
February	25	Tata Sons made a trial flight Bombay/ Nagpur/Jamshedpur / Kolkata with Fox Moth VT-ADZ (pilot Mr. Nevill Vintcent).
November	26	Experimental weekly mail service started on route Bombay/Goa/Cannanore/ Thiruvananthapuram with Miles Merlins. This connected with the Karachi/Bombay/Madras service.
		1936
December	-	During the year Tata Sons Ltd. introduced Waco YQC-6 biplanes.
		1937
April	16	Bhuj introduced as a stop on Bombay/ Karachi service.
November	6	Tata Sons began Bombay/Indore/ Bhopal/ Gwalior/Delhi service with Waco YQC-6 biplanes. The first flight by VT-AIX (pilots Mr. JRD Tata and Mr. Nevill Vintcent).

Contd...

Month	*Date*	*Event*
December	1	W/T facilities were brought into operation on the Karachi/Bombay/ Colombo route. During the year, Tata Sons introduced D.H. 89 Dragon Rapides equipped with radio.
		1938
January	22	Tata Airlines (successor to aviation division of Tata Sons) extended its Karachi / Bombay /Madras mail service to Colombo. Waco YQC-6 biplanes were used. Passengers and mail from Colombo were carried from January 29.
February	28	Government contract with Tata Air Lines came into effect for the carriage of first class un-surcharged mail between Karachi/Colombo under the Empire Air Mail Scheme. The route was Karachi/ Bhuj/Ahmedebad/Bombay/ Hyderabad/Madras/Tiruchirapalli/ Colombo.
March	2	Tata Air Lines extended its Bombay/ Thiruvananthapuram service to Tiruchirapalli.
		1939
-	-	Rapides and D.H. 86s requisitioned by the Government. Second-hand trimonitor Stinsons purchased. First Booking Office opened at Churchgate.
		1940
-	-	The Percival Q-6 aircraft joined the fleet. A twin-engine aircraft, manufactured by Percival Aircraft Ltd, it had a maximum speed of 190 mph.

1941 – 1950

Month	Date	Event
		1941
November	1	Tata Airlines began non-scheduled flights between Karachi and Baghdad via Jiwani, Sharjah, Bahrain and Basra. DC-2s loaned by the Government of India were used. During the year, Tata Airlines introduced three-engined Stinson Model A monoplanes.
		1942
February	-	Mr. Nevill Vintcent met with an accidental death when the plane which was travelling was shot down over the French coast.
August	-	Participation in the evacuation of Baghdad during the Rashid Ali revolt.
		1943
-	-	The Douglas DC-3, the mainstay of Air India's fleet in the immediate post-war period, joined Air India's fleet.
		1944
-	-	The Stinson Trimotor withdrawn from service.
March	1	Tata Airlines introduced DC-3s on twice-weekly Bombay/Karachi and weekly Bombay/Bangalore/Colombo service.
		1945
April	16	Tata Airlines began twice weekly Bombay/Nagpur/Kolkata service with DC-3s.

Contd...

Month	*Date*	*Event*
		1946
January	1	Indian Civil Aviation restored to commercial status.
July	29	Tata Air Lines converted into a public Company and renamed Air India Limited. Genell• Moots of TWA came from Kansas City to train India's first batch of Air Hostesses.
		1947
April	13	Air India received the first of its fleet of Vickers-Armstrongs Vikings. This was VT-CIY.
August	3	Mrs. Vijayalakshmi Pandit, first Indian Ambassador to the USSR, left India for Moscow in the Air India DC-3 VT-ATI (Late. Capt. A.C. Gazder). The DC-3 flew the Indian flag for the first time.
		1948
March	8	Air India International incorporated.
March	16	First L-749 Constellation VT-CQS "Mughal Princess" arrived.
June	8	Inauguration of a weekly Bombay / London service via Cairo and Geneva with Constellation VT-CQP "Malabar Princess". Special commemorative stamp issued by the Government of India.
		1949
January	1	The year opened with an aircraft fleet of three Constellations with a twice weekly service to London via Cairo and Geneva.
October	31	Arrival of L-749A Constellation "Maratha Princess" VT-DAR.

Contd...

Month	*Date*	*Event*
		1950
January	21	Inauguration of a fortnightly Bombay / Nairobi service via Aden.
March	12	Rome introduced as a halt on the UK route.
July	26	Karachi included as a halt on the Bombay / Nairobi service.
		1951
April	17	Paris introduced as a halt on the UK route.
		1952
December	7	Introduction of an All-Tourist Class service on the Nairobi route on every alternate Sunday with DC-4 aircraft leased from Air India Ltd.
		1953
February	21	Dusseldorf introduced as a halt on UK route.
March	-	Parliament passed The Air-Corporations Act (No. 27 Of 1953)
May	28	Air Corporations Act, 1953, ratified by the President of India.
June	15	Two Corporations - Air India International Limited and Indian Airlines Corporation (IAC) came into formal existence.
August	1	Nationalisation of Air India International Limited. Mr. JRD Tata appointed Chairman and Mr. B.K. Patel as Vice Chairman and General Manager.

Contd...

Month	*Date*	*Event*
October	3	Introduction of the mixed class (First Class-cum-Tourist Class) services to London and Nairobi. Frequency on Nairobi route increased to 2 flights a week.
		1954
June	6	Arrival of the first 1049-C Super Constellation, "Rani of Jhansi" (VT-DGL)
June	19	Inaugural flight of Super Constellation to UK July4Proving flight to Singapore with L-749A Constellation.
July	16	Inaugural flight to Singapore via Madras with L-749A Constellation VT-DAS on once-a-week basis.
July	25	Proving Flight to Tokyo with L-749A Constellation.
August	14	Inaugural flight to Hong Kong via Kolkata and Bangkok with L-749A Constellation VT-DAS on once-a-week basis.
November	16	A DC-3 Freighter (VT-CGP) purchased from I.A.C.
		1955
March	20	Arrival of first 1049E Super Constellation "Rani of Chittor" (VT-DHN)
May	7	Hong Kong service extended to Tokyo.
July	2	Introduction of an all-First Class Express service "Flying Rani" Bombay/Cairo/London.
July	4	Introduction of halts at Beirut and Zurich on the UK route.

Contd...

Month	***Date***	***Event***
July	6	Introduction of a weekly Round Robin Bombay/Kolkata/Delhi and Bombay/Delhi/Kolkata service as extensions to the UK- India route.
November	15	Introduction of Slumberettes on L-1049 Super Constellations in First Class on India/UK route.
		1956
January	6	Introduction of L-1049 Super Constellation once a week on Nairobi route.
April	1	Introduction of Slumberettes on L-749 Super Constellations in First Class on Bombay/Tokyo and Bombay/Nairobi routes.
April	3	Damascus introduced as a halt on the UK route.
April	4	Prague introduced as a halt on the UK route.
April	6	Introduction of L-1049 Super Constellations on the Singapore route.
June	11	Arrival of first L-1049G Super Constellation "Rani of Nilgiris" (VT-DHL).
October	5	Extension of the Bombay/Singapore service to Sydney via Darwin.
November	1	Halt at Karachi omitted from London/Bombay service.
December	25	Beirut reintroduced on all the six UK flights omitting Abadan and Istanbul.
December	27	Damascus reintroduced on two flights a week.

Contd...

Month	***Date***	***Event***
		1957
January	10	Super Constellations introduced on Tokyo route (flights diverted via Okinawa in the east-bound direction for technical reasons).
May	4	Karachi omitted as a stop on one Nairobi flight only, in east-bound direction.
September	1	Frequency on Nairobi route increased to thrice weekly; one via Karachi and Aden and two via Aden.
		1958
January	4	Jakarta introduced as a regular halt between Singapore and Darwin on Sydney route.
January	15	Withdrawal of L-749 Constellations from regular operations, due to their sale to Aeronaves de Mexico.
March	5	New Terminal Building at Santa Cruz opened.
August	15	Inaugural flight from Delhi to Moscow via Tashkent on once-a-week basis. Commencement of pool between Air India and Aeroflot for traffic between Delhi and Moscow.
October	11	Introduction of weekly once Bombay/ Jakarta terminator service via Madras and Singapore.
November	15	Introduction of once a week DC-4 freighter service, India/UK/India chartered from Messrs. Seaboard & Western Airlines.

Contd...

Month	Date	Event
		1959
October	4	Damascus discontinued to be an online station. Frequency through Cairo increased to four times a week.
		1960
February	21	Arrival of first Boeing 707-437 (VT-DJJ "Nandadevi") in Bombay, after a record breaking non-stop flight from London to Bombay in 8 hours and 5 minutes.
March	7	Arrival of second Boeing 707-437 (VT-DJI "Gaurishankar") in Bombay.
March	25	Arrival of third Boeing 707-437 (VT - DJK "Everest") in Bombay.
April	10	Frankfurt introduced as a halt on the UK route.
April	19	Inauguration of Bombay/London service with Boeing 707 "Annapurna" on a twice weekly frequency.
April	29	Dusseldorf discontinued as a halt on the India/UK route.
May	4	First 1049G Super Constellation (VT-DJW "Rani of Bijapur") sent to Ontario for conversion into a freighter.
May	14	Inaugural flight to New York via London with Boeing 707 on once-a-week frequency.
June	29	Super Constellations withdrawn from India/UK route. Introduction of a weekly Prague terminator service with 1049 Super Constellations.

Contd...

Month	*Date*	*Event*
July	22	Second 1049G Super Constellation (VT-DJX "Rani of Madurai") sent to Ontario for conversion into a freighter.
October	4	Introduction of a weekly Bombay/Kuwait service via Karachi and Bahrain with L1049 Super Constellations.
November	14	Introduction of weekly cargo service "The Flying Sherpa" to London with L-1049 Super Constellation aircraft. Termination of contract with Seaboard & Western Airlines.

9

The Great Tatas

Jamsetji Nusserwanji Tata

A pioneer, a visionary, a seer - perhaps these adjectives are not enough to describe a man of such extraordinary calibre and stature, who has secured a strong foothold in the map of industrialised nations of the world. The creative forces of his genius were harnessed to cater to the development of his own land and his dreams arising out of intense love of humanity. The same passion, ideals and vision went a long way in shaping an outstanding business conglomerate that, ever since, has been constantly nourished and nurtured to offer credence to this one man's novel dream, dreamt more than a century ago.

An inclination to envision really big was recognised in Jamsetji Nusserwanji Tata at a very young age. Born on March 3, 1839, in a small town of Gujarat, Navsari, he was the first child and only son of Nusserwanji Tata, in a family of Parsi priests.

It was only natural that Nusserwanji, would, as usual join the family priesthood, but the enterprising youngster broke the tradition to become the first member of the family to try his hand at business. The entrepreneurial acumen of Jamsetji coupled with his nationalistic outlook, which led him to believe that the fruits of his business success would enrich the nation as a whole, made him truly unique. Completing his education as a 'Green Scholar' (equivalent of today's graduate) from Elphinstone College, he joined hands with his father who ran a small firm. Jamsetji was only 20 then. The repression of the Indians in the hands of British rulers coupled with widespread poverty all across the nation at that time, was at the root of this entrepreneur's philosophy. This is what precisely set the stage for the Enterprise to plough back profits into various social-development initiatives – a direct fallout of the empathy set in the founder's philosophy of business.

An eager learner, Jamsetji soon became a skilful practitioner of various nuances of business. Armed with knowledge and experience of commodities and markets, trading and banking, in 1868, Jamsetji started a trading company with a capital of Rs. 21,000. He was just 29 then and wiser for the experience garnered by nine years of working with his father.

Jamsetji's knowledge expansion happened through successive trips abroad, mainly to England, and other places that convinced him that there was tremendous scope for Indian companies to forge through and make a foray in the British dominated textile industry. Jamsetji set his foot into the textile industry in 1869, first acquiring a dilapidated and bankrupt oil mill in Chinchpokli in the industrial heart of Bombay, then renaming the property Alexandra Mill and consequently converting it into a cotton mill. He subsequently sold the mill at a remarkable profit to start in a bigger way with the best men and machinery so that he could overcome the colonial masters.

Jamsetji, chose Nagpur for setting up the mill, a destination close to three crucial raw materials: close proximity to cotton-growing areas, easy access to a railway junction, and plentiful supplies of water and fuel. He floated his enterprise, the Central India Spinning, Weaving and Manufacturing Company in 1874 with a capital of 1.5 lakhs, and consequently the Empress Mills at the age of 37 years.

Perhaps, this has been the most significant of all times in Jamsetji's life as far as business development is concerned. From 1880 till his death in 1904, his entire being had concentrated solely on three missions of his life: setting up an iron and steel company, generating hydroelectric power, and creating a world-class educational institution that would enrich Indian minds in the field of the sciences. Though none of his dreams were fully realised during his lifetime, but the seeds were laid, and the pathway made, for his successors to take up, fructify and give a glorious expression to each of his dreams.

Interest in iron and steel stirred Jamsetji, when he attended a lecture by Thomas Carlyle in Manchester, where he went to check out new machinery for his textile mill. By the end of the trip, he was sufficiently excited by the prospects of setting up a steel plant and by 1880, his dream of building a steel plant that would compare with the best of its kind in the world was steadfast. Not only was it a gigantic task, it was even intimidating, as the contemporary Indian political scenario was not too optimistic as well. The industrial revolution that had touched and transformed most nations of the West, by passed India and made it difficult for this pioneer to make any attempt towards modernising and industrialising the East.

Steadfast in his determination, nothing was enough to deter this man with a mission. The motivation was strong enough to sustain the fruition of the steel project amidst a lot of adversity. In his tortuous journey, he had to suffer the scorn of people such as Sir Frederick Upcott, the chief commissioner of the Great Indian Peninsular Railway, who promised to "eat every pound of steel rail [the Tatas] succeed in making".

Though Jamsetji had passed away by the time, the first ingots rolled out of the production plant in 1912, his spirit and efforts were carried forward by his zealous son Dorab and cousin R. D. Tata, in the later years.

The enormity of Jamsetji's vision was apparent in the entrepreneurial quality of the man. Even long before the steel plant was established, Jamsetji had thought about the welfare of his employees. He was sensitive to the needs of his workmen, and laid out plans for them to have conducive workplace, shorter working hours and employee benefits such as provident fund and gratuity – long before they were made statutory in a work place the world over. Not only did he envision a contended and productive workforce, he also envisioned a planned city with a lot of greenery around. The city thus born out of his vision in the later years, under the aegis of Sir Dorabji Tata aptly came to be called Jamshedpur.

The humanitarian, charitable and humble principles that the industrialist followed made him believe that it was essential to nurture the fine brains of Indians in order to bring them out from the puddle of poverty. Jamsetji could never make his heart to believe in hands on charity. Therefore, he established the J.N. Tata Endowment in 1892 that helped Indian students to pursue higher studies abroad. One such success was followed by another and yet another until such a time when two out of every five Indians coming into the elite Indian Civil Service were Tata scholars. The Indian Institute of Science was established with similar focus where Jamsetji assured Rs 30 Lakhs from his personal fortune. But it was not before long years of wait that tangible results came out of the effort.

Amongst the various projects that Jamsetji had initiated but could not survive to bear the fruits of its success were the hydroelectric power plant project and the Taj Mahal Hotel in Bombay. The Taj Mahal Hotel is believed to have held a special corner in the entrepreneur's heart. If stories are to be believed then the root of the Taj Mahal project are beached on an incident where Jamsetji was denied entry into a city hotel for being an Indian. The incident left such deep scars on Jamsetji's heart that he decided to construct a place equally luxurious and lavish for all fellow Indians. By the time the Taj Mahal Hotel was completed in 1903, it was the finest luxury hotel and the first building in Bombay that used electricity. Endorsed with supreme luxury items from across the globe, Taj Mahal Hotel boasted American fans, German elevators, Turkish baths, English butlers and a whole lot of other innovative delights that the Indians were deprived of.

The true Indian that resided within the great industrialist shrouded an amasing assortment of passion and commitment that carried him along his pathway to success both in his personal and professional life. Nurturing his fascinating life, was Jamsetji's quest for knowledge that invariably bred in him a love for travel, which he passionately sought till he left for his heavenly abode in Germany in 1904.

Dorabji Tata

Following the footsteps of his father, Jamsetji Tata, Sir Dorabji Tata gave shape to his father's dream and took the Tata Enterprise to the peak from where it shone bright like a sparkling jewel. His optimism and keenness were the qualities that led him to the pinnacle of success.

Belonging to the legendary family of the Tatas, the eldest son of Hirabai and Jamsetji Nusserwanji Tata, Dorabji too inherited the family traits of being a pioneering force, a leader and an achiever. His visionary approach and farsightedness made it possible for him to materialise every dream that his father had seen. This versatility that was ingrained in him through Jamsetji's farsightedness, demonstrated a challenging approach in what ever he did.

Born in 1859 he received his primary education at Proprietary High School, Bombay after which he was sent to England where he was privately tutored. At the age of 18, he joined the Gonville and Caius College at Cambridge. His interest in sports excelled during the two years he spent at Cambridge. He received several awards in Cricket and Football. Abiding by the wish of his grandfather, Dorabji returned to India in 1879 and enrolled himself in the St. Xavier's College Bombay.

Starting as a journalist with the 'Bombay Gazette' Dorabji gradually grew a liking for his ancestral business, and it was in 1884 that he finally made his first entry into his father's business and joined the cotton division of his father's firm. He was sent to Mysore to study and investigate the possibility of an expansion in the area. Dorabji was swift in preparing his report and getting the Government sanction to set up mills there.

Jamsetji wished him to meet the learned and highly esteemed Dr. H.J. Bhabha who stayed there with his daughter Meherbai. When he met Meher as she was called then, he is believed to have fallen in love at first sight. Their marriage was solemnised in 1897 when he was 38 and Meherbai was just 18.

While into the family business, Sir Dorabji worked for the realisation of his father's vision. He always wished to give life to his father's dreams. In assistance with his cousin R.D. Tata, the abiding son got closely involved in materialising the project that his father had initiated. Thus began the saga of creating a modern iron and steel industry and the result was Tata Steel.

New challenges and difficulties would always be a source of inspiration for Dorabji. With his spirits high, he took on his shoulders the responsibility of powering the industries with hydroelectricity. And soon he was, credited for the establishment of 'Tata Power'. The two prime companies established by him 'Tata Steel' and 'Tata Power' are an integral part of the Tata Group industries today.

Dorabji had always been the motivating force behind every member of his team. Along with others, he too would get intensely involved in every aspect of the project that he would handle. His inquisitiveness and interest in every detail was so intense that he even accompanied the researchers and scientists who travelled to the mineral fields in search of iron. He encouraged researchers to survey every part of the field and made sure no portion is left unattended.

Under the leadership of Dorabji Tata, the Tata Group experienced immense expansion. From just three cotton mills and the Taj Hotel Bombay, the firm spread its wings rapidly and soon grew to become the largest private sector steel company. To name a few additions that were made under his management includes an integrated steel plant, three hydroelectric power companies, a large edible oil and soap company, two cement companies and also the aviation unit pioneered by JRD Tata. Dorabji also saw the establishment of the Indian Institute of Science, Bangalore, which became the pioneer scientific research centre in India.

Dorabji had an enduring love for sports. He took measures to enhance the athletic talent in India and also initiated to introduce the nation to the 'Olympic movement'. Holding the position of the president of the Indian Olympic Association, he financed the Indian contingent to the Paris Olympiad in 1924. He also became a member of International Olympic Committee.

Dorabji Tata established the 'Lady Tata Memorial Trust' in fond memory of his wife Meherbai Tata who died of leukaemia in 1931. The trust was established in order to advance the study into various diseases related to blood. In 1932, he established a trust fund, which was to be used for the advancement of research, for disaster relief and other humanitarian purposes. This trust came to be known as the 'Sir Dorabji Tata Trust'. It is believed that Sir Dorabji had invested all his assets and wealth into this trust.

Notable amongst his other deeds is the sizeable donation he gave in the field of education. He donated a considerable amount of money to the University of Cambridge for setting up laboratory equipments in the School of Engineering and also for the establishment of a Chair for Sanskrit studies at the 'Bhandarkar Oriental Research Institute', Pune. Dorabji is also known to have presented many of his paintings and artwork to the Prince of Wales Museum in Bombay.

The legend, Sir Dorabji Tata, who is known for his immense contribution to the progress and well being of the Tata Empire, breathed his last in Bad Kissingen, Germany on 3rd June 1932. He is buried alongside his wife in the Brookwood Cemetery, England.

Ratanji Dadabhoy Tata

Ratanji Dadabhoy Tata (R.D. Tata) was a great businessman who played a pivotal role in the growth of the Tata Group in India. He was a first cousin of Jamshedji Tata, the pioneering industrialist of India and the Founder of Tata Sons. He was one of the partners in Tata Sons founded by Jamshedji Tata. Ratanji was the father of JRD Tata.

Ratanji was born in Navsari in Gujarat in the year 1856. He studied at the Elphinstone College in Bombay. After graduating, he took up a course in agriculture in Madras. He then joined his family trade in the Far East.

Ratanji was married at an early age to a Parsi girl from the Banaji family. However, she died childless not too long after the marriage. Ratanji was in his forties when he remarried a French woman, Suzanne Brière, in 1902. This was considered revolutionary in his times and was not welcomed by everyone in the Parsi community. They had five children Rodabeh, Jehangir/JRD Tata, Jimmy, Sylla and Darab.

The families of a small band of Satyagrahis, who continued to court imprisonment in South Africa during Gandhi's campaign against racism and objectionable laws by General Smuts were given financial support by the Satyagraha association which was funded by the Indian National Congress, and many rich people in India like Ratanji Tata.

Tata Steel was conceived and commissioned by Jamsetji Tata. However, Jamsetji died before the completion of the project. Ratanji played an important role in the completion of the Tata Steel Project along with Jamsetji's son Dorab and thus Tata Steel was established in Jamshedpur.

The Tatas supplied steel to the British during the First World War. However, after the war Tata Steel went through a difficult period in the 1920s as steel was dumped in to India from Britain and Belgium. Ratanji, along with other directors successfully sought protection for the Indian steel industry from the colonial government of the day and steadied the operations of Tata Steel.

Ratanji died in 1926 at the age of 70. JRD Tata succeeded him as one of the permanent directors of Tata Sons. On his death Jamnalal Bajaj wrote: "If all businessmen in India would acquire half his love for things Indian, there is no reason why all our enterprises should not flourish."

Jehangir R. D. Tata

India's first pilot; established Air India International as India's first international airline; Chairman of Tata Sons for 50 years; recipient of Bharat Ratna in 1992... there are many personas of this one personality. Enterprising, indomitable and undaunted – JRD Tata is the pioneer who was driven by the spirit of the skies.

On the personal front, flying was a passion with JRD. He was the first person to qualify within India to fly. He got his license, which bore on it Number 1, on 10 February 1929. As an aviator and pioneer flier, he was the one who brought commercial aviation to India. JRD went on to establish Air-India International in 1948 and became the president of International Air Transport Association (IATA) within 10 years of its establishment. He remained at the helm of Air India till 1978, making it one of the most efficient airlines in the world.

Nobody could have guessed that this is how destiny would unfold, when JRD was born to R.D. Tata, a business partner and relative of Jamsetji Tata, and his French wife Sooni. JRD, the second of four siblings, was educated in France, Japan and England before being drafted into the French army for a mandatory one year period. JRD wanted to extend his stint in the forces (to avail of a chance to attend a renowned horse-riding school), but his father would have none of it. Leaving the French army saved JRD his life, because shortly thereafter, the regiment he served in was wiped out while on an expedition in Morocco.

JRD then set his mind on securing an engineering degree from Cambridge, but his father summoned him back to India (JRD would forever regret not being able to attend university). He soon found himself on the threshold of a business career in a country he was far from familiar with.

JRD entered the Tatas as an unpaid apprentice in December 1925. His mentor in business was John Peterson, a Scotsman who had joined the Group after serving in the Indian Civil Service. At 22, soon after his father passed away, he was on the board of Tata Sons, the Group's flagship company. In 1929, aged 25, he surrendered his French citizenship to embrace the country that would become the central motif of his life. In the same year on February 10, JRD became the first Indian to pass the pilot's examination. With this distinctive honour of being India's first pilot, he was instrumental in giving wings to India by building Tata Airlines, which ultimately became Air India. His passion for flying was fulfilled with the formation of the Tata Aviation Service in 1932.

At the age of 34, in 1938, JRD was elected Chairman of Tata Sons making him the youngest head of the largest industrial group in India. His leadership at Tata Sons, at the beginning, had 14 enterprises which half a century later had expanded to a conglomerate of 95 enterprises. During his tenure, the group expanded into diverse fields such as chemicals, automobiles, tea and information technology. Breaking with the common practice of having members of one's own family run different operations in a business, JRD urged to bring in professionals to the table. He turned the Tata Group into a business federation, where entrepreneurial talent and expertise were encouraged to flower.

During his tenure, JRD initiated a programme of closer "employee association with management" to give workers a stronger voice in the affairs of the company. He, for the first time, pioneered the system of developing 'employee welfare schemes' in corporate India and steered the principles of an eight hour working day, free medical aid, workers' provident fund and accident compensation schemes, which were later, adopted as statutory requirements in India.

Under JRD's aegis, in the year 1979, Tata Steel instituted a new practice; a worker is deemed to be "at work" from the moment he leaves home for work till he returns home from work. Hence the company is financially liable to the worker if any mishap takes place on the way to and from work.

JRD stepped down from his position as Chairman in 1991, to handover the baton to Ratan Tata.

Self-effacing, modest, wistful and endearing are a few of the adjectives used to describe JRD. During the 89 years of his life and as an established corporate citizen of India.

JRD Tata was honoured with a number of awards. He received the Padma Vibhushan in 1957 for his remarkable contribution to the aviation industry, the Guggenheim Medal for aviation in 1988. In 1992, because of his selfless humanitarian endeavours, JRD Tata was awarded India's highest civilian honour, the Bharat Ratna — one of the rarest instances in which this award was granted during a person's lifetime. In the same year, JRD Tata was also bestowed with the United Nations Population Award for his crusading endeavours towards initiating and successfully implementing the family planning movement in India, much before it became an official government policy.

JRD and his wife, Thelma, whom he married after a Paris romance in 1930, did not have any children, but JRD always appeared most comfortable with kids. Be it adult or children, to him, it was people who mattered. With his demise on November 29, 1993, in a Geneva hospital, an epoch had come to an end. A noble bit of India—and Indianness—was gone forever.

Naval Hormusji Tata

Born in August 1904, Naval H. Tata joined the Tata Group in 1930, and by 1933 he was the secretary of the Group's Aviation division. In 1939 he was made the Managing Director of the Group's textile companies and in 1941 was made the Director of Tata Sons. Mr. Naval Tata was actively engaged with the Tata Charities and served as the Chairman of the Sir Ratan Tata Trust from 1965 to the time of his passing. He was the founder president of the Indian Cancer Society and held the position from 1951 through 1989.

His most valuable contribution outside of business was in the domain of labour relations. He believed in responsible negotiations between employers, workers and governments in the search for equitable solutions to labour issues. For over four decades he provided a voice of reason, consideration and conciliation to national and international organisations working to minimise employer-employee friction. He was an employer who always regarded himself as a trustee of the rights and interests of workers.

Mr. Naval Tata became part of Geneva-based International Labour Organisation governing body in 1951 and continued in the post till 1989. He was also a member of the International Organisation of Employers for 38 years and was the president of the Employers' Federation of India from 1959 to 1985. Naval Tata symbolised all that is best of the Tata spirit of giving back to society and the communities in which its enterprises grow.

He was also an avid sports lover and Indian field hockey was another beneficiary of his capabilities. He was the administrative head of the game in India when the country won gold in three successive Olympics. Mr. Naval Tata's caring and endearing nature, his abiding concern for the poor, his love of a good laugh and his instinct to trust even those not worthy of it, made him one of a kind. He married Simone in 1955. Mr. Naval Tata passed away in 1989.

Ratan Naval Tata

When Ratan Tata became group chairman in 1991, he ushered in an era of change. A Company or business that remains static is a business that will die. A company that constantly changes and accepts that there are better way to do things than the ways to do things than the way they are done today, is a company that will survive in the global market that we face.

A Business Legend: Ratan Tata is the chairman of the Tata Group, India's largest corporation.

- He is the latest in a long line of Tatas to head the family owned company.
- Born into an old Parsi family of Bombay on 28th December, 1937.
- He received a Bachelor's degree in Architecture from America's Cornell University in 1962.
- He returned to India and joined the Tata Group.
- Tata is single and leads a modest lifestyle in his bachelor apartment.
- The US educated bachelor lives alone with his two German shepherds in an apartment in Mumbai.
- He is known to be a supporter of the traditional Parsi way of life.
- He has a passion for home cooked food and is known to indulge reply in art collection.
- A trained pilot who still takes to the skies on his own aircraft has picked a number of awards.
- He is known to slip into the front seat alongside his driver to and from work.

Ats the helm of Tata Group since the retirement of JRD Tata in 1991, Mr. Ratan Naval Tata, the son of Naval H. Tata, has made the Tata Group a global player. The January 10, 2005 issue of Forbes Asia, named Ratan Tata as Asia's Businessman of the Year. Under Mr. Ratan Tata's guidance, the Tata Group has grown rapidly and made forays into new industries and areas of business.

Mr. Ratan N. Tata is the Chairman of Tata Sons Limited, the holding company of the Tata Group, and the Chairman of major Tata operating companies. In addition, Mr. Tata serves on the central board of the Reserve Bank of India and is on the Prime Minister's Council on Trade and Industry. He also heads the Investment Commission, which he recently set up with the Government of India.

A leader in the worldwide business community, Mr. Tata serves on the international advisory boards of Mitsubishi Corporation, the American International Group, JP Morgan Chase and Booz-Allen Hamilton Inc.

He is also a member of the International Investment Council of the President of South Africa, the Asia Pacific Advisory Committee to the Board of Directors of the New York Stock Exchange and chairs the Advisory Board of Rand's Centre for Asia Pacific Policy.

Mr. Tata is a role model in both his personal life and professional career. He serves as the Chairman of two of the largest private sector philanthropic undertakings in India: the Sir Dorabji Tata Trust and the Sir Ratan Tata Trust. He is also a member of the board of trustees of the Ford Foundation and of the programme board of the Bill and Melinda Gates Foundation's India Aids Initiative.

The Tata Group

- The Tata Group consists of nearly 100 Companies.
- Tata Group is a multinational conglomerate and one of the largest private companies in India.
- Today, it has strength of 3, 50,000 employees all over the world and an estimated annual turnover of $62 billion USD.

- Tata's contribution to India's GDP is nearly 5.5 per cent and 60 per cent of its revenue comes from foreign countries.
- Tata group was always known for its business ethics and corporate governance.
- The Tata group has spread its operations across six continents and more than 80 countries

Ratan Tata: India's Industrial Architect: Ratan Naval Tata, the Chairman of the Tata Group, one of the largest group of industries; something he inherits from his earlier generation. Brought up by his grandmother due to separation of his parents, Ratan Tata did his schooling from Cathedral and John Cannon School in Mumbai. Later on he got his Architectural and Engineering Degree from Cornell University. From here he joined his family business. After turning down a job offer from IBM, he joined the Jamshedpur Tata Steel plant working with the Blue Collar employees handling blast furnaces.

Peek in the Past: In 1971, Ratan Tata joined Nelco and turned it into a profit churning company. Later on when he joined the sick unit of Tata's Empress Mill, he turned it into a dividend declaring company. In 1981 he was declared the Chairman of the Tata Group of Industries. Today the Company has been listed in New York Stock Exchange.

The Story So Far: The young lad who left the IBM job and brewed the corridors of his own company, is today the Chairman of Tata Group of Companies and has his company listed in New York Exchange. His latest expedition is the Tata Elegante the latest Tata four wheeler he presented at the Geneva Car Expo.

The Recognition: Honoured with Padma Bhushan he is a member on Prime Ministers Council on Trade and Industry. Ratan Tata was also honoured by Cornell University as the 26th Robert S. Hatfield Fellow in Economic Education, considered to be the highest honour by the Cornell University. He is also a member of the board of trustees of the RAND Corporation. He is board member on the Republic of South Africa's International Investment Council and is a Asia-Pacific advisory committee member for the New York Stock Exchange.

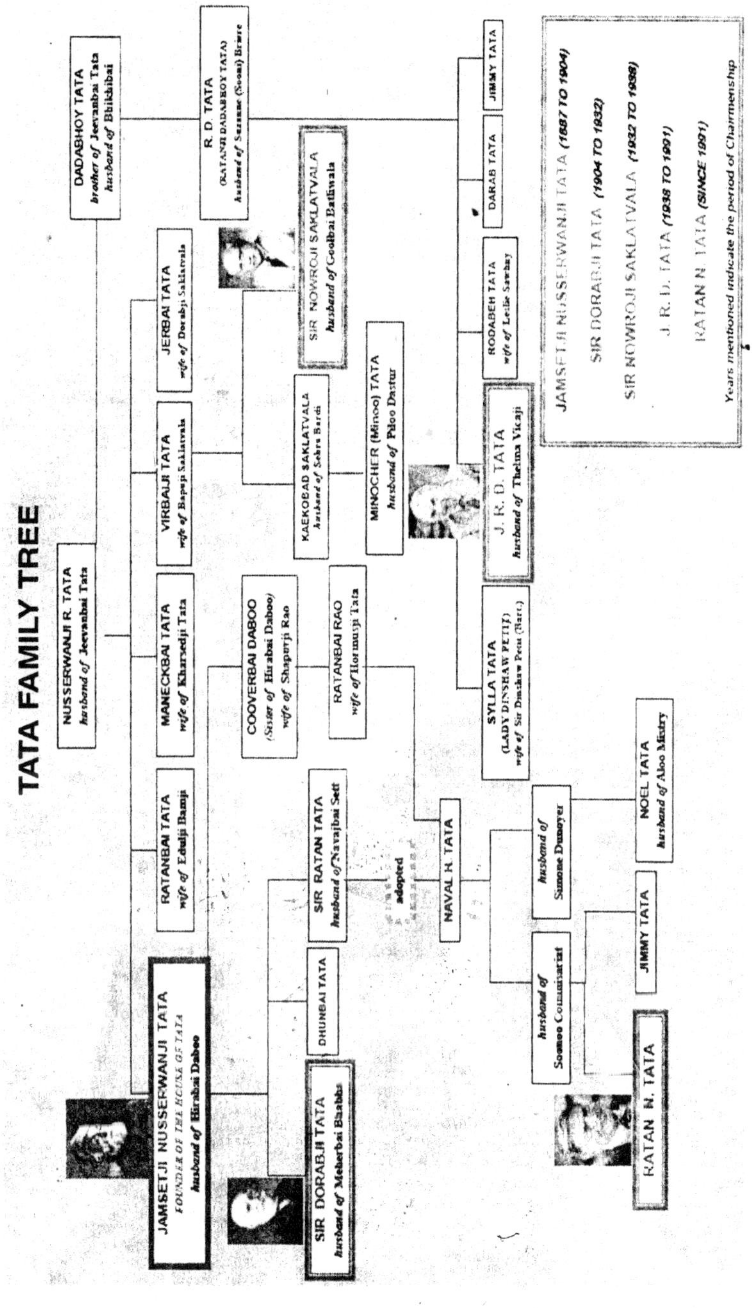
TATA FAMILY TREE
JAMSETJI NUSSERWANJI TATA
FOUNDER OF THE HOUSE OF TATA
husband of Hirabai Daboo
NUSSERWANJI R. TATA
husband of Jeevanbai Tata
DADABHOY TATA
brother of Jeevanbai Tata
husband of Bhikhibai
R. D. TATA
(RATANJI DADABHOY TATA)
husband of Suzanne (Sooni) Briere
RATANBAI TATA
wife of Edulji Bamji
MANECKBAI TATA
wife of Khursedji Tata
VIRBAIJI TATA
wife of Bapuji Saklatvala
JERBAI TATA
wife of Dorabji Saklatvala
SIR NOWROJI SAKLATVALA
husband of Goolbai Batliwala
KAEKOBAD SAKLATVALA
husband of Sehra Bardi
COOVERBAI DABOO
(Sister of Hirabai Daboo)
wife of Shapurji Rao
RATANBAI RAO
wife of Hormusji Tata
MINOCHER (Minoo) TATA
husband of Piloo Dastur
SIR DORABJI TATA
husband of Meherbai Bhabha
DHUNBAI TATA
SIR RATAN TATA
husband of Navajbai Sett
adopted
NAVAL H. TATA
SYLLA TATA
(LADY DINSHAW PETIT)
wife of Sir Dinshaw Petit (Bart.)
J. R. D. TATA
husband of Thelma Vicaji
RODABEH TATA
wife of Leslie Sawhny
DARAB TATA
JIMMY TATA
husband of
Sooni Commissariat
husband of
Simone Dunoyer
NOEL TATA
husband of Aloo Mistry
JIMMY TATA
RATAN N. TATA
JAMSETJI NUSSERWANJI TATA (1887 TO 1904)
SIR DORABJI TATA (1904 TO 1932)
SIR NOWROJI SAKLATVALA (1932 TO 1938)
J. R. D. TATA (1938 TO 1991)
RATAN N. TATA (SINCE 1991)
Years mentioned indicate the period of Chairmenship

10

Golden Words of JRD

- I do not want India to be an economic superpower. I want India to be a happy country.
- No institute of science and technology can guarantee discoveries or inventions, and we cannot plan or command a work of genius at will. But do we give sufficient thought to the nurture of the young investigator, to providing the right atmosphere and conditions of work and full opportunity for development? It is these things that foster invention and discovery.
- Growing organisations in any field must constantly evolve, accept or even seek new ideas, new visions, and new enthusiasms.
- (The) Future belongs to the young. We must not only trust them with responsibility but must thrust it upon them whilst they are still young and full of energy, zest, hope and even illusions. However heartbreaking it may be to ourselves, we must make way for the new generations even when we feel we are still in our prime.
- If I were to attribute any single reason to such success as I have achieved, I would say that success would not have

been possible without a sustained belief that what I did or attempted to do would serve the needs and interests of our country and our people and that I was a trustee of such interests.— JRD Tata, In reply to a letter by Prof. Sahni, IIM Bangalore, who requested him to share his philosophy of life with his students.

- As I lay down office as chairman of the firm, I do so in the conviction that the future of the Tata group, its continuing growth and prosperity, are in safe hands.
- We have to find the intermediate ways and means of restoring a degree of stability to our politics and more than a degree of safety to our citizens.
- Money is like manure. It stinks when you pile it; it grows when you spread it.
- Never start with diffidence, Always start with confidence.
- To be a leader, you've got to lead human beings with affection.
- I never had any interest in making money. None of my decisions were influenced by whether it would bring me money or wealth.
- Uncommon thinkers reuse what common thinkers refuse.
- When you work, work as if everything depends on you. When you pray, pray as if everything depends on God.
- Cleanliness is the Hallmark of perfect standards and the best quality inspector is the conscience.
- Quality is first engineered; only then it is inspected.
- Making steel may be compared to making a chappati (tortilla). To make a good chappati, even a golden pin will not work unless the dough is good.
- Common people have an appetite for food; uncommon people have an appetite for service.
- Nothing worthwhile is ever achieved without deep thought and hard work.

- One must think for oneself and never accept at their face value slogans and catch phrases to which, unfortunately, our people are too easily susceptible.
- One must forever strive for excellence, or even perfection, in any task however small, and never be satisfied with the second best.
- No success or achievement in material terms is worthwhile unless it serves the needs or interests of the country and its people and is achieved by fair and honest means.
- Good human relations not only bring great personal rewards but also are essential to the success of any enterprise.
- While I usually came back from meeting Gandhiji elated and inspired but always a bit sceptical, and from talks with Jawaharlal, fired with emotional zeal but often confused and unconvinced, meetings with Vallabhbhai were a joy from which I returned with renewed confidence in the future of our country. I have often thought that if fate had decreed that he, instead of Jawaharlal, would be the younger of the two, India would have followed a very different path and would be in better economic shape that it is today.
- I wish, I were big enough, like Einstein, to do what he did on one occasion. A hundred-dollar-a-plate dinner was organised for him to speak, and leaders of America in all fields, particularly in the field of science, were invited to hear the great man. When his turn came, he rose and said: 'I've nothing to say,' and sat down. You can imagine the consternation, quite apart from the wasted cost of the dinner! Realising the frightful effect his remarks had on the audience, Einstein got up again and said: 'When I've something to say, I'll let you know.' (Address to the Lions Club of Jamshedpur, August 22, 1963.)
- The essence of air transport is speed, and speed is unfortunately one of the most expensive commodities in the world, principally because of the disproportionate

amount of the power required to achieve high speed and to lift loads thousands of feet into the air. This is strikingly illustrated by the fact that while an average cargo ship, freight train and transport aeroplane are each equipped with engines totalling about 2,500 H.P., the ship can carry a load of about 7,000 tons, the train 800 tons and the plane only two and a half tons. ('On November 2, 1943, JRD Tata spoke to the Bombay Rotary Club.)

- There is today hardly any country in the world outside the communist bloc which does not have a mixed economy. In fact, even countries which call themselves socialist would object to theirs not being described as a mixed economy, for it would imply that it was a totalitarian one, while countries like Germany or Japan, usually thought of as having typically free enterprise economies, would do the same; for, otherwise, it would imply that theirs was a nineteenth century laissez-faire economy. (Address on 'Why a Mixed Economy?' to the Associated Chambers of Commerce and Industry of India, New Delhi, April 4, 1975.)

- The Psychology of Delay. Some of the causes of delay in coming to economic decisions in our country seem to lie in the psychological realm. There is such a thing as the psychology of power which motivates people: power of control and patronage, power to delay an application, power to hold up a file, power to keep people waiting in an anteroom, all of which are consciously or subconsciously treated as symbols of prestige and hallmarks of importance. (To The Central Advisory Council of Industries, New Delhi, January 3, 1969.)

- At the Crossroads. The effective execution of a Plan is what counts and not mere planning on paper; it is not what we put on our plate or even what we eat that provides nourishment and growth, but what we digest. (The Central Advisory Council of Industries, New Delhi, August 13, 1965)

- Road to Social Justice. The first and perhaps the most important of the factors which have contributed to our failure to make real impact on poverty expressed in terms of total number who live below the poverty line has clearly been the uncontrolled growth of our population... First, we must, at all costs, make a much more earnest effort at controlling the growth of our population. As it is, we are running out of time and there is no longer any possibility of preventing it from exceeding 1,000 million souls by the end of the century. (At The International Seminar of Economic Journalists, New Delhi, December 5, 1972.)

11

Great Life at a Glance

1904, July, 29: JRD Tata was born in Paris, France. His father was Ratanji Dadabhoy Tata, a Parsi and his mother was Suzanne "Sooni" Briere, a French.

1907: Dorabji Tata established Tata Iron and Steel in 1907.

1910: The Tatas spread their wings further with the formation of Tata Hydro Electric Power Supply Co., the first venture in the power sector.

1911: The Tata Memorial Library, better known as the Indian Institute of Science Library was established, and is the best library for Science and Technology in India.

1921: In Male village in Mulshi taluka a satyagraha was led by freedom fighter Senapati Bapat against a dam built by Tatas.

1922: JRD Tata returned to India to join the family business. He also became the first Indian pilot to qualify for a British private license.

1926: Ratanji died at the age of 70. JRD Tata succeeded him as one of the permanent directors of Tata Sons.

1929: JRD became the first pilot to have qualified in India with No. 1 on his flying licence.

1931: JRD Tata was the first to make a solo flight from Mumbai to Karachi, (Now in Pakistan).

1932: Tata Aviation Service, the forerunner to Tata Airlines and Air India , took to the skies. The first flight lifted off from Drigh Road in Karachi with JRD Tata at the control of a Puss Moth. The Tata Airline was conceived by a former officer of the Royal Airforce, called Nevill Vincent. It was he who offered JRD Tata a project to start an airline. The initial investment was small — Indian Rupees 200000.

1933: Tata Airlines started full operations. It had one Puss Moth and one Leopard Moth aircraft, one palm-thatched shed to operate from and one whole time pilot, assisted by JRD Tata and Neville Vintcent.

1937: Ratan Tata was born in Mumbai.

1938: JRD Tata, 34 and relatively unknown, took over from Nowroji Saklatvala as group chairman, as per the will of the late Dorabji Tata.

1941, Mar 20,: The Tata Institute of Fundamental Research was planned.

1945: JRD, with Homi J. Bhabha established Tata Institute of Fundamental Research (TIFR).

1952: Lakme was started as a 100 per cent subsidiary of TATA Oil Mills (Tomco), part of the TATA Group. It was named after the French Opera-Lakme, which itself is the French form of Lakshmi, the goddess of wealth, also renowned for her beauty.

1953, Aug 1: Air India began as the new Airlines. The Indian government exercised it's option to purchase a majority ownership in Air India and Air India International, Ltd. was born.

1957: Tata Administrative Service was conceived by JRD Tata.

1974: Tata Energy Research Institute (TERI) was established, in Delhi.

1979: On JRD's instance, Tata Steel instituted a new practice; a worker is deemed to be "at work" from the moment he leaves home for work till he returns home from work.

1984, Dec.: When the Government of India arrested Union Carbide Chairman Warren Anderson for his role in causing the Bhopal gas disaster, JRD Tata was one of the few Indians to condemn the arrest.

1991, March 25: Ratan Tata's name was proposed and seconded by Pallonji Mistry and JRD Tata decided to hand over charge to Ratan Tata.

1991, Oct.: In a move executed in the characteristically quiet and unobtrusive style of the Tatas, JRD Tata stepped down from the Chairmanship of Tata Industries to make way for Ratan Naval Tata to take his place.

1992, March: The country's highest civilian award, the Bharat Ratna was presented to JRD Tata for his great contribution in building modern India.

1993, Nov., 29: JRD Tata passed away in distant Geneva and his death caused an emotional upheaval in the entire group, which he had led for 53 years.

Appendix

(JRD Tata Memorial Award)

The Man and His Vision

Bharat Ratna, the late Mr. JRD Tata, was among those handful of world citizens whom destiny itself so shaped to become an institution in a lifetime. He had been regarded as one of the stalwarts among Indians in the 20th Century, who stamped his personality on the country's affairs both before and after independence. He was the crusader for the promotion of family planning, both as a tool of curbing India's rapidly increasing population, and an entirely new way of life in a developing society in which a family is not mere numbers but valuable relationships of shared growth.

The late Mr. Tata had promoted and fostered several causes in the service of science and nation. His holistic view of the population problem had turned him into an equally strong humanist, concerned no less with the problems of poverty and environment, intertwined with population. Mr. Tata was the first to raise an alarm in 1951, in the course of a speech, about the continuous and fast growth of the India's population and its serious potential consequences to the country's economy and progress. Realising later the need for non-governmental action, he founded the Family Planning Foundation in 1970, of which he was the founder Chairman. Family Planning Foundation was rechristened as the Population Foundation of India in 1993 to reflect the wider dimensions of the population issue in a changing world. Mr. Tata's unique services in the cause of population had been recognised by the United Nations who had chosen him for their prestigious Population Award for 1992. For his many splendoured achievements, India also conferred on him 'Bharat Ratna', the highest civilian award of the Nation in 1992.

The Population Foundation

The Population Foundation of India (formerly known as Family Planning Foundation) was established in 1970 by a dedicated group of industrialists and population activists led by Bharat Ratna the late Mr. JRD Tata who guided it as the founder Board Chairman until his death in 1993.

After his demise, Dr. Bharat Ram, noted industrialist and a founding member of the Foundation, was its Board Chairman. After his demise in 2007, Mr. Hari Shankar Singhania, renowned industrialist took over as the Board Chairman of the foundation.

The Foundation has been in the forefront of non-governmental efforts at population stabilisation and establishing a balance between resources, environment and population. Social development including population stabilisation in India should not and cannot remain the sole concern of the Government.

It ought to be supported and supplemented by private voluntary enterprises. In this regard, the Foundation has always worked in close cooperation and coordination with official agencies and programmes, both at the Centre and in the States.

In its independent role, it has tried to guide and influence the National Population Policy and to serve as a catalytic agent to promote programmes at different levels directed towards the ultimate goal of population stabilisation.

The Foundation supports innovative research, experimentation and social action to further the cause of population stabilisation and provide a forum for pooling of experiences and sharing of professional expertise to strengthen and enlarge the operational base of the Reproductive and Child Health (RCH) programmes.

The Award

When the founder Board Chairman of the Foundation Mr. JRD Tata passed away in 1993, having laid a strong base for a social movement to stabilise the growth of population in India as an essential prerequisite to attain higher qualities of life for the Indian people, the Foundation felt that it would be a fitting tribute to the great man if national awards were instituted in his name to further the cause for which he was a champion acknowledged all over the world.

In February 1996, the PFI Governing Board formally decided to institute national awards for the best State and the best districts with outstanding performance in population and reproductive health and family planning programme.

The Significance of the Award

The process of integration of related programmes of maternal and child health initiated with the implementation of the Child Survival and Safe Motherhood (CSSM) Programme was taken a step further in 1994 when the International Conference on Population and Development (ICPD) in Cairo recommended that the participant countries should implement unified programmes for reproductive health.

India took the lead by introducing the target-free approach to family welfare programmes from April 1996. During the 9th Plan, the RCH Programme, accordingly, integrated all the related programmes of the 8th Plan on maternal and child health, family planning, adolescent sexual health, etc. The concept of RCH is to provide to the beneficiaries need based, client centred, demand driven, high quality and integrated RCH services.

It is a legitimate right of the citizens to be able to experience sound Reproductive and Child Health and therefore the RCH Programme seeks to provide relevant services for assuring Reproductive and Child Health to all citizens. RCH is even more relevant for obtaining the objective of population stabilisation in the country.

The selection of winners for the Awards is not dependent just on the current levels of performance in a number of crucial indicators. Emphasis has been given on the change factor signifying the pace of progress achieved over a period of time. It is well known that despite the relatively slow performance in the field of RCH for the country as a whole, there are States within the country, which have made significant strides in the field of Reproductive and Child Health and their achievements are comparable to the best even in advanced societies.

These demonstrate that, given the leadership, will and conditions, such success can be repeated in other regions. The awards are recognition of this sustained effort and will hopefully generate the much needed impetus and confidence amongst the others that they could also achieve the same standards. The criteria adopted for the selection cover various aspects of human development and reproductive health.

Accordingly, the first JRD Tata Memorial Awards were announced on July 29, 1997 and were given to the winning State and districts by the Prime Minister of India, in a function organised by the Foundation on 13th November 1997.

The first JRD Tata Memorial Award for the best performing State was given to Kerala. Awards for the best performing districts were given to three districts, namely, Palakkad in Kerala (in the large population size category), Toothukudi in Tamil Nadu (in the medium population size category) and Kurukshetra in Haryana (in the small population size category).

The second JRD Tata Memorial Awards were announced on 28th July 2000 and were given to the winning state and districts by the Union Minister of Health and Family Welfare in a function organised by the Foundation on 3rd January 2001.

The second JRD Tata Memorial Award for the best performing State was given to Tamil Nadu. Awards for the best performing districts were given to three districts, namely, Chennai in Tamil Nadu (in the large population size category), Alappuzha in Kerala (in the medium population size category) and Jorhat in Assam (in the small population size category). Awards were also given to the best performing district in the not so good performing states. In this category, the districts of Dehradun in the then Uttar Pradesh, Purbi Singhbhum in the erstwhile Bihar and Cuttack in Orissa were adjudged the winners.

The third JRD Tata Memorial Award for the best performing state was given by Vice-President of India to Himachal Pradesh on November 7, 2003. Awards for the best performing districts were given to three districts, namely, West Godavari in Andhra Pradesh (in the large population category), Churu in Rajasthan (in the medium population category) and Lahul & Spiti in Himachal Pradesh (in the small population category).

Awards were also given to the best performing districts in the not so good performing states. In this category, the districts of Ri Bhoi in Meghalaya, Ranchi in Jharkhand and Bhagalpur in Bihar were adjudged the winners.

The Methodology

For the selection of states for the 4th JRD Tata Memorial awards, it was decided by the award committee to institute two state level awards, one among the bigger population category (population of 10 million and above) and another among smaller population category (population of less than 10 million).

The selection of the states for the state level award 2008 has been done on the basis of 14 indicators, for which data were compiled from various published sources. These indicators were finalised on the basis of recommendations of the Technical Advisory Committee.

These indicators have a strong bearing on reproductive health, gender equity, family planning and fertility levels of the population.

While selecting the 4th JRD Tata Memorial Awards for the states, it was decided by the award committee to defer the district level awards till the availability of next round of DLHS data as due to large reorganisation of districts the change was not accessed while selecting the best districts.

Indicators

Sl. No.	*Indicator*	*Source*
1.	Women (20-24 years) married before age 18	NFHS II & III
2.	CPR (Contraceptive Prevalence Rate) –any methods NFHS II & III	
3.	Full Immunisation	NFHS II & III
4.	TFR (Total Fertility Rate)	NFHS II & III
5.	At least 3 ANC (Antenatal check ups) visits	NFHS II & III
6.	Safe Delivery	NFHS II & III
7.	% Children underweight (weight for age)	NFHS II & III
8.	IMR (Infant Mortality Rate)	SRS (Sample Registration System), 1999 and 2005
9.	Under Five Mortality Rate Indirect Estimates, Census 2001	(Male/Female Ratio)
10.	Child Sex Ratio (0-6 years)	Census, 1991 and 2001
11.	Girls School Attendance Rate (6-14 years)	Census, 1991 and 2001
12.	Female Youth (15-24 years) Literacy Rate	Census, 1991 and 2001
13.	Literacy Rate (7 and more years)	Census, 1991 and 2001
14.	Planned Expenditure on Social Sector, 1997	National Human Development and 2004 Report, 2001 and Statistical Abstract India, 2001

Sources of Data

The first seven indicators have been derived from the last two rounds of the National Family Health Survey (NFHS-II & III). The data on child sex ratio, girls school attendance rate, female youth literacy and literacy rate are from the Census of India 1991 and 2001 and IMR is from the SRS. The M/F (Male/Female) ratio of under five mortality is based on the indirect estimate from 2001 Census by Brass method. Social Sector includes education, health, water supply and sanitation, urban development, information and welfare & labour. Planned expenditure on social sector for the year 1997-98 is an average of 1996-98. Similarly, planned expenditure for the year 2004-05 is an average of 2003-06.

As data are compiled from different sources, the base year and final year are not the same for all the fourteen indicators. Efforts have been made to compile data for the most recent year and making the indicators comparable. The base and final years of the different state level indicators are as follows:

Source	*Base Year*	*Final Year*
Census	1991	2001
NFHS	1998-99	2005-06
SRS	1999	2005
National Human Development Report & Statistical Abstract, India, 2001	1997-98	2004-05

Selection of the Best Performing State

Step 1:

At first step, as it has been followed by UNDP for Human Development Index (HDI) each variable is converted into an index ranging from 0 to 100. The index is computed as: For *positive indicators* (like use of family planning and utilisation of ANC):

$$\text{Index}=\frac{(\text{State value - Minimum value})}{(\text{Maximu value - Minimum value})}\times 100$$

For *negative indicators* (like TFR and IMR):

$$\text{Index}=\frac{(\text{Maximum value - State value})}{(\text{Maximu value - Minimum value})}\times 100$$

Step 2:

Secondly, a composite index is computed for base year and final year on the basis of these fourteen indices. This composite index is the simple average of fourteen indices.

Step 3:

Thirdly, a score is obtained for each state by combining the recent levels and changes over the base and final years in the composite index in the ratio of 1:4.

The Winners

After final ranking of the nineteen bigger states (population of 10 million and above) on the basis of composite index, Chhattisgarh emerged as the best state and among the ten smaller states (population of less than 10 million) Sikkim emerged as the best state. Chhattisgarh got a high score among all the bigger states in the composite index as the change is observed to be the highest among all the 19 bigger states. Similarly among 10 smaller states, Sikkim emerged as the winner state, as the change in between the base year and the final year for Sikkim is observed to be the highest.

Profile of the Winners

The best performing States have their distinct characteristics, which have led to their success. These relate varyingly to the historical past, the geographical location, the ethnic composition, the social structure, political commitment to development such as population policies, bureaucratic efficiency and other determinants which contribute to the achievement. A study of some of these factors would be rewarding for other comparable areas.

Winner among Bigger States

The 4th JRD Tata Memorial awards for execellence in reproductive health & population programmes for the year 2008 is own by Chhattisgarh. The State with a score of 115.8 ranked first among the bigger states, followed by Rajasthan & Andhra Pradesh with scores of 103.5 & 100.6 respectively.

Chhattisgarh is one of the bigger states of India with a population of about 21 million persons according to the 2001 Census. Chhattisgarh was carved out from Eastern part of Madhya Pradesh and the State of Chhattisgarh came into existence on 1st November 2000 as the 26th states of the Union of India. The State has made significant strides in developing an educational and health infrastructure and transport and communication networks. These advances had a significant impact on the socioeconomic and demorgraphic status of the state.

Chhattisgarh ranks favourably in many of the indices used to determine the performance of reproductive and child heath programmes in the states.

Chhattisgarh has made improvement in almost all the indicators considered for the 4th JRD Tata Memorial award. Full immunisation for the state improved from 20.0 in 1998-99 to 48.7 in 2005-06. Similarly for at least three ANC visits, the figure got a boost from 33.2 in 1998-99 to 54.2 in 2005-06. The state has also shown improvement, in safe delivery, children underweight and infant mortality rate.

Winner among Smaller States

Sikkim attained statehood as the 22nd state of the Indian Union in 1975. It is one of the smaller states of India. It is having population of half million according to the 2001 Census. Among the smaller states (population of less than 10 million), Sikkim has done well in relation to all the indicators considered for the 4th JRD Tata Memorial award. The state has shown remarkable improvement in terms of couple protection rate (53.8 to 57.6), full immunisation (47.4 to 69.6), at least three ANC visits (42.6 to 70.1) in between two successive National Family Health Surveys (1998-99 and 2005-06). The state has also made substantial reduction in infant mortality rate and percentage of children underweight. The change in between the overall index of final year and base year was found to be highest for the State of Chhattisgarh (13.5) among bigger states. For Sikkim change was found to be second highest (9.6) among smaller states. This resulted in selection of the two states under bigger and smaller population category states for the 4'th JRD Tata Memorial Awards.

Sikkim on the Path of Development

P.D. Rai

Deputy Chairman, Sikkim State Planning Commission, Government of Sikkim, Tashiling, Gangtok

This article is less about numbers and more about ideas and the political economy – it captures the essence of the direction of development, the policy instruments and indeed the flow of

Government funds to the people of Sikkim and its impact, as has been studied by independent institutions. There are many discrepancies and downsides, but as all development is about trade-offs, these are being handled albeit in a way by acknowledging their import.

Sikkim's leap into the 21st Century

Sikkim joined the national mainstream as the 22nd State of the Indian Union in 1975. Since then it has taken up the development in total coordination with the policies set out by the Planning Commission of India, participating fully from the 5th Five Year Plan onwards.

Today it has attained spectacular growth in an atmosphere of peace and communal harmony, growing at a per capita GSDP of Rs. 26,215 (2004-05)1 and maintaining rate of growth at about 10 per cent per annum.

So the ups and downs of development that has persisted in India have also affected the State. Sikkim's accelerated growth in the last ten years is indeed visible. Whether it has been done in a significantly different manner than others is a matter of debate.

Sikkim is always described in glowing terms by nearly all visitors who happen to come here on one pretext or other. They find this place gloriously calm. The hills and mountains dazzle. The peace and tranquillity thrill. However, they also report a sudden disquiet especially after they have visited Nathula and gone through the major part of Gangtok in some detail. Pinpointing it may not be politically correct. So we hear sentences like "Gangtok could have been better planned!" or "The traffic is quite something!"

The State is, geopolitically, highly strategic even though it is so small an area in the Eastern Himalayas. The mountain passes of Jelepla and Nathula make it prized in terms of access to the Tibetan Plateau and to the economic, social and political exchanges. It offers the shortest route to Lhasa, the capital of Tibet, from Kolkata and its sea ports – a mere 1350 Km or so. The British conquered Sikkim by the late 1800s for this very strategic reason and Sikkim became part of India in 1975.

Always a bone of contention with China, Sikkim is now acknowledged as part of India by that country but not after extracting some major concessions. Tibet has been recognised by India as part of China. Dalai Lama is not to be highlighted, not even his vision of a free autonomous Tibet under China.

Size Matters

The State's land size is miniscule. With a population of a little more than half a million it is sparsely populated, one of the specificities of mountain communities. Indeed access to and for villagers is always a challenge. Sikkim has but only 7 per cent land out of our 7096 Sq Km which can be made habitable by world standards. The rest is too steep or wilderness. Little wonder then that it has over 80 per cent of the land as Forests. Forest cover is increasing and at about 40 per cent. Sikkim is proud of this great biodiversity reserve contributing significantly to India's overall reserve.

Sikkim's forests have been regenerated after policies which can be considered perhaps the greenest in India. Two most important initiatives of the Government have been the Green Mission and the removal of graziers from high altitude pastures, since this was becoming unsustainable. Alternative livelihoods have been provided though implementation is still an issue.

How can a small mountain state make it thus far? Only from generous plan and non-plan funding from Government of India. Sikkim's own resources are limited and only ecotourism and Hydro power is the key to generate any real level of State resources. If and when Nathula pass opens up fully for trade then the State will have to find a mechanism of getting a share of the trade surpluses that will inevitably accrue. So, Sikkim's annual plan size and non-plan component is mainly funded by assistance from the Centre. The State is a special category one. Furthermore, in 2002 Sikkim was assimilated into the North Eastern Council as the eighth member. This has opened up another pool of assistance from the NEC as well as the non-lapsable pool of resources of Government of India through the Ministry of Development of North-Eastern Region (DONER).

Not all sections of society are happy with the Hydro Power projects that are being implemented in the State. However, dialogue has always been welcomed with dissenters. Many projects have then been modified or degraded suitably to take into account the concerns. However, it is important to realise that there is justifiable opposition to the implementation of these projects. On the other hand Sikkim has very little options if it wants to become free of dependence on central funding, even for running the Government machinery on a day to day basis. The overheads of Governance are indeed very high!

The objective is that by 2015 the State should be able to take care of the resource requirements through aforementioned routes.

Political Power Facilitation

The Government in the State is formed by the leader of the Sikkim Democratic Front Party, Dr. Pawan Chamling. Now a very well known politician in India and is also known as the 'greenest' Chief Minister. The recent IFMR/CDF 2008 award of being the second in terms of Environmental Sustainability Index (ESI) among 28 States in India is in line and correlates positively with the green policies of the State.

Chief Minister Chamling has been at the helm of affairs for the last 14 years and into concluding his third term in office. Political stability has led to an enabling environment where deepening and indeed widening of reach of various schemes of State and Central Government has been facilitated.

The State also has the lowest crime rate and so today it is best known for being the most peaceful State in India. Even though it is strategically placed with eyeball to eyeball contact with China (Tibet) the integration with the mainstream is not really a problem.

In response to the wishes of the people and during this time in office there has been a huge fillip given to rural development, health and universalisation of education. Right from the start about 70 per cent of the Plan allocation has been used in the villages of Sikkim. The rural population is over 85 per cent and so in many ways this is truly targeted spending.

Just recently Dr. Chamling personally received the *Rashtriya Nirmal Gram Puraskar*, for 100 per cent coverage in sanitation within the State. This is a clear indication that there is both depth and reach in terms of scope of the projects that are being carried out in the State. This is aided in part by the network of roads that have been built up over the last thirty years. Being a mountain State it tries its best to fit the programs offered from Delhi to the mountain issues of the State. Mountain specificities are unique. Only recently have mountain issues have been given some thought and mind space in the Planning Commission. Is there now scope for better policy mechanisms that can be worked out uniquely for mountain States? This question is going to receive further impetus in the time to come as Government grapples with an 'inclusive growth' agenda.

So, with a strong leadership and clear cut people-centric direction, policies have been formulated to enable opportunities for people. Access to funds and programs, for remote villages, are also facilitated by respective MLAs and Panchayat leaders. The way democracy has panned out here makes this possible. This accounts for much of the appreciation that Sikkim is currently receiving in the fields of environment management, health and education. The downside is that the rural people of Sikkim are far more dependent on Government largesse. This is not a healthy situation for sustainable growth.

Policy Planning Initiatives

Sikkim was perhaps one of the early adopters of assessing its Human Development Index in 20015. Sikkim's HDI is close to the national index if not better. It was 0.532 in 1999 and should have increased in the last eight years. Furthermore, Government commissioned the making of a Vision Document in 1999 to understand the goals that needed to be achieved over a sustained period of fifteen years. Much of it has been achieved though all have not been fulfilled and lots more work is still to be done.

One of the key initiatives has been for Government to set out the direction for growth. This was documented in the Sikkim: The People's Vision Report authored by Ashok K. Lahiri *et. al* from the NIPFP, New Delhi.

'An accelerated path of eco-friendly sustainable development' – this was to be Sikkim's growth paradigm. "The aim is to build on the state's strengths, benefit from post-liberalisation spurt in growth in the rest of the country and, with judicious use of modern technology, in less than two decades, leave the centuries of underdevelopment rapidly behind."

Another important aspect was the stabilisation of population. This was to achieve by 2050 constant population of half a million. This goal however seems unlikely to be achieved. Even at that time the demographic dividend has been well articulated in the document. We see some of it playing out today as we find that many of the young people are working in all different parts of the country and abroad in television and media, BPO and IT industry and emerging financial businesses. These augers well for a pronounced impact back in Sikkim in the years to come. Sikkim will reap its share of this dividend but a policy to facilitate this will have to be crafted out.

The means for achieving the overall vision has been well argued in the document. This definitely formed the basis on which much of the growth has happened. Policies of Government were aligned to the means as is thought through and stated.

The Government also constituted a State Planning Commission and requested Prof. Muchkund Dubey to take the post of Deputy Chairman of the Commission in 2002. He led the team for two consecutive three year terms. The Commission has been able to make planning in the State more professional and capable. Capacity building of the officers was also done especially in bringing out much needed reports.

This has allowed for much debate and better articulation of needs of the people. One of the best things that came out of the Commission was the devolution of powers and functions to the Panchayats. District planning bodies have been constituted and bottom up approach of planning is now a reality. Sikkim has today achieved the status of being recognised as the 3rd best State to implement the 73rd and 74th Amendments of the Constitution of India. In fact more than 40 per cent of women now participate in the Panchayati Raj system of local governance.

Meanwhile, the Millennium Development Goals (MDG) is another important set of goals towards which Government works in synchronisation for achievement by 2015. Sikkim is doing better than most of the other States in achieving these goals. Some of them have already been achieved. More research and surveys will be done in the course of the next one year to ascertain the exact position and status of the State.

Future Challenges

Future challenges faced by Sikkim in the short and medium term relate to some fundamental issues facing India and the world today. New economic outlooks will have to be factored in even as globalisation and its attendant problems kick in. Then there is the whole issue of climate change and making carbon friendly if not carbon neutral policy frameworks.

Food security can be looked at the first major challenge in the short term leading to large scale vulnerability of Sikkim's population. Since about 75 per cent of our food is imported the State faces the twin challenges of increasing domestic production as well as importing food without hindrance. We have the national highway 31A as the only reliable entry to Sikkim. This is not without hassles from our neighbours, West Bengal and the Gorkhaland agitators. Furthermore, severe landslides also have contributed to this especially after the start of the construction of Teesta Stage 6 low dam project in West Bengal.

Access is also a major issue when trying to bring high value tourists into the State. The long route from Delhi or Kolkata and then a four hour journey puts many people off. People would like to come over the weekend and holiday and get back as soon as possible, especially those who can afford to pay rather large sums. This has to be explored as a market option and tourism positioning in the years to come. Sikkim will have its own airport by 2012.

The third challenge is that Sikkim cannot grow in isolation. The region adjoining us also has to prosper in equal measure. For this to happen, the tussle between the Darjeeling political movement for autonomy and the West Bengal Government has to be sorted out amicably. The problem which is simmering is having a huge negative impact in the region as a whole.

The fourth challenge is about the Nathula Pass and how to make commercial sense of it all. This is where there are different schools of thought. There is the perception of security and how does India trade with our neighbour. The question of Tibet is always a ticklish one. Then there are issues of scaling up the items and having movement of people for tourism.

The final thought in this is, of course, are the people of Sikkim ready? There is great concern on all fronts and so Government of Sikkim is indeed taking a cautious approach. However, in the future this pass will be one which will perhaps change Sikkim forever.

The fifth challenge is to achieve a major breakthrough in the quality of delivery and access of education and health. The Government and the Planning Commission is seized of this all important issue facing the delivery system of Government. Governance will have to take this up with greater focus in the next five years. One of the ways to deliver greater coverage for health is to usher in Universal Financial Inclusion, for the entire population of the State using hitherto unavailable technologies. This would enable bank accounts to be opened up for every household. This would be very useful for cutting down on middlemen for delivering pensions and payments for NREG Scheme.

Furthermore, all families would be linked to some form of health and life insurance as well. There is also the issue of ensuring that the civil society plays a constructive role in the furthering quality transformation that is required in all spheres of social development. There are high hopes that this will be possible but the key would be to deliver high quality primary education. Moreover, making enough opportunities available for the youth of Sikkim to be able to come back and contribute to the growth and development of the State is a must.

Finally, there is the greatest challenge of fiscal transformation. From a dependent State on Central funds and grants to that of being independent on a fiscal basis would be possible by 2015. Till then the Centre has to prime the pump. Sikkim would be able to harness enough of Hydro Power as well as make other fiscal arrangements to be able to pay for its development agenda on a sustainable basis.

Achievements of Chhattisgarh during the Last Decade

T. Sundararaman, *Executive Director, National Health System Resource Centre, New Delhi*

K.R. Antony, *Director, State Health Resource Centre, Chhattisgarh*

V.R. Raman, *Faculty, State Health Resource Centre, Chhattisgarh*

Introduction and Summary

Chhattisgarh is among the newest states of India, formed on 1st November 2000, by carving it out from the then Madhya Pradesh State. Throughout these seven years the state's health sector has recorded very good improvements, though, given the baselines with which it started up, it has still a long way to go to catch up to national averages on most parameters. One of the major contributors to this advance were the health sector reforms in the state that led to a significant increase in public health expenditure, that improved the delivery of quality health services and in improving the public health infrastructure and above all that increased community awareness and support for health programmes.

Of the various health outcome indicators, only Infant Mortality Rate (IMR) and death rates are measurable and reliable on an annual basis and these showed significant declines in rural areas-though they remained relatively unchanged in urban areas where these reform measures had not reached. In 2003, the Rural IMR was as poor as 77 per 1000 live births whereas presently it is 62 which is equal to the national average.

Table: Mortality Trends in Chhattisgarh

Indicators	*Chhattisgarh*	
	2003	*2007*
Infant Mortality Rate(Total)	79	61
Infant Mortality Rate(Rural)	95	62
Infant Mortality Rate (Urban)	49	50
Crude Death Rate(Total)	8.5	8.1
Crude Death Rate (Rural)	9.1	8.5
Crude Death Rate (Urban)	7.1	6.3

Source: SRS, GoI

On service delivery indicators the most reliable are the National Family Health Survey (NFHS) data and a comparison between the NFHS-2 done in 1998-99 (the figures for Chhattisgarh were pulled out of Madhya Pradesh sample and were sufficient for the purpose) and the NFHS-3, done in 2005-06, further supports such a trend.

Thus complete immunisation rates more than doubled (from 21.8% to 48.7%), children getting all three polio vaccines rose from 57 per cent to 85 per cent and antenatal coverage went up also from 57 per cent to 89 per cent. The other parameter that correlates closely to declining IMR was the community level achievement in breast-feeding. In all aspects of breast feeding – in colostrum feeding, in early initiation of breast-feeding and in exclusive breast-feeding, the state is now well above national averages. Both NFHS-3 and District Level Household Survey (DLHS) and the independent coverage evaluation survey done by UNICEF bears this out. DLHS- 3 not only confirms these general trends but shows further steep gains in some areas. For example, children receiving measles vaccine went up from 21.1 per cent in 2002-03 to 79.9 per cent in 2007-08. This outcome was a result of comprehensive community level health education drives that the state government was able to gear up through various measures like folk art based communication programmes followed up together by health department staff and the central role played by the Mitanin.

Also malnutrition made a modest decline, much less than the improvement in service parameters. More important child malnutrition still remains impermissibly high with over 52 per cent of children below 3 years being malnourished. Though this improvement, reflects a much better inter departmental coordination and better access to services, the challenge of addressing the social determinants of such high malnutrition and a much more effective outreach to these children remain.

Improvement in Contraception prevalence rate was also good, but not good enough to contain the birth rate, which is now at 26.9. Much of the problem is in access to services as unmet needs remain at a high 20.9 per cent (DLHS-3).

Apart from above, the state was able to record major achievements in disease control - like:

- YAWS- Disease of the underdeveloped areas- has been eliminated from the state and it is marching towards eradication. There were 15 identified cases of YAWS in the state in 2003, whereas within a year, this was brought down to zero. The Chhattisgarh efforts on this has been highly appreciated by World Health Organisation (WHO) and our officials are now been invited to support the YAWS operations in countries like Indonesia.
- The Polio scene has also been controlled very well during this period. During the initial days of the state, a threat of polio was prevalent as some cases were reported in the state during that time. With effective surveillance systems, management and immunisation initiatives, the disease has been prevented as much as possible and "no case" has been reported till date.
- Leprosy is another disease which is reaching the elimination stage. In 2003, the prevalence rate was 7.20 per 10000 populations which have been brought down to 1.99 through persistent efforts. In 6 out of 16 districts national goal of less than 1 prevalence rate has been achieved and the remaining districts are moving quickly to achieve this. Though better case detection criteria would probably show a higher prevalence, there is no denying an overall decrease and an almost complete absence of new leprosy caused deformities.
- In TB control, Malaria control and in HIV/AIDS the programmes inch forward. The TB control programme, is now extended to all districts. In Malaria control, the major achievement the Annual Parasite Incidence (API), which was 10.6 in 2003, has been brought down to 5.6, and epidemics with deaths which were almost an annual feature in the past are much less now. Still, three of the southern districts where API is high are critical. Blindness control too has done well and the performance is comparable to the best amongst the states.
- A special programme to control Sickle Cell Anaemia, a specific disease prevalent in the state is also being run.

Operational research, mass screening and counselling as well as other measures initiated where support from Red Cross society is also availed.

- One of the areas where the state has been most challenged and constrained is in the improvement of institutional deliveries under the Janani Suraksha Yojana (JSY). The institutional delivery level has stagnated at about 16 per cent and this is reflective of the constraints the state is facing with facility based secondary services. With the improvement in facilities and human resource becoming available within a year of two, even these parameters should start showing considerable improvement.

Innovations that have Contributed to Chhattisgarh's Achievements

When the achievement of Chhattisgarh are judged, they need to be seen against a baseline. At the time of its formation about 40 per cent of the sanctioned posts were vacant. And each facility had less than one thirds of the staff it should have by Indian Public Health Standard (IPHS) recommendations and further almost one fifth of sub-centres, one third of Public Health Centres (PHCs) were not created at all. Indeed the lack of infrastructure and development was one of the reasons for creating a new state. The new state had also got to create its own institutional framework for management and training of health staff and expand its educational capacities.

That the state was able to do all this was largely due to innovative and indigenous planning efforts linked to a wide variety of partnerships and trust in community processes. Not all innovations and efforts have given immediate results and especially in improved service delivery in facilities the states efforts must be strengthened and sustained for one year before its impact would be measurable. We describe below some of the key innovations- many of which we note are today mainstreamed into the National Rural Health Mission (NRHM) at the national level. Indeed the focus on strengthening public health systems as the centrepiece of health sector reform, relegating public private partnerships to a supplementary role, a major feature of the NRHM, was the approach that Chhattisgarh took at a time when that had not yet become the major framework of reform.

- *Optimising the Community Level Measures-The Mitanin Programme:* The Mitanin Scheme of community health volunteers, which began with much hesitation and teething troubles has grown over the last few years into a state level programme which serves as an inspiration and an example for the entire country. Today about 60000 Mitanins or voluntary health activists are giving their voluntary services in every hamlet and in every nook and corner of the state. They have undergone 10 rounds of trainings including one on essential new born care and an integrated management of the sick neonate and child. They provide first level curative care using drugs provided as part of Mukhyamantri Dawa Peti Scheme. Learnings from the Mitanin Scheme have had a major influence on the design of ASHA (Accredited Social Health Activist) scheme under the National Rural Health Mission launched by Government of India. There are seven important ways in which the Mitanin programme differed with earlier large scale community health worker programmes organised by the government. Firstly – all the Mitanins are women. Secondly the area of coverage was a habitation, which meant less problem of heterogeneity and more access and what is most important a decreased work load making voluntarism feasible. Thirdly selection was by the community, but through a defined process and facilitated by a trained prerak who not only ensured that the community made an informed decision but also articulated the views of weaker sections. Fourthly, a strategy where the main motivation was social recognition and the spirit of service, where the honorarium in the form of incentives for specific tasks, didn't become central to her work. Fifth, training was considered and recurrent and continued activity for the entire duration of the programme and not just an initiating event. Sixth and what was important was a full time dedicated, specifically trained cadre of trainer facilitators who provided not only training, but also monitoring and much needed on the job support. And finally management of the programme through state civil society partnerships at every level. The precise contribution that this programme made to, the visible improvement in so many health outcomes and service delivery outcomes, as desegregated from other changes happening in this period, will forever remain difficult to determine. However, undeniably, five years after its initiation the attendance at each round of training continues to be undiminished, Mitanins in the vast majority of hamlets continue to make modest daily contributions to better community health with undiminished enthusiasm, and tens of thousands of women have become empowered to articulate a variety of health and related issues. These are in itself reasons for optimism and hope and the programme has become a flagship for health sector reform, drawing not only local leaders to attend to health issues, but also finance departments to sanction more funds for the health sector.

- *Improving Performance of the Hospitals:* The Jeevan Deep Approach: In order to improve the quality of management of the government run hospitals and to change the perceptions of general community about the poor quality of services in government hospitals, a pioneering hospital reform scheme called the Jeevan Deep Scheme has been put in place in the state. Under this novel scheme a more responsive, more representative, more people oriented and more target centric hospital management committees called Jeevan Deep Samitis have been created for every level of government hospitals up to the PHC. These committees will also have the power to recommend disciplinary action against non-performing officials. Under this scheme, every hospital in the state will be graded on the basis of its service quality and best hospitals will be given Jeevan Deep gold stars, silver stars and bronze stars respectively. The best hospital in every district will get Rs. 2 lakh as reward for good services. Chhattisgarh is the pioneer state to have launched such a peoples friendly target oriented scheme. It will be a marked departure from the old Rogi Kalyan Samitis which were running the hospitals earlier. Korba, Ambikapur and Durg are Silver Star hospitals. The Korba District Hospital has been since through a further process of quality improvement been certified for ISO 9001:2000- one of the very few public hospitals in India to have been so certified.

- *Developing FRU Facilities and Bridging Specialist Gaps:* the Equip Initiative: In terms of closing the gaps in infrastructure, skilled manpower and equipment in parallel to addressing quality and adequacy of utilisation of services, a new block by block approach has been adopted by the state. This approach goes by the acronym "EQUIP"-Enhancing Quality in Primary health care- and it focuses on reduction of maternal mortality as the quality index around which health services are rationalised. 32 blocks each has been taken up in the first two years and the entire state is planned to be covered in another 3 years. So as to address the specialist gaps, an innovative training programme for multiskilling doctors, particularly in Emergency Obstetric Care (EmoC) and Anaesthesia, has been designed which has been replicated nationally now. These trainings are conducted in 3 top medical institutions of the state and so far 96 MBBS doctors has been built capacities to impart EMoC services as well as anaesthesia. However only about 25 per cent of this converted into functional First Referral Units (FRUs), due to various operational constraints. Despite this, the number of FRUs rose sharply and way forward on this difficult goal became clear. Training on essential neonatal care and some other disciplines are also started very recently. This way the FRU service provision has been marked a much better status in the state if compared to past. We would like to note that these facilities are now becoming available even in some of those facilities situated in conflict-ridden areas of the state.

- *Placing Health into Panchayats Agenda- The Swasth Panchayat Scheme:* This is a programme to support local health planning and to enhance Panchyat Raj Institutions (PRI) role in health. An indicator based health & human development index has been prepared for all Panchayats of the state which is hamlet centred so as to capture even the intra-panchayat variations. At present, the HHDI is ready for 9141 Panchayats out of 9820 Panchayats in the state. Honble Chief Minister of the state has declared an award for two top Panchayats of each block based on this index and also provisions are made to support weaker Panchayats identified under this process. The Programme is now in the second year of implementation. This programme builds on the community mobilisation initiated by the Mitanin programme and takes it forward into village level comprehensive health planning.

- *Reaching Out to the People in Every Corner- The Mobile Medical Units:* Chhattisgarh is a tribal state where 44 per cent of the area is covered with forests. Reaching out to the far-flung corners of the state for providing health services is major challenge. In order to overcome this challenge and to provide uninterrupted health services in tribal blocks, as many as 74 mobile medical units have been operationalised in the state. They are providing valuable services in the haat baazars of tribal blocks in the state.
- An innovative institutional model has been set up in the form of state-civil society joint initiative, the State Health Resource Centre (SHRC) to shape the reform processes and to initiate them wherever it is necessary. The important innovation is not only that it is partnership between government and civil society, but also that it has built a model of technical assistance which is based on indigenous technical strengths, largely operates within a government financial rules and what is most important is based upon institutional capacity building and not on external consultancy alone. Though this has been one of the earliest innovations picked up for replication, similar SHRCs have been slow to emerge, and in retrospect one begins to appreciate the level of innovation and change that setting this up required.

Core Improvements

Other than these major innovations, there are various "reform" milestones set by the NRHM that have been achieved by this state as well. These are not innovations that they represent well known, almost routine measures of a functional health department. Yet it is often the implementation of these core measures that would have the maximum impact. We list a few of these below:

- *Formation of State Health Mission and Driving towards the NRHM Goals:* Moving towards health for the poor, a state health mission has been constituted under NRHM, Chaired by the Hon. Chief Minister. State and District and Block programme Management Units are supporting the mission activities at respective levels. Decentralised planning and management of resources to address local needs has become a reality.
- *Major Infrastructure Expansion:* The inadequacy in number of facilities has been met during this period by sanctioning health facilities: apart from district hospitals sanctioned and in most cases built new for all districts, 17 new Community Health Centres (CHCs), 200 new Primary Health Centres and 874 new sub-centres have been sanctioned. By this, the state has achieved population norms for creation of facilities except in the case of CHCs. In terms of filling the building gaps, 26 CHCs, 39 PHCs and 201 sub centre buildings are under construction though the vast majority of sub-centres still need to be provided with a building. During the last 3 years, Rs 20 lakh per block allocations are made under various schemes for refurbishment of available buildings in all 146 blocks. Under the ongoing European Union State Partnership, infrastructure development is a major focus.
- *Creation of the State Institute of Health & Family Welfare (SIHFW):* A Human Resource Development policy for health has been adopted and SIHFW has been created to take forward the implementation of this policy. A state of the art building for SIHFW has been completed and the institution has given adequate manpower and logistical support in terms of achieving its goals. It is aimed that the capacity and motivation gaps among the field force be addressed through systematic planning and implementation of training programmes initiated by SIHFW.

- *Sanction of Staff Setup for the Health Department:* A revised administrative set up was adopted in 2006 under which adequate number of posts was sanctioned in every health facility. Though still short of the IPHS norms, for Chhattisgarh it was a major step forward.

- *Recruitment of Medical Officers:* For the first time after the state formation, and almost after a period of 15 years, 449 doctors were appointed through Public Service Commission, and of these 250 of them have joined the services. In addition AYUSH doctors have been used to fill up medical officer posts in over 150 primary health centres. Rural posting of medical graduates as a mandatory condition of consideration for post-graduation has also led to over 150 doctors becoming every year on a contractual basis. In addition to all of this all districts are empowered to fill up vacancies on a contractual basis. To expand the pool of medical officers available for recruitment, two more medical colleges, one in 2002 in Bilaspur, and another in 2007 in Jagdalpur have been added to the existing medical college at Raipur. More colleges are planned. In order to meet the doctor deficiency, as an immediate measure the state has pooled 398 "rural medical assistants" in PHCs from the ongoing 3 year medical course.

- *Mainstreaming of Indian Systems of Medicine:* The Indian Systems of Medicine has been given top priority by the state. The Raipur Ayurveda College has been developed into a model college and then as a University. Drug testing facilities, for ayurvedic drugs are now available. Panchakarma therapy centres and speciality clinics has been started in a number of Allopathic health facilities so as to provide choice between systems for the community in chronic illness. As many as 86 Primary Health Centres and Ayurvedic Dispenseries have been merged. And all 60000 Mitanins are being trained on household herbal remedies.

- *Control of Food & Drugs:* A state of the art Drug Testing Laboratory is ready for inauguration at Raipur city until now it was necessary to sent food/drug samples to external laboratories for getting the sample tests done. In addition to this, mobile laboratories have been made operational in order to make collecting samples from remote and village areas possible. Smoking and tobacco use has been banned in public places.

Emerging Policies and Initiatives: After an extensive process of discussion with a wide variety of stakeholders, the State Health & Population Policy has been prepared and this shall be notified soon. A new act for regulation of clinical establishments under private sector is drafted and awaiting approval. There is a major plan being put in place to rapidly increase nursing education and nurse availability within the system. A Bal Hruday Suraksha Yojna (literally meaning Child Heart Protection Scheme) is proposed as a special school health programme to help poor children with congenital cardiac diseases. A state wide urban health programme and a scheme for building dharamsalas in every government hospital are also being rolled out. 5000 telephone connections through BSNL to connect all Sub Centres, PHCs, CHCs and district hospitals are under installation and an emergency ambulance system is under consideration.

A Comparative Chart on Health-Showing Growth on Various Health Sector Reform Areas

Area	*Status 2003*	*Status 2008*	*Purpose/Achievement*
Policies and Programmes			
Health and Population Policy	Nil	Finalised, awaiting approval	Policy Governance
HRD Policy	Nil	Notified	Planned HR Development
Drug Policy	Nil	Finalised, awaiting approval	Towards rational drug use
Policy for Medically Underserved Areas	Nil	Under Preparation	Reaching the unreached
Delegation and decentralisation of powers	Upto District	Upto Block	Grassroots governance
Mainstreaming of AYUSH	Not done	Achieved	Holistic approach
YAWS Control (No. of cases)	15	0	Towards Elimination
Polio Control (No. of cases)	2	0	Towards elimination
Leprosy Control (Prevalence Rate)	7.2	1.99	72.36 % reduction
TB Control (District Covered)	4	16	100 % coverage

Contd...

Area	*Status 2003*	*Status 2008*	*Purpose/Achievement*
Mitanin Programme (No. of Mitanins)	Nil	60092	100 % coverage of rural areas
Medical Facilities in Public Sector			
No. of Medical Colleges	2	3	1
No. of District Hospitals	9	15	6
No. of 100 bedded Civil Hospitals	8	16	8
No. of Community Health Centres	114	129	15
No. of Functional First Referral Units	0	64	64
No. of Primary Health Centres	512	727	215
No. of Primary Health Sub centres	3818	4728	910
Manpower			
No. of Posts sanctioned of medical officers	1455	1737	282
No. of Posts sanctioned of Specialists	247	637	390
No. Doctors promoted as specialists	0	250	250
Doctors sanctioned for a PHC	1	2	2 times
Doctors sanctioned for CHC	4	8	2 times
Selection of Doctors through PSC	0	448	448
Completion of Buildings			
New District hospital	0	6	6
New CHCs	0	36	36
New PHCs	0	73	73
New Sub centres	0	203	203
Fund Allocations			
Budget outlay for Health Department	235.23 crores	485.7 crores	Almost 2 times
Assistance Under Sanjeevni Kosh	2.49 crores	13.29	crores Almost 5 times
External Assistance Mobilised	Less than 50 crores	More than 300 crores	Almost 3 times
Inpatient dietary allocations per head	8.00 Rs	16.00 Rs	2 times hike
Additional Untied Funds per District Hospital pa	0	5.0 lakh	5.0 lakh for 16 facilities
Additional Untied Funds per CHC pa	0	2.0 lakh	2.0 lakh for 117 facilities
Additional Untied Funds per PHC pa	0	0.5 lakh	0.5 lakh for 517 facilities
Additional Untied funds per Sub centre	0	0.18 lakh	0.18 lakh for 4692 facilities

Indicators, Indices and Ranking of States for the 4th JRD Tata Memorial Awards

Table: Inputs for Base Year in the States of India

	Census, 1991	*NFHS II*	*NFHS II*	*NFHS II*	*NFHS II*	*NFHS II*	*NFHS II*	*NFHS II*	*SRS*	*Census, 1991*	*Census, 1991*	*Census, 1991*	*National Human Development Report, 2001*
State	*Sex Ratio (0-6)-1991*	*Women (20-24) married by age 18*	*CPR any methods*	*Full Immunisation*	*TFR*	*Atleast three ANC Visits*	*Safe Delivery*	*% Children Underweight*	**IMR, 1999*	*Girl school attendance rate (6-14),*	*Female Youth (15-24) Literacy*	*Literacy Rate(7+)*	*% of Plan Expenditure on Social Sector, 1991 1997-98*
Andhra Pradesh	975	64.3	59.6	58.7	2.3	80.1	65.2	37.7	66	46.1	41.0	44.1	22.46
Arunachal Pradesh	982	27.6	35.4	20.5	2.5	40.5	31.9	24.3	35	40.6	42.4	41.6	29.65
Assam	975	40.7	43.3	17.0	2.3	30.8	21.4	36.0	76	48.7	52.9	52.9	45.89
Bihar	953	71.9	23.5	12.5	3.7	15.6	25.3	54.4	63	29.1	28.3	37.5	17.26
Chhattisgarh	984	61.3	45.0	20.0	2.8	33.2	32.3	60.8	78	43.5	35.5	42.9	32.74
Delhi	915	19.8	63.8	69.8	2.4	68.2	65.9	34.7	25	76.3	75.0	75.3	51.9
Goa	964	10.1	47.5	82.6	1.8	95.7	90.8	28.6	17	84.3	85.7	75.5	42.83
Gujarat	928	40.7	59.0	53.0	2.7	60.2	53.5	45.1	63	58.0	58.4	61.3	22.97
Haryana	879	41.5	62.4	62.7	2.9	37.4	42.0	34.6	68	58.6	50.5	55.8	34.26
Himachal Pradesh	951	10.7	67.7	83.4	2.1	60.9	40.2	43.6	54	75.0	72.3	63.9	35.24
Jammu & Kashmir**	917	22.1	49.1	56.7	2.7	66.0	42.4	34.5	45	46.4	43.7	44.1	28.86
Jharkhand	979	64.1	27.6	6.5	2.8	24.5	17.5	54.3	71	34.2	30.1	41.4	17.26
Karnataka	960	46.3	58.3	60.0	2.1	71.4	59.1	43.9	58	56.1	54.8	56.0	32.31
Kerala	958	17.0	63.7	79.7	2.0	98.3	94.0	26.9	15	91.9	96.8	89.8	18.88
Madhya Pradesh	941	64.0	44.1	23.2	3.5	26.3	28.8	53.1	90	41.6	35.8	44.7	32.74
Maharashtra	946	47.7	60.9	78.4	2.5	65.4	59.4	49.6	48	66.5	67.0	64.9	20.69
Manipur	974	9.9	38.7	42.3	3.0	54.4	53.9	27.5	23	54.9	62.2	59.9	32.44

Contd...

Census,	*NFHS II 1991*	*NFHS II*	*NFHS II*	*NFHS II*	*NFHS II*	*NFHS II*	*NFHS II*	*SRS*	*Census,*	*Census, 1991*	*Census, 1991*	*National 1991*	*Human Development Report, 2001*
State	***Sex Ratio (0-6)-1991***	***Women (20-24) married by age 18***	***CPR any methods***	***Full Immunisation***	***TFR***	***Atleast three ANC Visits***	***Safe Delivery***	***% Children Underweight***	****IMR, 1999***	***Girl school attendance rate (6-14),***	***Female Youth (15-24) Literacy***	***Literacy Rate(7+)***	***% of Plan Expenditure on Social Sector, 1991 1997-98***
Meghalaya	986	25.5	20.2	14.3	4.6	31.3	20.6	37.9	61	42.6	56.9	49.1	37.83
Mizoram	969	11.6	57.7	59.6	2.9	75.8	67.5	27.7	14	68.2	87.2	82.3	30.35
Nagaland	993	22.9	30.3	14.1	3.8	23.1	32.8	24.1	32	54.4	70.0	61.6	36.73
Orissa	967	37.6	46.8	43.7	2.5	47.3	33.4	54.4	97	47.4	45.5	49.1	32.38
Punjab	875	11.6	66.7	72.1	2.2	57.0	62.6	28.7	53	65.4	66.5	58.5	20.67
Rajasthan	916	68.3	40.3	17.3	3.8	22.9	35.8	50.6	81	27.7	25.9	38.6	24.22
Sikkim	965	22.3	53.8	47.4	2.8	42.6	35.1	20.6	46	62.0	61.7	56.9	45.38
Tamil Nadu	948	24.9	52.1	88.8	2.2	91.4	83.8	36.7	52	71.1	63.9	62.7	38.89
Tripura	967	37.7	55.5	40.7	1.9	47.2	47.5	42.6	27	56.6	62.4	60.4	43.18
Uttar Pradesh	927	64.3	27.3	20.5	4.1	14.7	21.8	52.2	84	30.4	31.6	40.7	29.6
Uttarakhand	949	25.9	43.1	34.6	2.6	19.7	34.6	41.8	52	55.2	55.9	57.8	29.6
West Bengal	967	45.9	66.6	43.8	2.3	57.0	44.2	48.7	52	47.3	56.1	57.7	22.83
Maximum	1000	100.0	100.0	100.0	6	100.0	100.0	100.0	150.0	100.0	100.0	100.0	100
Minimum	700	0	0	0	2.1	0	0	0	5	0	0	0	0

Table: Input for the Final Year in the States of India

State	Census, 2001 Sex Ratio (0-6)	NFHS III Women (20-24) married by age 18	NFHS III CPR any methods	NFHS III Full Immuni-sation	NFHS III TFR	NFHS III Atleast three ANC Visits	NFHS III Safe Delivery	NFHS III % Children Underweight	SRS IMR, 2005	Under Five Mortality Rate, Census, 2001 M/F Ratio	Under Five Mortality Rate, Census, 2001 M/F Ratio (Truncated at 1)	Census, 2001 Girl school attendance rate (6-14)	Census, 201 Female Youth (15-24) Literacy Rate	Census, 2001 Literacy Rate(7+)	Statistical Abstract, India, 2001 % of Plan Expenditure on Social Sector, 2004-05
Andhra Pradesh	961	54.7	67.6	46.0	1.8	85.4	74.9	32.5	57	1.09	1.0	74.3	64.7	60.5	30.0
Arunachal Pradesh	964	40.6	43.2	28.4	3.0	35.5	30.2	32.5	37	1.03	1.0	56.7	61.6	54.3	31.6
Assam	965	38.0	56.5	31.4	2.4	39.3	31.0	36.4	68	1.05	1.0	62.5	68.1	63.3	32.5
Bihar	942	50.3	34.1	32.8	4.0	17.0	29.3	55.9	61	0.88	0.9	40.6	42.8	47.0	33.3
Chhattisgarh	975	51.8	53.2	48.7	2.6	54.2	41.6	47.1	63	1.07	1.0	69.9	68.8	64.7	39.9
Delhi	868	21.2	66.9	63.2	2.1	75.1	64.1	26.1	35	0.96	1.0	83.4	85.2	81.7	50.6
Goa	938	11.7	48.2	78.6	1.8	94.9	94.0	25.0	16	0.98	1.0	89.4	91.0	82.0	43.2
Gujarat	883	33.5	66.6	45.2	2.4	67.5	63.0	44.6	54	0.99	1.0	71.4	72.4	69.1	37.3
Haryana	819	39.8	63.4	65.3	2.7	59.2	48.9	39.6	60	0.89	0.9	75.7	75.3	67.9	44.1
Himachal Pradesh	896	12.3	72.6	74.2	1.9	62.6	47.8	36.5	49	1.09	1.0	90.5	89.3	76.5	46.9
Jammu & Kashmir	941	14.0	52.6	66.7	2.4	73.5	56.5	25.6	50	0.96	1.0	60.3	57.4	55.5	29.7
Jharkhand	965	51.2	35.7	34.2	3.3	35.9	27.8	56.5	50	0.98	1.0	51.2	50.3	53.6	29.2
Karnataka	946	41.2	63.6	55.0	2.1	79.5	69.7	37.6	50	1.06	1.0	74.2	73.7	66.6	29.6
Kerala	960	15.4	68.6	75.3	1.9	93.6	99.4	22.9	14	0.87	0.9	95.1	98.1	90.9	22.3
Madhya Pradesh	932	53.0	55.9	40.3	3.1	40.7	32.7	60.0	76	0.95	1.0	65.7	62.6	63.7	30.3
Maharashtra	913	38.8	66.9	58.8	2.1	75.1	68.7	37.0	36	1.01	1.0	84.7	84.9	76.9	44.7
Manipur	957	12.7	48.7	46.8	2.8	68.6	59.0	22.1	13	0.96	1.0	77.9	79.5	70.5	36.2
Meghalaya	973	24.5	24.3	32.9	3.8	54.0	31.1	48.8	49	1.03	1.0	60.3	74.0	62.6	38.0
Mizoram	964	20.6	59.9	46.5	2.9	59.3	65.4	19.9	20	1.01	1.0	81.2	92.6	88.8	28.1
Nagaland	964	21.1	29.7	21.0	3.7	32.7	24.7	25.2	18	0.83	0.8	70.0	73.3	66.6	33.6

Contd...

Census,	*NFHS III 2001*	*NFHS III*	*NFHS III*	*NFHS III*	*NFHS III*	*NFHS III*	*NFHS III*	*SRS*	*Under Five*	*Census, Mortality Rate,*	*Census, 2001*	*Census, 2001*	*Census, 201*	*Statistical 2001*	*Abstract, India, 2001*
State	***Sex Ratio (0-6)***	***Women (20-24) married by age 18***	***CPR any methods***	***Full Immuni-sation***	***TFR***	***Atleast three ANC Visits***	***Safe Delivery***	***% Children Underweight***	***IMR, 2005***	***M/F Ratio***	***M/F Ratio (Truncated at 1)***	***Girl school attendance rate (6-14)***	***Female Youth (15-24) Literacy Rate***	***Literacy Rate(7+)***	***% of Plan Expenditure on Social Sector, 2004-05***
Orissa	953	36.3	50.7	51.8	2.4	61.8	44.0	40.7	75	1.05	1.0	64.9	66.3	63.1	29.0
Punjab	798	19.4	63.3	60.1	2.0	74.8	68.2	24.9	44	0.96	1.0	79.4	81.1	69.7	25.4
Rajasthan	909	57.1	47.2	26.5	3.2	41.2	41.0	39.9	68	0.92	0.9	60.9	54.9	60.4	31.4
Sikkim	963	30.1	57.6	69.6	2.0	70.1	53.7	19.7	30	1.03	1.0	81.2	79.8	68.8	40.9
Tamil Nadu	942	21.5	61.4	80.9	1.8	95.9	90.6	29.8	37	0.99	1.0	86.9	84.2	73.5	46.5
Tripura	966	41.0	65.7	49.7	2.2	60.0	48.8	39.6	31	1.01	1.0	75.0	78.7	73.2	44.3
Uttar Pradesh	916	53.0	43.6	23.0	3.8	26.6	27.2	42.4	73	0.89	0.9	57.8	53.2	56.3	30.6
Uttarakhand	908	22.6	59.3	60.0	2.6	44.9	38.5	38.0	42	1.00	1.0	80.0	78.1	71.6	41.4
West Bengal	960	53.3	71.2	64.3	2.3	62.0	47.6	38.7	38	1.02	1.0	69.3	70.8	68.6	36.0
Maximum	1000	100	100	100	6	100	100	100	150	1	1	100	100	100	100
Minimum	700	0	0	0	2.1	0	0	0	5	0.83	0.83	0	0	0	0

Table: Index Values for Base and Final Years and Ranking

State	Composite index, NFHS III	Rank of NFHS III	Composite index (U5 excluded), NFHS III	Composite index, NFHS II	Rank of NFHS II	Change (NFHSIII-II)	Rank Change (NFHS III-II)	4*Change	Rank of 4* Change (NFHS III-II)	Final Index	Final Rank
Chhatisgarh	61.8	19	58.9	45.4	24	13.5	1	54.0	1	115.8	1
Sikkim	73.5	5	71.5	61.9	12	9.6	5	38.3	5	111.8	2
Uttarakhand	66.4	15	63.8	53.8	19	9.9	3	39.7	3	106.1	3
Rajasthan	51.0	26	50.8	37.7	27	13.1	2	52.5	2	103.5	4
Manipur	70.7	9	70.3	62.8	9	7.5	11	30.0	11	100.8	5
Andhra Pradesh	68.9	11	66.5	58.5	13	7.9	9	31.8	9	100.6	6
Tamil Nadu	78.6	3	77.5	72.2	5	5.2	17	21.0	17	99.6	7
Jammu & Kashmir	66.0	16	65.2	57.7	16	7.5	12	30.0	12	95.9	8
West Bengal	67.2	14	64.7	57.9	15	6.8	13	27.4	13	94.6	9
Maharashtra	71.6	8	69.4	63.6	8	5.7	15	23.0	15	94.5	10
Madhya Pradesh	53.3	24	52.0	42.0	25	9.9	4	39.7	4	93.0	11
Orissa	62.0	18	59.1	51.5	22	7.6	10	30.3	10	92.4	12
Karnataka	69.8	10	67.5	62.1	10	5.4	16	21.5	16	91.3	13
Meghalaya	57.7	22	54.4	46.4	23	8.1	8	32.3	8	90.0	14
Jharkhand	50.8	27	48.0	39.3	26	8.6	7	34.6	7	85.4	15
Kerala	79.1	2	83.3	82.2	1	1.1	25	4.5	25	83.6	16
Tripura	68.3	12	65.9	62.1	11	3.8	21	15.2	21	83.5	17
Gujarat	65.2	17	62.9	58.5	14	4.4	20	17.7	20	82.9	18
Uttar Pradesh	44.6	28	45.3	36.2	28	9.1	6	36.5	6	81.1	19
Himachal Pradesh	72.5	6	70.3	68.7	6	1.6	23	6.5	23	79.0	20
Assam	59.6	20	56.4	51.8	21	4.6	19	18.5	19	78.0	21
Goa	80.4	1	79.8	80.5	2	-0.7	27	-2.8	27	77.6	22
Haryana	58.5	21	60.4	55.7	17	4.7	18	19.0	18	77.6	23
Punjab	67.3	13	67.2	65.5	7	1.7	22	6.6	22	74.5	24
Mizoram	74.0	4	72.0	73.3	3	-1.3	29	-5.3	29	68.7	25
Delhi	71.6	7	71.3	72.4	4	-1.2	28	-4.6	28	67.0	26
Bihar	40.9	29	41.8	35.8	29	5.9	14	23.8	14	64.7	27
Nagaland	52.4	25	56.4	54.8	18	1.6	24	6.5	24	58.9	28
Arunachal Pradesh	57.0	23	53.7	53.3	20	0.4	26	1.7	26	58.7	29

Table: Ranking of States on Reproductive and Child Health Programmes in India

Bigger States			Smaller States		
S.No.	States	Rank	S.No.	States	Rank
1.	Chhattisgarh	1	1.	Sikkim	1
2.	Rajasthan	2	2.	Uttarakhand	2
3.	Andhra Pradesh	3	3.	Manipur	3
4.	Tamil Nadu	4	4.	Meghalaya	4
5.	Jammu & Kashmir	5	5.	Tripura	5
6.	West Bengal	6	6.	Himachal Pradesh	6
7.	Maharashtra	7	7.	Goa	7
8.	Madhya Pradesh	8	8.	Mizoram	8
9.	Orissa	9	9.	Nagaland	9
10.	Karnataka	10	10.	Arunachal Pradesh	10
11.	Jharkhand	11			
12.	Kerala	12			
13.	Gujarat	13			
14.	Uttar Pradesh	14			
15.	Assam	15			
16.	Haryana	16			
17.	Punjab	17			
18.	Delhi	18			
19.	Bihar	19			

Bibliography

Arvind, Mambro S.A. Sabavala and R.M. Lala: *J.R.D. Tata : Letters and Keynote*, Rupa, 2004.

Bakhtiar, K. Dadabhoy: *A Life of J.R.D. Tata*, Rupa, 2005.

Bakshi, S. R.: *Indian Freedom Fighters: Struggle for Independence*, Hardcover, 2002.

BBC News: *India's Tata wins race for Corus*, 2007.

Bhagwan, V.: *Indian Freedom Movement and Constitutional Acts*, Atma Ram, 1999.

Bhattacharya, B. K.: *India's Freedom Movement: Legacy of Bipin Chandra Pal*, Deep and Deep, New Delhi, 2007.

Chakravarty, Shachi: *Quit India Movement: A Study*, New Century Publication, 2002.

Chandra, Bipan: *India's Struggle For Independence*, Penguin Books India (P) Ltd., New Delhi, 1989.

Chandra, Shailesh: *90 Years of India's Struggle for Independence: 1857-1947*, Alfa Pub, 2008.

Dubey, Rajiv: *Interview with Ratan Tata*, Businessworld, 2005.

Ganjoo, S.: *Muslim Freedom Fighters of India*, Anmol Publication, New Delhi, 2002.

GEO and GCC: *Tata Group*, Retrieved 2009.

Ghosh, Ratna: *Netaji Subhas Chandra Bose and Indian Freedom Struggle (2 Vols-Set)*, Deep and Deep, 2006.

Goyal, P. K.: *Battle of India's Freedom Movement*, Vista International, 2005.

Gupta, Shantinath: *Great Freedom Fighters of India*, Anmol, 2006.

Hari Hara Das: *The History of Freedom Movement in India (1857-1947)*, National, 1998.

Huggler, Justin: *From Parsee Priests to Profits: Say Hello to Tata: The Independent*, Retrieved, 2009.

India's Tata Group: *Empowering Marginalized Communities*, 2008.

Indu Dave: *Indian Personality in Its Developmental Background*, Himanshu, 1991.

Iyengar, A. S.: *Role of Press and Indian Freedom Struggle: All through the Gandhian Era*, APH, 2001.

Kailash Khanna: *History of Indian Freedom Struggle*, Commonwealth Publication, 2004.

Kaushik, A. S.: *Great Freedom Fighters of India*, Indian Publication, 2007.

Khairul Anam, Md.: *Indian Freedom Movement and Murshidabad District 1905-1947*, Bagchi, K. P., 2008.

Kneale, Klaus: *World's Most Reputable Companies: The Rankings*, Forbes Retrieved, 2009.

Krishan Mohan: *Encyclopaedic History of Indian Freedom Movement (4 Vols-Set)*, Book Enclave, 1999.

Kumar, Prafulla Pattanaik: *The First Indian War of Independence: Freedom Movement in Orissa, 1804-1825*, APH, 2005.

Kumar, Raj: *Essays on Indian Freedom Movement*, History and Culture Series, Discovery, 2003.

Kumar, Ravindra: *Champaran to Quit India Movement*, Mittal, 2002.

Kumar, Sirisa Shadangi: *The Prisons of South Orissa and the Freedom Fighters in Incarceration, 1900 - 1947*, Punthi Pustak, 2005.

Lala, R. M.: *Beyond the Last Blue Mountain: the Authorised Biography of J.R.D. Tata*, Viking, 1992.

Leadership with Trust: *Tata Group*, Retrieved 2009.

Lion Agrawal, M. G.: *Freedom Fighters of India (4 Vols-Set)*, Isha Books, 2008.

Magubira, Patty: *Tanzania: UK Activists Pile Pressure Against Soda Ash Project*, Retrieved, 2008.

Majumdar, R. C.: *History of the Freedom Movement in India (3 Vols-Set)*, Firma KLM, 1997.

Malhotra, Sumiti: *Thoughts of Great Personalities in 20 Century*, Raj Publishing, 2003.

Mambro, Arvind: *J.R.D. Tata Letters*, Rupa, 2004.

Maulana Syed Mohammad Mian: *The Prisoners of Malta (Asira'n-E-Malta): The Heart-Rending Tale of Muslim Freedom Fighters in British Period*, Manak, 2005.

Mazhar Kibriya: *Gandhi and Indian Freedom Struggle*, APH, 1999.

Muthaiah, S.: *Women Freedom Fighters*, The Hindu, 2004.

Nanda, S. P.: *Freedom Movement and Constitutional Development in India*, Dominant, 2004.

Nityanand, Jayaraman: *CorpWatch : Stolen for Steel: Tata Takes Tribal Lands in India*, 2006.

Om Prakash: *Encyclopaedic History of Indian Freedom Movement (12 to 21 Vols)*, Anmol, 2003.

Omesh Saigal: *Shaheed Bhagat Singh: Unique Martyr in Freedom Movement*, Gyan Publication, 2002.

Parashar, Parmanand: *Kashmir and the Freedom Movement*, Sarup, 2004.

Pathak, Maulik: *Tata Chemicals' African Safari Hits Green Hurdle*, The Economic Times, 2007.

Piramal, Gita: *Business Maharajas*, Penguin, New Delhi, 1997.

Pradhan, K. B.: *Freedom Movement in India*, Arise Pub, 2007.

Rafiya, Nisar: *Shaikh-Ul-Hind Maulana Mahmud Hasan and Indian Freedom Movement*, Manak Pub, 2008.

Ram Sharma, S.: *Education of Women and Freedom Movement*, Discovery, 1996.

Ram, S. and Kumar, R.: *Encyclopaedia of Indian Freedom Struggle (10 Vols-Set)*, Commonwealth Pub, 2008.

Ram, S. and Kumar, R.: *Quit India Movement: 1942-1945*, Commonwealth Pub, 2008.

Ramanathan, K. V.: *The Satyamurti Letters, Vol. II: The Indian Freedom Struggle Through the Eyes of a Parliamentarian*, Dorling Kindersley for Pearson Longman an Imprint of Pearson Education, 2008.

Ramu, P. S.: *Azad Hind Fauj (I.N.A.) and The Freedom Movement*, Freedom Movement Memorial Comm, 1998.

Ratan Tata wins 2010 Business Leader of the Year Award at The Asian Awards in London

Sharma, S. K.: *Eminent Indian Freedom Fighters (2 Vols-Set)*, Anmol Publication, New Delhi, 2004.

Sharma, Subramaniam: *India's Tata Takes Leap With $7.6 Billion Corus Bid*, Bloomberg, 2006.

Sinha, Suveen K.: *Ratan Tata: The Man with Steely Resolve*, 2007.

Sirkin, Harold L. James W. Hemerling and Arindam K. Bhattacharya *GLOBALITY: Competing with Everyone from Everywhere for Everything*, Business Plus, New York, 2004.

Sundaram, V.: *Great Crusader for Women's Emancipation*, News Today, 2005.

Sundararaja, Saroja: *March to Freedom in Madras Presidency, 1916-1947,* Lalitha Publication, Chennai, 1989.

Taneja, Anup: *Gandhi, Women and the National Movement, 1920-47,* Har-Anand Publications, Delhi, 2005.

Thebault, Pierre: *French Compressed Air Car Set for Take-Off in India,* Retrieved, 2009.

Thomson, Reuters: *Tata Motors Completes Acquisition of Jag,* Land Rover, 2008.

Timmons, Heather: *Tata Pulls Ford Units into Its Orbit,* The New York Times, Retrieved, 2008.

Tony, Lewin: *Classic Names are Part of Tata Deal,* Crain Communications work=Automotive News, 2008.

Index

N

P

R

S

T

U

Z

❑❑❑